Fast Track to Quality

A 12-Month Program for Small to Mid-Sized Businesses

Roger Tunks

McGraw-Hill, Inc.

New York   St. Louis   San Francisco   Auckland   Bogotá
Caracas   Lisbon   London   Madrid   Mexico   Milan
Montreal   New Delhi   Paris   San Juan   São Paulo
Singapore   Sydney   Tokyo   Toronto

Library of Congress Cataloging-in-Publication Data

Tunks, Roger.
    Fast track to quality : a 12-month program for small to mid-sized
businesses / Roger Tunks.
        p.   cm.
    Includes index.
    ISBN 0-07-065476-X :
    1. Total quality management.   2. Small business—Quality control.
3. Small business—Management.   I. Title.
HD62.15.T86   1992
658.5'62—dc20   92-12143
                                                                              CIP

1 2 3 4 5 6 7 8 9 0   DOC/DOC   9 8 7 6 5 4 3 2

ISBN   0-07-065476-X

*The sponsoring editor for this book was Theodore Nardin, the editing supervisor
was Fred Dahl, and the production supervisor was Pamela Pelton. It was set in
Baskerville by Inkwell Publishing Services.*

Printed and bound by R. R. Donnelley & Sons Company.

Contents

Part 3. Fine-Tuning and Putting the Fast-Track Paradigm to Work   149

16. Four Steps to Building Employee Commitment   195

17. Five Steps to Empowerment   205

18. Eight Communication Channels for Fast Tracking TQM   213

Preface

This book provides managers with the action plan to develop and apply Total Quality Management (TQM) in small to mid-sized companies. This plan provides understanding of a *proven new technology called Fast Track to Quality*. It has been applied by hundreds of managers in small to mid-sized companies with dramatic results. In describing the Fast-Track method, emphasis is on the many practical "How to's." It will instruct and empower managers to:

1. Understand and become effective communicators of TQM principles.

2. Understand and apply the vital leadership skills to guide their companies to full TQM effectiveness.

3. Avoid the mistakes other managers have made as they sought to advance their companies to TQM success.

4. Become more competitive in the marketplace.

5. Above all—to increase profits.

In writing this book, the underlying requirement has been to keep it practical. Theory and intellectual bantering has been minimized with the focus clearly on practical, real life applications. My greatest frustration as a Quality consultant is getting managers to accept the simplicity of TQM. Somehow TQM has developed a mystique, with many managers convinced it is a complicated process. It isn't. Simply described: everyone in an organization consistently seeks to improve the quality of products and services by performing error-free work the first time and every time. The results include: on-time delivery; minimal waste; no rework; reduced expense; and of course, satisfied customers and increased profits.

It's easy to describe TQM and understand the requirement of quality success. The tough part is "how to do it." That's what this book is all about. It is divided into four parts:

1. Fast Tracking for the small and mid-sized companies.

2. The Fast-Track Paradigm for TQM success—elements and events that make the Fast-Track method work.

3. Making the Fast-Track process work... key actions for Fast-Track success.

4. Fast-Track success stories... real-life examples of the Fast-Track process at work in different companies.

The step-by-step process described here is designed to advance your company to full TQM status within a relatively short time frame and with minimal cost. Each of the concepts, principles, and key actions has been carefully thought out and tested for impact and practicality. In a word, they work.

This book will become a valuable resource for you as you advance the Quality of your company's products and services. You'll have the experience and input of many consultants at your fingertips. You'll realize the benefits of the experience of companies who have spent thousands and even millions of dollars to advance Quality.

The greatest benefit of this book can be realized by discussing its concepts, key actions, and exercises with others. Invite others as traveling companions on your journey to advance quality in your company. Treat this book as your private Quality consultant. Challenge and test its concepts. Read and reread it as you apply its principles.

My colleagues and I have conducted numerous studies to confirm and validate the techniques and methods in the new process of Fast Tracking to Quality. Many of those studies and experiences have become the grist for this book. I guarantee that every concept, principle, and key action in this book has been validated and successfully used by many companies across the country. They've seen their market share and their profits increase as they've improved the quality of their products and service using the "Fast Track to Quality." It can work for you too.

Acknowledgments

In my life there have been many influences stimulating growth and change. Early training from parents, Homer and Leah Tunks, developed my personal value system for hard work and devotion to serving in the Lord's way. My companion for over thirty years, Patricia, has been the inspiration to seek the best things in life and beyond. Her support has given me confidence to experiment and move on to new challenges in advancing from mediocrity to something special. My four children have taught me patience and understanding of what truly matters in life. To each of these choice people I say, "Thank you!"

With the support of staff, Tracey Hogan, Fran Leavitt, and Ed Vachal, in transcribing and preparing the manuscript, this book has become a reality. I am indebted to Bobby Hasselbring for her editing talents and support.

To the reader, I hope you catch the vision of the Fast-Track concept and can move the true value and importance of the Quality improvement from the head to the heart. I wish you well as you advance your organization to World Class.

Roger Tunks, President
The Richard-Rogers Group, Inc.
Portland, Oregon

PART 1

A Place for Fast Track

This first section of the book is about the principles of Total Quality Management (TQM) and what Quality advancement can do for your organization. Typically, people make the concept of TQM more complicated than it has to be. Common sense says that customers want Quality products and services. TQM delivers that Quality in a cooperative and consistent way through an organization's employees.

After reading this section, you should be able to describe:

1. What the Fast-Track Method to Quality is and is not.

2. What being a TQM organization means.

3. The benefits of being a TQM organization and its application in your company.

4. How much poor Quality is costing your company.

5. How to define, and who defines, Quality products and services.

6. How organizations change.

1
Fast Track...
the Right Track

When someone describes a process as being "Fast Tracked," the phrase that comes to mind is "quick and easy." It sounds good. But Fast Tracking does not mean leaving something out; that is "Short-Cutting." So when I describe the process of Fast Track to Quality, let it be very clear that I am in no way suggesting any short-cuts or that you are to leave anything out. Short-cuts are not what I am talking about.

What I am talking about is a more efficient way to achieve the desired outcome of Quality improvements with measurable results and in less time.

The concept of Fast Tracking originated years ago in the building industry. Under the previously accepted building practices, complete sets of plans were prepared prior to beginning construction. Every detail was worked out in the planning process to meet the expected needs of the customer. Once the plans were completed, they were signed off by the customer and the construction would begin. This planning process could take years and frequently got bogged down in the complexities of predicting needs and responses to the many variables. Costly change orders, brought about by the changing needs of customers and planning errors, became commonplace. Something was needed to break old thinking, something that would get the job done without incurring so many errors, something that would speed up the process.

The Fast-Track process was born and the building industry was never the same. According to this method, first the basic requirements for the building are defined, i.e., number of floors required, use for each floor, and necessary space requirement for each function. Then the foundation is designed and construction begins. While the site is prepared and the foundation is being constructed, the planning proceeds with the floor design and layout. While the floors are under construction, the utilities are designed. As each phase is constructed, the next is being designed.

It's easy to see how, under the Fast-Track system, months and in some cases years are shaved off the design/construction schedule. Not only is the end result a completed building constructed much quicker, but the planning process becomes more visual for the customer and for the designers working together on the way to the finished construction. The final benefit of Fast Track is a lower error count, which reduces cost.

The benefits of applying the Fast-Track method to other types of organizations are basically the same as in the construction business: faster, almost immediate, results; fewer errors; reduced cost; and ultimately more satisfied customers. Also, Fast Track can bring you and your organization the benefits of Quality advancement that are actually measurable in dollars.

Many managers have envisioned these benefits, but they are frustrated with the "how-to's." Much is written on the "why" and "what" to do. Many of the same managers know that the process and techniques associated with Quality improvement have been around for years. Now, however, a refined and proven technology utilizing the same Fast-Track techniques that revolutionized the construction industry is available to develop Quality-driven organizations. This process clearly provides the all-important "how-to's" to develop a successful Quality-driven organization.

Fast-Track Tip 1

The processes and techniques associated with Quality improvement have been around now for many years. Fast Tracking sets new priorities and eliminates the processes that waste time and resources.

Unfortunately some of the techniques still being applied to advance Quality in American industry are just plain trash. For example, I recently visited a senior manager of an organization who had embarked on a Quality improvement process eighteen months earlier. He described a scenario I have heard many times over the past few years. They began their Quality process by sending three of their respected managers for instruction in "Quality Advancement." They were to learn how to train other managers and employees in Quality-related concepts. After five days of training, they purchased several hundred course manuals for their managers and employees. Then they conducted multiple training sessions throughout the organization. As expected, some managers caught the vision of the Quality concept better than others and promptly took action to make Quality improvements. Does it sound good so far?

Eighteen months later, their program was barely a memory and, for many, a bad one at that. To date they've spent more than $50,000 in direct costs for trainer training, travel expense, manuals, and on-site consulting. I asked the penetrating question, "What have you received from your investment of money and time?" The room became very quiet. Finally, they told me they planned a management meeting in a few weeks to review the progress and results of their Quality Program. After this update meeting I was told they were able to document less than $20,000 in annualized performance improvements and no evidence that customer satisfaction was improved. This is after more than eighteen months of effort.

What went wrong? Everything! Every principle associated with the Fast Track to Quality method had been violated: commitment and involvement of senior management were missing; leadership capability was missing; and finally senior managers lacked a vision of what Quality improvement is all about.

In direct contrast, another organization invested $20,000, applied the Fast-Track method—and demonstrated more than $500,000 in annualized performance improvements, along with an 8% expansion of their customer base all within six months. Still another organization applying the Fast-Track method recorded over $4,000,000 in annualized performance improvements in only six months, with an investment of less than $100,000. All these facts and figures can perhaps best be summed up by one of the company presidents who said, "What a return on investment!"

The Fast Track to Quality process is proven. It works. It produces quick and measurable results to confirm advancement in product and service Quality to the customer.

Ten Principles to Fast Tracking Quality Improvement

The Fast-Track method is based on ten principles for fast, effective, and efficient Quality improvement. The principles are not just a description of the method, but the very foundation of what makes the process work. Power is a function of applying leverage where it will do the most good. Violate any one of the ten Fast-Track principles, and the process loses leverage, reducing or even losing the benefits.

REQUIREMENTS FOR FAST TRACKING

_____ 1. Involve the maximum number of managers and employees in every key action along the way.

_____ 2. Be clear, and frequently communicate to all employees and customers your motive, intent, and progress in developing a Quality-driven organization.

_____ 3. Clarify and define every manager's, supervisor's, and employee's role in the Quality process.

_____ 4. Frequently communicate realistic expectations to employees, and hold people accountable for their achievement.

_____ 5. Focus on changing how the organization conducts business and not on changing the people.

_____ 6. Celebrate major successes and recognize personal and group accomplishments for exceptional achievements.

_____ 7. Demand that every manager and employee knows who his/her customers are and their expectations.

_____ 8. Empower employees to meet or exceed customer expectations.

_____ 9. Strengthen the Quality of management before trying to manage Quality.

_____ 10. Establish accountability at all levels to ensure that the principles are being consistently applied.

Individually, each principle is simple. Combined and consistently applied together, they become the Fast-Track Method to Quality.

I take care not to call the principles in the Quality improvement process "steps." The word steps implies a sequence of events with a beginning and an end. In contrast, "key actions" are important accomplishments along the way that are often repeated many times for continuing success. The journey to Quality with the Fast-Track Method certainly has a beginning, but it has no end. To continually compete and be successful in meeting your customers' expectations requires ongoing effort in becoming better and better at what you do.

Fast-Track Tip 2

Use the ten principles of Fast Tracking to Quality as a checklist to confirm your understanding and direction in leading for Quality advancement.

Small Differences Make a Big Difference

In life, a small difference can make a significant impact on an outcome. An example is a thousandth-of-a-second difference in the outcome of a race or a decimal point in a check register. This is equally true in developing a Quality-driven organization. Small differences can and do make a significant impact on the success. Some of the differences are subtle and even hard to detect, but they still exist and have direct impact. The application of the ten principles adds the leverage in which small differences make the difference.

2
Understanding the Quality Initiative

Becoming a first-rate Quality-driven organization is serious business. It requires thoughtful and careful planning at all levels. As CEOs lead their companies into the twenty-first century, the decision to become a Quality-driven company may be the most critical and difficult one they'll ever make.

Four Obstacles to Quality Advancement

Four obstacles lie along the path leading the way to Quality improvement. All of them involve the attitudes many managers have about Quality.

1. The first and perhaps most pervasive obstacle is the limited under-standing most managers have about Quality improvement and how it relates to organizational effectiveness. Over the past few years, there have been many remarkable Quality success stories. Unfortunately, there have also been many dismal failures. Too often, managers draw all of their information about the Quality initiative from the failures, without ever really finding out what leading for Quality involves or how it can help their organizations.

2. The second obstacle involves believing the naysayers who call leading for Quality a fad, cult, or even a religion. While they shake their heads and joke about Quality leadership, their competition is quietly moving ahead and proving them wrong. As any manager knows, once a company falls behind, it becomes difficult, if not impossible, to catch up.

3. The third obstacle to Quality exists because many managers are short-sighted, believing that Quality improvement processes relate to a "special program." The danger in referring to Quality improvement as a "program" is that all programs have a beginning and an end. They are admitting before they begin that there will be an end to Quality improvement. In truth, Quality improvement is a never-ending journey, a continuous process of becoming better and more competitive.

4. The fourth obstacle to overcome is the narrow vision of viewing Quality improvement only as a management system of statistical process controls (SPC). While statistical measurements become an important element of Quality, they are only a part of the process of leading for continuous Quality improvement.

Overcoming these four obstacles to leading for Quality improvement involves knowledge and understanding on the part of managers. The common denominator for success and/or failure among companies that have employed Quality management is the extent to which the managers at all levels understand, commit to, and become involved in the Quality process. I have counseled many managers by telling them, "Success occurs because it is planned and prepared for." And so it is with Total Quality Management (TQM). Quality planning begins with a thorough understanding of what Quality improvement is about and how to apply the necessary leadership skills.

Simply put, Quality improvement is an overt way of consistently leading people. It is not a "system" or a "program." It is certainly not a "fad." It requires changes in leadership methods that are based on proven technologies. When effectively installed and utilized, leadership for Quality can advance organizational success despite today's keen competition and often shrinking markets.

So...What's Different?

Becoming a Quality-driven organization and consistently applying Quality improvement processes requires an understanding of what drives Quality in an organization. Clearly and without question,

> Quality improvement is a leadership issue—not an employee issue.

If Quality were an employee issue, management would simply have to get out of the way and Quality would improve. Of course, in some companies where there is poor leadership, this may be the best solution. But regardless of whether management is good or poor, Quality improvement is still a leadership issue.

Leading for Quality is truly a different management philosophy than we typically find in American business. Continuous Quality leadership embodies a different mindset about how leadership is applied, particularly in setting organizational direction and the ordering of priorities. It is a unique way of running a company. *In leading for Quality, management puts Quality on an equal priority footing with cost and schedule.*

Making Quality as important as cost and scheduling is a major change for managers driven by the bottom line. They may know the right words to describe the importance of Quality, but their behavior frequently does not put it on the same par as expenses and delivery. Their attitude is, "Quality is important, but. . . ." The "but" becomes an excuse for sacrificing Quality for cost and schedule. Keeping costs down and being on time have little value if Quality is missing.

In contrast, when managers catch the vision of how Quality improvement can benefit their company, they behave and apply leadership differently. They become actively involved in developing an organizational culture in which every action and process is under scrutiny to minimize or eliminate the cause of poor Quality.

Why Get Involved in Quality Improvement?

At a management training session on Quality improvement, Noel Watson, President of Jacobs Engineering in Pasadena, California, gave his senior staff this clear message: "There is only one reason for us to get involved in a Quality improvement process... money. Quality improvement will make it easier to sell our services to our customers and to expand our market share... and to make money."

Noel Watson's pronouncement is a simple and profound answer to the question, "Why get involved in Quality improvement?" He clearly understands his role as a corporate leader and his responsibility to the company's shareholders.

But other leaders offer different perspectives. The CEO of another service company said the purpose of applying Quality improvement principles in his company was "to build employee morale and create job satisfaction." Another leader said, "It's a matter of survival. Our competition has made marked improvements in their products. We must be even better."

Which executive is right? Should a company invest in Quality improvement for money, for staff morale and job satisfaction, or for staying competitive—perhaps for all three? Certainly Quality improvement can improve revenue, market share, and customer and employee satisfaction.

For many CEOs, revenue generation and survival become immediate and overriding concerns. Why else might you become involved in Quality improvement?

Think about the question, rephrased: "Why should your company get involved in a Quality improvement process?" Whatever reasons you come up with, it's important that you be clear about your motives in initiating a Quality improvement process. A questionable or poor reason makes it difficult to get others to buy into the process.

Fast-Track Tip 3

Be clear about your reason or purpose in getting involved in the Quality advancement process. Communicate your purpose to your staff clearly and frequently.

Total Quality Management (TQM): What Is It?

Total Quality Management (TQM) emerged in 1988 as a generic title for the process of Quality improvement. (Throughout this book, I'll use the terms "Total Quality Management," "TQM," "Quality advancement," and "Quality improvement" interchangeably.) But what does the phrase really mean? As the words imply, TQM is a way of managing an organization; it describes the processes and interventions that continuously support Quality improvement.

Most companies adopting TQM establish their own title or acronym for their Quality improvement process. It gives the company "ownership" of the process and removes the "not invented here" resistance. But be careful about making up a name. One company, in their zeal to establish their own Quality identity, adopted the title Quality Advancement Process or QAP. If you say QAP a few times to yourself out loud, you'll soon see, as did the company, that the acronym had a problem and had to be changed.

Regardless of the title your company uses, including the word "leadership," rather than "management," in the title probably better describes what is required for Quality improvement. After all, we manage things, projects, resources, and time. In direct contrast, we lead people. Leading people, not managing them, is what Quality improvement is about.

To understand and utilize TQM, we need to establish a common understanding of what TQM really is. Try the following complete, yet simple, Fast-Track TQM definition:

> Total Quality Management is the involvement and commitment of both management and employees to conduct business by consistently meeting or exceeding customer expectations.

This definition includes three important components:

1. Management and employees are directly involved and committed.
2. TQM is a way of doing business, not just a program.
3. The "target" of Quality improvement is the customer and his or her expectations.

Together, these components of TQM become a management philosophy or a management ethic. It becomes a way of describing how the organization functions internally to advance Quality.

Who Defines Quality?

What is Quality? Who defines Quality for your company's services or products? There's no question that as a consultant I should be the last person asked to define Quality for your company. By the same token, you as a manager of your company, even with all your experience and wisdom, are limited in your ability to define Quality. Certainly we can define parameters, standards, and our beliefs regarding Quality. But something is missing—the fact that the one you must please, the "king," is the customer. *Ultimately, the customer decides whether the Quality of a product or service is worthy of his/her hard-earned resources.*

Customers, in all businesses and industries, have the final say in defining Quality and in determining what they're willing to pay. A good example is the Yugo automobile. At one time, it was the lowest-priced new car in North America. The importer believed the low price would guarantee that they would sell every automobile they brought into the country. But the Yugo was a dismal marketing failure. It didn't take long for word to get around to prospective buyers that the cars had multiple defects and needed frequent repairs. The Yugo company and its importers learned a basic lesson: *Quality sells, not just lower cost.*

About the same time the Yugo was introduced, another new automobile, the Hyundai, made its appearance in showrooms. But the Hyundai is a success story. It sold well and is still selling. Why? The reason is that it is a Quality product in the eyes of consumers. The Hyundai's cost started at a modest level to catch the attention of the buying public and to interest them in the new, unfamiliar automobile. As the Hyundai market became established and matured with the automobile's proven Quality, the cost edged up to a level comparable to its competition. The message is unmistakable: Customers believe in Quality. They demonstrate it by what they are willing to accept and what they are willing to buy.

Fast-Track Tip 4

Don't try to define Quality. Look to your customers for the real definition of Quality in your products and services.

Who Are Your Customers?

Consider the question, "Who are your customers?" Both managers and employees are quick to describe the external customer, the one outside the company who receives the final product or service. It may be a government agency, a broker, a retailer, or perhaps the buying public. But the answer is only half correct. What about your internal customers? Every company has both internal and external customers. External customers are easy to define. They are the eventual users of your product or service outside of the company. Internal customers are a little trickier to identify. They are people within your organization who use your product or service as input for their own processes or services. They may be the purchasing department, the accounting department, the shipping department, or the next process in an assembly line that adds value to the product or service.

Internal and external customers define Quality in the context of what they are willing to accept. In working to meet or exceed customers' expectations, companies must be concerned with both external and internal customer needs and expectations.

But how do you know what your customers want? The easiest and most effective way is to ask each customer. The difficulty comes in quantifying customer expectations so that measured progress can be made in meeting those expectations. This is a skill in itself and will be covered in detail in Chap. 10.

The Three Dimensions of Quality

Put yourself in the role of customer, the purchaser of a product or service. What do you look for when you're assessing a possible purchase for Quality? My staff and I have asked that question to thousands of managers, employees, and consumers. We've narrowed the responses to three major descriptors that customers look for to achieve satisfaction:

1. Fit for use

2. Defect-free

3. Perceived Quality

Test each dimension from your own experience, and see how closely they fit your requirements for Quality.

Descriptor 1: Fit for Use

"Fit for use" means the service or product performs as expected immediately after purchase and throughout the extended life of the product. If the product meets this expectation, the customer will probably say the product has Quality. For example, a customer purchases a new knife to cut vegetables and fruit. In the beginning, the knife cuts almost any food item and can be described as "fit for use." As time goes by, the blade becomes dull and the knife is unable to cut tomatoes without squishing them. From the customer's perspective, the knife has lost its fitness for use. The longer the knife retains a sharp edge and is fit for use, the higher the Quality is in the customer's view. Any product or service that is successful must be viewed by the customer as fit for use—and the longer the better.

Descriptor 2: Defect-Free

Often when people hear the word "defect," they think we're talking only about manufacturing. Not so! The word "defect" is a descriptive way of referring to an error, a mistake, or failure in any industry. Consumers begin with the expectation that a product or service they purchase will work every time with no exceptions. Industry would call this condition "defect-free." What the customer doesn't see is the number of products reworked or rejected by the manufacturer before the "defect-free" product or service reaches them.

External customers define Quality as zero defects, both in extended use and in deterioration of appearance. In other words, a Quality product is expected to work correctly for an extended period of time and continue to look good during its service life.

For the internal customer, the expectation of zero defect should be the same. Of course, the reality may be different from the expectation. In most companies, individuals or work teams pass on a small percentage of defects. The problem is that the small number of defects becomes compounded. If five production teams pass on only 1 percent of defective work, the 1 percent has multiplied to a 5-percent defect rate. Now, with a 5-percent level of defect, do we have a Quality product? Truly any defect suggests questionable Quality.

Fast-Track Tip 5

The word "defect" is a descriptive way of referring to an error, failure, or something broken without placing blame. The word "mistake" draws the question, "Who did it?" Change your language and begin using the term "defect" in conversations with your staff and colleagues. The change will foster cooperative solutions to problems without placing blame.

Descriptor 3: Perceived Quality

Customer perception is the most elusive and difficult dimension of Quality to define. Perception is in the eye of the beholder and is driven by each individual's personal value system. At best, perceptions can be categorized rather than quantified because the calibration of a "scale" of perceptions is at best fuzzy.

A friend has a business appraising and setting precious stones for retail jewelers. When asked how he values diamonds, he likes to pull out two stones that are identical in size and cut. One diamond is worth $4,000; the other $2,500. Which one is the higher quality? As an untrained gemologist, I can only hold each up to the light. Both look the same, but which is the higher quality? For me, it's a guess. A trained gemologist can easily use an eye piece to examine each stone for clarity and color and to confirm which is the more valuable diamond.

Which diamond would you buy? Given that they appear the same, most people would say the less expensive stone. For them, small imperfections that do not affect appearance do not affect the Quality. Yet some people would purchase the higher-grade stone for its clarity and brighter color as reported by the gemologist. Why? For some people, the clarity and brightness represent Quality, and they're willing to pay for it. It's a difference in the perception of Quality. For any manager to advance their success the message becomes obvious: *Clearly understand the perceptions of your target customers.*

Fast-Track Tip 6

Memorize the three dimensions of Quality:
    Fit for use
    Defect-free
    Perceived Quality
    Use these dimensions in your language as you discuss Quality with your staff and your customers.

The Quality Advantage

Quality improvement processes that produce products and/or services that meet or exceed customers' expectations will have a direct impact on your organization's success. Fast-Track TQM improvement can impact at least the following six areas:

1. **Increased customer satisfaction:** Since Quality is designed for the customer's benefit, the result of all Quality improvement processes is ultimately increased customer satisfaction. However, one danger in working for customer satisfaction is that you could "give away the store" to some customers, and they still might not be satisfied.

How far to go in meeting or exceeding customer expectations is a tough question. If you meet their expectations and even exceed them by a small margin, is this enough? Certainly you've satisfied the greatest percentage of customers, but what about the others? What about the relatively small percentage of customers whose needs go unmet? What should be done to satisfy them?

This last question goes to the heart of Total Quality Management. The answer is that you go a step further. You seek to build customer satisfaction in all customers, even in the small percentage who are especially demanding. In TQM, every customer receives services and products that exceed their expectations. They receive services and products that surprise and delight them. In TQM, there's no "yes, but." Simply put, TQM is about satisfying customers.

2. **Enhanced image and reputation:** It's important to clarify the distinction between image and reputation. Image is how the customer sees the company. Reputation is what they tell others about the company. If you have a choice between improving image or improving reputation, which would you invest in to enhance your success? Reputation, of course.

An example will convince you of this important difference. Recently, a large discount retailer spent millions of dollars refurbishing their stores with new lighting, shelving, floor plan, and decor. They hired television personalities and movie stars to present their products and their company in advertising. No doubt, their image as a successful retailer was enhanced. But what about their reputation in the marketplace with consumers? Customers still complained about the difficulty in finding sales help. If they found a clerk, the service was hostile or indifferent. The store's return policy was still a bureaucratic nightmare. Although millions of dollars had been spent to improve the company image, little or no change was made in affecting what customers told others about their shopping experience.

In contrast, a prominent grocer in Alaska directed the company's resources to improving the reputation of their retail stores. Every employee was trained in ways to serve their customers. Displays were rearranged more attractively and more practically on existing shelves. Product Quality was increased through joint efforts between the company and its suppliers. The store image wasn't changed appreciably, but its reputation underwent a complete transformation! People talk about the courtesy of the staff, the excellent service, the fresh produce. Stories are told about produce managers tossing out wilted lettuce and air freighting fresh lettuce for next-day display to ensure customer satisfaction. With this kind of reputation, it's easy to project an increase in repeat and new customers.

3. **Increased customer loyalty:** Organizations earn customer loyalty through the consistent efforts of every employee to satisfy customers. Loyalty translates into trust in the eyes of customers who consistently have their expectations met for Quality products and services. The unspoken customer message is clear: "I trust that you will continue to provide Quality service and products. If you violate that trust, I will go somewhere else." While this may sound harsh, it is the reality of customer loyalty. Customers who experience Quality products and service will return time and time again, even to the point of going out of their way. Such customers become more forgiving of occasional "human errors" that occur in every business.

How do you create internal customer loyalty? The central issue is still trust. Internal customers may not have the option of going elsewhere for the product or service they need. But they can sabotage products or processes, or they can increase their inspections to make the provider look incompetent. Relationships become adversarial. It becomes a game of "gotcha." In contrast, internal customers who receive Quality products and service develop high levels of loyalty and trust. The need for constant inspections decrease, and relationships within the workplace become more positive and cooperative.

4. **Higher productivity levels:** As employees become partners in TQM, productivity automatically increases. Does this sound too good to be true? With Quality services and products, there is less rework and delays. When every process is completed right the first and every time, wasted time doing rework is minimized or completely eradicated.

5. **Improved employee morale:** A fundamental part of TQM is increased employee participation in work-related decisions. This helps unleash the creative and technical potential of employees. They have a greater sense of control and enjoy the satisfaction of helping improve their company. They are empowered to become actively involved in identifying and solving work problems. As employees become partners in improving the Quality of products and services to customers, their job satisfaction and morale naturally increase.

6. **Greater profitability:** TQM increases productivity, accountability, and commitment at all levels in an organization. The reductions in errors, rework, waste, and inventory shrinkage show directly in the bottom line as greater profitability. As profits increase, they can be distributed to shareholders, passed on to customers, or used to expand products/service capacity.

Most managers would be pleased to have any one of these six benefits of TQM. With the Fast-Track method for Quality improvement, you can have all six. Using Fast Track to Quality unleashes unlimited creative power in your employees and provides you with a distinct advantage over the competition.

Fast Track at a Glance

✔ The decision to become a TQM-driven company may be the most critical and difficult one senior management can make.

✔ Four attitudinal obstacles lie along the path to TQM: (1) limited understanding about TQM; (2) believing TQM is a fad, a cult, or a religion; (3) seeing TQM as a short-term program; and (4) viewing TQM only as a system of statistical process controls (SPCs).

- ✔ TQM is not a program, but a different way of doing business on an ongoing basis.
- ✔ Quality improvement is a leadership issue, not an employee issue.
- ✔ Quality must be as important to management as cost and schedule.
- ✔ Be clear about the reason or purpose for getting your company involved in TQM.
- ✔ TQM is a way of managing an organization whose processes and interventions support continuous Quality improvement.
- ✔ Total Quality management means managers and employees are committed and involved in consistently meeting and/or exceeding customer expectations.
- ✔ Customers define Quality.
- ✔ Every organization has both internal and external customers. Both types must be satisfied.
- ✔ Quality has three dimensions: (1) fit for use, (2) defect-free, and (3) perceived Quality.
- ✔ Fast-Track TQM can impact six areas: (1) increased customer satisfaction; (2) enhanced image and reputation; (3) increased customer loyalty; (4) higher productivity levels; (5) improved employee morale; and (6) greater productivity.

3

Is Quality for You and Your Organization?

I often begin my Quality training seminars by testing the audience to ensure their openness and readiness to examine the Quality process. The test centers around four premises. If they respond with a "yes" to each premise, they are ready to examine the Quality process and begin planning for change. A "no" answer to any of the premises indicates a block to Quality in the manager's personal value system.

Take a moment to test your own beliefs about the value and importance of Quality improvement. "The public" described in each premise is the end user or external customer.

Premise 1: The public wants Quality products and services, and they are willing to pay more for them.

With a few exceptions, most managers quickly agree with this premise. "Yes, of course, people want and even demand Quality products and services," they say. However, the real test is in the statement, "Are they willing to pay more for quality?" Perhaps a more accurate response is that people generally want and will buy the highest Quality they can afford.

Premise 2: A Quality emphasis reduces waste, rework, and expense.

Again, we usually get a big "yes" from both manufacturing and service industry managers. In manufacturing, performing each process correctly the first and every time certainly takes away the need for rework. Without rework, wasted material, time, and labor are all minimized. (It's important to point out that the waste is not at zero, but it is minimized.) Of course, the key to waste, labor, and time reduction is performing each process correctly every time. Any variance from this standard will produce the need for additional rework, waste, delays, and ultimately increased expense.

A former client who produced flexible sealing compounds had a 40-percent material waste problem. Forty percent of all the product they produced had to be discarded because of errors in accurately mixing chemicals. The cost was actually even higher because they had to reconstitute the defective product so that it could be disposed of safely. Even with this high level of waste and the associated costs, the company was able to achieve a good return on investment for their stockholders.

The opportunity for increased profit and market share, however, by controlling their errors and waste problem was clear. By becoming involved in a Quality Improvement Process, this company, in one year's time, was able to reduce their waste from 40 percent to 31 percent, nearly a 10-percent improvement. And they're still improving! Clearly, the management of this company recognized the need for, and the benefits of, Quality improvement. The struggle was in how to make it happen. TQM principles provided the technology to overcome a vexing problem of Quality improvement.

Service industry companies are equally challenged with minimizing rework and associated costs. A client in a financial institution was confronted with a tremendous amount of rework in processing home mortgages. Before sending the completed paperwork to the escrow offices for the purchaser/seller signatures, their final inspection revealed rework was needed in 68 percent of their documents. While the rework took place, the company and its customers incurred needless delays and expenses. After applying the Fast-Track process to Quality improvement, the company was able to reduce its defect rate to 7 percent in a matter of months. While this isn't defect-free, they're continually working to achieve zero defects.

Premise 3: A Quality emphasis improves service, image and reputation, employee morale, and profits.

Image: Imagine how satisfying it would be to deliver a product or service defect-free every time and on time—not only defect-free on delivery, but defect-free as intended for years to come. The customer's view of the company would certainly be positive. If this were a consistent experience by every customer, imagine the positive *image* (how customers view the company) and *reputation* (what customers say to others about the company) it would create.

Reputation: A good example of how Quality enhances reputation is the recent increase in warehouse-styled grocery retailers. Their image is austere, with concrete floors and open ceiling rafters. It's certainly not the glitter and glamour of a shopping mall decor. Yet their reputation is positive. After shopping in the warehouse setting, people say that the products are of good Quality and priced less than at local grocery stores. They say little about the image or setting because the Quality products and low prices override the austere setting.

Employee morale: Quality increases employee morale because everyone likes to be a winner. Winning teams generate high morale.

Profit: If we combine premise 2 (A Quality emphasis reduces waste, rework, and expense.) and premise 3 (A Quality emphasis improves service, image and reputation, employee morale, and profits.), we can graphically show the full impact of applying a Quality emphasis in Fig. 3.1.

Premise 4: Successful Quality improvement processes increase employee productivity.

I've saved the most difficult premise for last. Typically, industrial engineering, work simplification, and system analysis interventions focus on increasing the productivity of employees. The emphasis is on getting more work produced with less resources expended. For employees, the perceived motive is "you want me to work harder." That's not a very popular position in today's labor market.

In contrast, Fast-Track principles bring an alternative that employees quickly accept and even seek out. *With Fast Track to TQM, employees*

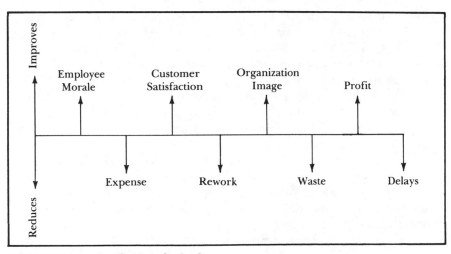

Figure 3.1. What Fast Track to Quality Impacts

1. Less rework is required by "doing it right the first time." More units are produced in the same time frame.

2. Employee morale improves through the elimination of rejected work and the associated worker discouragement.

3. Employees take personal initiative to look for ways to improve the Quality of work produced.

4. Employees enjoy greater self-esteem through personal and group recognition of their accomplishments.

Figure 3.2. Fast Track increases employee productivity

increase their productivity because they want to. They see that Quality improvement makes their jobs easier.

Quality improvement process increase employee productivity as outlined in Fig. 3.2.

If you had any doubts about finding value in applying TQM principles, I hope they have vanished. The message of Fast Track to TQM is logical and simple: *If you do it right the first time and every time, and if you consistently meet or exceed the expectations of internal and external customers, improved productivity is bound to follow.*

Is TQM the Right Business Issue?

Every organization can benefit from the application of Quality improvement principles. (I believe this statement to be a given.) But not every organization should embark on a proactive process to improve the Quality of its products or services. Why not? The issue has to do with timing or organizational readiness.

At a management forum, Marty Goldberg, Director of Organizational Development at Imperial Bank in Los Angeles, offered this insight into the importance of organizational readiness: "Managers should only embark on Quality improvement when it is the right business issue." This is sound advice, but how do you know if it's the correct business issue for your company?

I frequently give the test in Fig. 3.3 to CEOs and presidents to help them decide if Quality is the right business issue for their companies. Test yourself, and assess your company's readiness to embark on a course leading to major Quality improvement.

The first seven items relate to the need for Quality improvement as a business issue. If you answered "yes" to each of these items, it makes sense from a business perspective to seriously consider incorporating Quality

Write "yes" for statements that are true for your organization, "no" for statements that are not true.

_____ 1. My company needs improved competitiveness in the market.

_____ 2. Customers are talking about and requesting Quality improvements.

_____ 3. Material waste and rework costs are too high.

_____ 4. Our image and reputation in the marketplace need improving.

_____ 5. We have too many delays in serving our customers.

_____ 6. Poor Quality is costing us too much.

_____ 7. Managers and employees recognize changes are needed.

_____ 8. One of my greatest concerns is our Quality.

_____ 9. Quality is as important as cost and scheduling.

_____ 10. Managers can make time to improve our Quality.

Figure 3.3. Test of readiness to embark on a Quality process

processes. Even one or two "no" responses raise serious questions about whether Quality improvement is the right business issue for your organization at this time.

The real test lies in items 8 through 10. They relate to how you personally rate Quality improvement as a methodology in leading your organization to increased profits and stability. Without a clear "yes" for each of the last three questions, the probability for success is questionable. A "no" for any of the three questions indicates that you have a questionable personal commitment to Quality improvement at this time. When you can give an honest "yes" to all 10 questions, Quality improvement is clearly a correct business issue for your organization.

Fast-Track Tip 7

Clarify the correctness of TQM as the right business issue for your organization. Confirm your personal commitment to Quality improvement, and proceed only when you are willing to champion the Quality cause.

Taking Your Company's
Quality Temperature

"It's easier to get where you want to go if you know where you're starting from." This adage applies well to Quality emphasis in your company. Determining where you are begins with establishing a benchmark, a reference point against which you can measure your progress as you move ahead. Fast-Tracking involves the Measurement of Quality advancement. It is firmly believed, "If you can't measure it, it can't be improved." You must always have a reference point to confirm change, up or down.

In the human body, the reference point is a temperature of 98.6 degrees. Any deviation either up or down is cause for concern. The greater the variance, the greater the concern. Without this benchmark, any point of measurement would only have value in comparison to other measurements. The benchmark establishes a point with which all other measurements are compared.

So it is with advancing the Quality in your company. A reference point is needed to confirm progress. A reference point also reflects *the present level of importance your management and supervisory staff place on Quality as a valued way of doing business*. It can also be described as the present "climate" in your organization toward Quality as a way of doing business.

Establishing a benchmark is not the same as measuring Quality. That comes later. The focus is to confirm the extent to which managers and supervisors overtly accept the responsibility of providing consistent Quality products and services as a way of doing business. Ultimately, their commitment to Quality is based on actions, not on words. Words express intent. Actions express commitment. Understanding your organization's climate toward Quality improvement provides insight into the organization's commitment and priorities.

On a periodic basis, a company's "temperature" should be taken to confirm the progress toward creating an organization in which every action supports the advancement of Quality improvement. In examining your company's present climate and in establishing a benchmark from which to measure progress, pay particular attention to the following three questions:

1. What is the present level of concern (with supporting evidence) that Quality is an important part of your company's business practices?

2. Who defines Quality in your organization, and to what degree are we meeting those expectations at any given time?

3. What actions lead or detract from Quality advancement in your company?

A minisurvey, taken from your management and supervisory staff, can be used to establish a benchmark of your company's present Quality climate. The instrument provided in this chapter examines the *actions* and *specific behaviors* of managers, supervisors, and employees. You can use it to provide a more objective way to quantify present behaviors that support Quality improvement and to periodically measure progress. Overt behavior can be measured and recorded for future comparison. It assesses "what is happening" instead of the usual "how people are feeling."

The following survey instrument was prepared for clients to easily confirm the present focus of management in applying the Fast Track to TQM principles in his/her organization. It is also used as a benchmark to monitor future progress in Quality advancement.

To support the integrity of the survey process, we provide written instructions that are read to each group prior to distributing the instruments for marking (see Fig. 3.4). The questionnaire is typically marked by all managers and supervisors, or by a sample of them in large organizations. Data can be established by division or level of management in the organization.

VERBAL INSTRUCTIONS FOR CLIMATE SURVEY

Each of you has had many opportunities to observe how the company is operating. You are asked to report those observations at this time. Please report your observations without judging the actions as good or bad, just what you have observed. Before you mark each question, be cautious about basing your response on a single incident. Keep your perspective to the big picture in how the organization generally operates. You will be asked to mark each question on a scale of 0 to 10, with a 10 rating being at the "fully" or "consistently" operating level; a 0 rating would be "not at all." Mark your score in the blank by each question. Take as much time as you need. There are no time limits. The first area to mark is your job classification on the line provided as "manager," "supervisor," or "employee." Are there any questions before we start? [Provide time to respond as needed.] Okay, proceed.

Figure 3.4a. Instructions for survey

COMPANY RATING QUESTIONNAIRE

Your present status: Manager ___ Supervisor ___ Employee ___

Instructions: Based on your observations, rate our company in each of the following categories on a scale of 0 to 10 (0 = "not at all," 10 = "fully" or "consistently").

____ 1. Our managers' daily actions reflect their involvement and commitment to consistently improve the Quality of our products and customer service.

____ 2. We determine the precise needs of our customers and frequently update our understanding of them.

____ 3. We consistently conform to our customers' needs and expectations 100 percent of the time.

____ 4. We achieve Quality improvement through "prevention" rather than "inspection."

____ 5. We consistently support our employees' endeavors to achieve Quality through training in areas of awareness, detection, measuring, and evaluation.

____ 6. Our company is always flexible in adapting to changes in our customers' needs and expectations.

____ 7. Our employees are regularly informed of the company's progress in meeting or exceeding customers' expectations.

____ 8. Every employee is committed and consistently takes action to meet or exceed customers needs and expectations.

____ 9. Employees receive recognition for their contribution to Quality improvements.

____ 10. Quality improvement is a goal every employee understands, supports, and works to achieve.

____ Sum of your scores

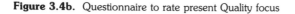

Figure 3.4b. Questionnaire to rate present Quality focus

A perfect score is 100 points, so that the sum scores can quickly be converted to percent scores. The average of the group can be computed by adding the sum scores and dividing by the number of tabulated surveys. The average score provides a simple, yet effective data point to compare present and future performance, and it can be used as a tool for explaining the need for organizational change in specific areas.

How Other Companies Stack Up

Nearly 40,000 managers and supervisors have answered the Quality survey over a two-year period. Participants have come from a variety of private industries and various governmental agencies. Analysis of the data has produced some insights that may be useful for your company. Compare your company's scores with the following:

1. The average of the sum scores from all participating managers and supervisors is 58.68. (With the exception of 125 managers, respondents marked the survey without any Quality awareness or skill training.) In each participating company, the individual score became the established benchmark for measuring future progress.

2. From a statistical standpoint, any variance in the pre- and post-testing larger than $+/-$ 4.34 points proved to be statistically significant.

3. There is no statistical difference between the responses of public and private sector companies. Eight or ten years ago, this may have been untrue, but with government agencies becoming more cost conscious and more accountable for demonstrating quantifiable results, the gap between the two worlds has narrowed. In addition to having to achieve the same or more with less, government agencies are feeling the competitive spirit of privatization.

4. We conducted a comparative analysis to determine if there were unique responses to particular questions by specific industries. Setting aside the statistical detail, question 1 ("Our managers' daily actions reflect their involvement and commitment to consistently improve the Quality of our products and customer service.") proved of particular importance. It's been repeatedly proven statistically that, in companies where the CEO and/or vice president of operations was directly involved in leading the Quality advancement process, average scores were consistently higher than in companies where this was not the case. Mid- and lower-level managers consistently supported the Quality process more when senior management was directly involved in leading the Quality improvement.

A new area of organizational research we are studying is the impact on Quality advancement in organizations having a senior manager appointed as Quality Manager versus organizations using the existing management structure to lead their units in TQM principles. Preliminary conclusions indicate that better results can be achieved *without a designated Quality manager*. It's easy to see why this might be so. Appointing a

Quality manager typically dilutes the focus of responsibility from every manager and supervisor to one individual. *The common denominator in Quality advancement success is that every manager and supervisor must be directly involved and accountable for improving Quality.*

Fast-Track Tip 8

Be ready to show quantifiable "before-and-after" data on your Quality progress. Conduct a brief, semiannual climate survey with managers and supervisors to monitor behavior changes. Measured improvements in Quality will provide evidence to confirm advancements in organizational climate as Fast-Track principles are applied.

How Much Is Poor Quality Actually Costing Your Company?

The usual response to this question is "too much." But how much is "too much"? You can answer the second question only when you know the actual dollars involved. Let's go together through a process you can use with your senior staff that can not only open their eyes to the dollars lost due to poor Quality, but also demonstrate the real opportunity Quality improvement holds for increased profits and expanded market share. You can use this process to help change old attitudes and to build intrinsic commitment to Quality improvement at all levels.

As an example, I'll use a client in a service industry from a real-life situation. The company's revenues were $100 million with 250 employees working out of four geographic locations in the same state. We gathered 28 of the company's managers in a hotel conference room as part of a planning session to develop a master plan on how and where to lead for Quality advancement. (The master planning process will be discussed further in Chap. 9.)

Early that morning, I'd asked the company's president, "How much is the company losing because of poor Quality service?" Without hesitation, he said, "$20 million." I wrote the figure on a chart pad, but couldn't help noticing that many of the other managers were negatively shaking their heads and rolling their eyes. I intentionally let the matter drop, knowing the managers would continue to think about and discuss among themselves the president's $20 million figure. That afternoon, I put up the chart in Fig. 3.5. Not only does the chart break the cost of poor Quality into categories, it provides a structured thought process to examine costs within specific work units.

Following an explanation of the chart in Fig. 3.5, the group was divided into functional teams (i.e., marketing, finance, operations, administration, etc.). Each group was assigned the task of determining the actual dollars spent or lost due to poor product or service Quality in their functional area, and to provide examples.

After 20 minutes, the groups reconvened. I prepared a matrix on a chart pad and recorded their lost dollars data. The sum was $19.8 million! Without comment, I turned to the sheet with the president's $20 million figure, adding the figures and their sources. As might be expected, the room was very quiet. Then I asked them, "What is the message for your company?"

This group of managers came to their own realization that they had both the need and an opportunity for Quality improvement. In less than an hour after reaching that conclusion, these managers were exploring options in how to pursue Quality improvement. The seeds for individual commitment to Quality advancement had been planted.

THE COST OF POOR QUALITY

1. **Cost of appraisal:** These are costs associated with internal testing, monitoring, policing, inspection, supervision, and reporting.

2. **Cost of mistakes:** These are costs associated with defects produced during the manufacturing processes or in the preparation of the service to be delivered. These mistakes are mixed/repaired/rejected before delivery and unseen by the external customer. In the eyes of the external customer, the product or service is defect-free.

3. **Cost of failure:** These are costs associated with the failure of a product or service after it's been received by the external customer. Direct costs are for repair or replacement.

4. **Cost of lost business:** These are costs associated with not meeting external customers' expectations and their going elsewhere for the product or service.

5. **Cost of prevention:** These costs are necessary to ensure that work is correctly performed and consistently conforms to customers' expectations every time. Employee skill training is included.

Figure 3.5. The cost of poor Quality

You can follow this model with your own company. Try the exercise with your senior staff. One of the keys to facilitating this process is not to make declarative statements or critical judgments. Allow the group to explore and reach their own conclusions. The data they come up with will pack a powerful message. Remember, "If you have good data, the data will speak for itself." Let the data help your managers develop their individual and group commitment to do something about Quality. Let them answer the question, "What is the message for our company?"

Fast-Track Tip 9

Challenge your staff to determine the cost of poor Quality.

- Have each work unit put a dollar figure on the cost of appraisal, mistakes, failure, lost business, and prevention.

- Record and total the figures. Then ask, "What is the message for our company?"

Discuss each item, and challenge, "Is this acceptable?"

Quality for You and Your Company—It's Your Choice

By now, you've undoubtedly thought through the concept of Quality improvement and have reached some personal conclusions. Read the 10 statements in Fig. 3.6 that describe how Quality fits into an organization. See if they come close to your present views.

Fast Track at a Glance

- ✔ Management's beliefs about the value and importance of Quality have a direct impact on achieving Quality advancement.

- ✔ Before pursuing TQM, you must be sure that it is the right business issue for your company at this time.

- ✔ To know where you want to go, you have to establish a "benchmark," a point from which to measure your Quality advancement progress. The present level of importance that your management and supervisory staff place on Quality can be this reference point.

_____ 1. Quality begins with the direct involvement and commitment of senior managers to plan and direct a supporting leadership culture.

_____ 2. Quality is driven by indicators of customer satisfaction, both internal and external.

_____ 3. Quality requires the consistent conformance to customer needs and expectations 100 percent of the time.

_____ 4. Quality is achieved through prevention rather than inspection and correction.

_____ 5. Quality requires a labor force thoroughly trained at all levels in awareness, defect detection, problem solving, and measurement.

_____ 6. Quality requires continued flexibility in adapting to changing customer needs and expectations.

_____ 7. Quality is an attitude or state of mind in which every employee seeks to achieve his or her best.

_____ 8. Quality requires consistent conformance to defined behaviors by every employee.

_____ 9. Quality requires continual scrutiny and is measured to confirm advancement.

_____ 10. Quality requires the input from every employee to ensure continuous improvement.

Figure 3.6. Fundamental principles of Fast Track to TQM

✔ Periodically, take your company's "temperature" with regard to progress in advancing Quality.

✔ Give your management staff the observation questionnaire to monitor their Quality-advancing actions.

✔ Every manager in the organization must be directly involved and accountable for improving Quality.

✔ You should be able to calculate in actual dollars how much poor Quality is costing your company.

✔ Determining the cost of poor Quality must take into account the cost of appraisal, mistakes, failure, lost business, and prevention.

4

How Organizations Change

Becoming a Fast-Track TQM company requires change. Even if you're present Quality of products and services is high, there's always room for improvement. There will always be a competitor willing to deliver a product or service that is better. In the Quality game, you don't have to be sick to get better. But you do have to be willing to change.

Some companies pride themselves on consistency and lack of change. "It's always worked for us." While that kind of attitude may have worked 10 or 15 years ago, today's market expects and even demands change. Organizations unwilling to adapt to ever-changing standards and customer expectations are destined to become anachronisms, outdated and outmoded by competitors who stay on top of changing demands in the marketplace.

There's no question that change can be frustrating. But even worse is living with the results of no change. Like the adage says, "If I do tomorrow what I've done today, I'll have tomorrow only what I have today." A better tomorrow requires doing something different today. Change is about making a better tomorrow.

"Quality" as a Way of Doing Business

People talk about the "culture" of a society. What they are really talking about is how people live together. When we talk about an organization's culture, we are talking about how it conducts business. It's common to hear people talk about how difficult it is to change the culture of an organization. But it doesn't have to be difficult. *Change the way a company does business and you've changed the organization's culture.* This kind of change becomes even easier to envision when you break the company's culture into its subparts. Every organization's culture has subcultures, such as a social subculture, a service subculture, a leadership subculture, etc.

In developing a Quality-driven company, we are particularly concerned about the leadership culture, specifically how leadership can be applied in leading employees to produce Quality products and services every time. The emphasis on Quality must become embodied in the leadership culture in such a way that every operational process involved in providing a product or service is under scrutiny to make it the best possible. The ultimate aim is for Quality improvement to become ingrained in the organization as the driving force in how business is conducted every day. A step-by-step guide on the process of change and developing a Quality-driven leadership is included in Chap. 7.

Unfortunately, human beings are creatures of habit. We resist change even when it yields positive results. We love our old sneakers even though they're torn and leaky. We love the predictability of our routines. We embrace stability and predictability even when they're not good for us. It's as if there were some universal law to maintain the status quo. In this kind of stagnant, change-resistant climate, it shouldn't be a surprise that most managers and employees resist organizational change.

Start talking about change in your organization and observe what happens. While a few forward-looking managers embrace change, you'll find that most managers and employees are less receptive.

- "We've always done it this way. Why do we have to change?"
- "Just when I was getting to know this system, we're changing it again."
- "I think they change things just to hassle us."

People resist change because they're afraid. They fear what they don't know and what they don't understand. They fear what they can't control. They fear they might fail at something new. It makes perfect sense that your employees and managers will resist change. They fear it. To put it another way, "People are down on what they're not up on."

If people are "up on" change, they are less likely to fear and resist it. Managing for Quality means managing change by getting people "up on change." The ultimate goal, of course, is to develop employees to look for and even ask for Quality-enhancing changes. To that end, it's management's responsibility to help managers, supervisors, and employees understand:

- Why change is necessary.
- The benefits of the change.
- What's required.
- The likely outcomes.
- The kind of support they'll have making the change.
- The actual process of change.

Fast-Track Tip 10

Avoid the inevitable employee question, "Why is change needed?" by stating the need for change and backing up the statement with hard data. Instead of simply announcing the change in a memo or meeting, hold discussion groups to confirm staff understanding and acceptance of the change.

The two most critical factors in getting people to accept and embrace change are:

1. A clear understanding of the need for change.
2. A clearly defined process to make change happen.

If your employees and managers clearly understand these two factors, you'll have minimized their questioning and criticism.

Understanding the Need for Change

Perhaps the greatest challenge to change is answering that inevitable employee question, "Why do we have to change?" Failing to adequately address this critical question can sabotage your Quality improvement efforts and make it much more difficult for your staff to buy into Fast-Track TQM principles.

Change is usually stimulated by one of two factors:

1. A business crisis, that is, an event or events that are seen by management as hindering business.
2. A leader's vision of what an organization might be.

Crises as a Spur to Change

An event that causes a business distress in its ability to conduct business is a crisis that warrants change. The crisis may be a key employee who is lured away by a competitor, loss of trade secrets, new competition moving into the marketplace, or any number of similar events. Usually the force behind a crisis is external and beyond management's control. The change taken by the organization is reactive rather than proactive.

It's interesting that, during times of crisis, change becomes expected, even welcomed. Often managers and employees rise to the occasion and meet the challenge with enthusiasm. After successfully surviving the event, many managers and employees look back on it with pride and satisfaction. Later, they may even believe that they need another crisis.

A crisis can be valuable to an organization when it's turned into an opportunity. Too often, managers view crisis as a negative force for change. While management should not create such a situation to effect change, it's important to recognize the valuable opportunities in any crisis. Fortunately, the positives in many crisis situations often outweigh the negatives.

An example is the company that faced a business crisis when the local legislature was on the verge of passing laws that would have given a direct advantage to the competition in getting goods to market. Recognizing the threat, the firm's management and employees met and developed a unified argument to present to the voting public. Since their very livelihood was at stake, the company's management and employees worked together like never before. The result of their efforts was that the proposed laws were resoundingly defeated.

Perhaps even more important was the fact that the crisis unified the company's management and labor unions. By working together toward a common goal, the crisis became a positive by demonstrating how the two groups, often seen as adversaries, could work effectively together. Six months later, they were able to enter into a new labor contract with remarkable speed and satisfaction for all concerned. While the crisis was long past, the positive benefits of the experience will be felt by the company for years to come.

In another crisis situation, a company president was dissatisfied with the allocation of company automobiles. He realized the number of company cars used by managers was creating too great an expense. He also knew that taking away automobiles and replacing that perk with mileage reimbursement wouldn't be met with much enthusiasm. About the same time, the local economy went into a slump. Instead of moving ahead with the automobile policy change, the president decided to wait until the deteriorating conditions in the local economy became widely known by company employees. When he finally made the announcement regarding the automobile allocation, the managers clearly understood that the company had to make such changes in order to maintain operating stability. While his announcement wasn't met with wild enthusiasm, the managers clearly understood the "why" of the change and accepted it willingly. Timing for change is critical to acceptance and success.

The Power of a Leader's Vision

A second driving force for change comes from a leader's vision for the organization. Dissatisfied with the organization's current operating conditions or direction, the leader—the CEO, president, or senior officer—forms a mental picture, a vision, of where the organization could be and initiates changes to make that vision a reality. Unlike crisis-initiated change, a leader's visionary change is internal and within management's control. The key, of course, is management's ability to recognize the opportunity in the vision and to have the courage to go for it. The challenge becomes getting others to buy into that vision and to do the work needed to make the appropriate changes.

One of the most common mistakes visionary managers make is failing to clearly express their vision to others. Unless they are questioned or challenged, they keep their dream of what the organization could be to themselves. As I said earlier, "people are down on what they're not up on." For managers with vision, clearly describing their vision to others can prove to be key to an organization's successful change.

Fast-Track Tip 11

Be open and clear with others regarding your vision of the organization. Instead of spending time describing the "how-to's" of your vision, involve your staff in the development of a "how-to" plan.

Over the years, I've facilitated many planning and team-building retreats with senior managers. I always allow time for the senior executives to describe their vision of the organization and where they see it going in the upcoming few years. Usually the best time is in the evening after dinner, when everyone is relaxed and receptive. Before the event, I coach the presidents in how to express their vision for the organization. The key points in expressing a vision for the future are shown in Fig. 4.1.

- The business they are currently in and how that may change.
- Present and future opportunities for new markets.
- The current organizational structure and how that might change.
- Strategies the organization must consider in order to be successful 5 to 10 years from now.
- The critical issues that must be faced to remain competitive.
- The need for effective planning.
- Strategies for improving customer satisfaction.

Figure 4.1. Key points in describing the leader's vision

Generally, such sessions take one or two hours, including the discussion and question phase. But it's wisely invested time. Watching the energy level and enthusiasm of the audience rise as they gain new insights and understandings into the organization is very exciting. If the leader's vision is expressed clearly, managers typically begin taking notes and are soon caught up in the opportunities that change can provide.

Effecting Change Through a Leader's Vision

While crisis-oriented change is often a "seat-of-our-pants" kind of reaction, change stimulated by a leader's vision can be carefully planned. Three key actions are required to successfully effect visionary change:

1. A clear expression of the leader's vision.
2. Second party validation of the vision.
3. A clear explanation of the elements of change and employee involvement in that change.

1. Clear Expression of the Leader's Vision.   A leader's vision for an organization isn't a fantasy or fortune teller's tale. It's an intelligent picture of possibilities based on the company's capabilities and the leader's experience. It's a new definition of the business and how it defines success.

A CEO of a multimillion-dollar milk processing facility expressed his vision for the company this way: "We're going to become the best dairy in the industry." This brief, simply statement caused intense questioning and discussion by the company's managers. What does "best" mean? How should they go about achieving that? The leader's few words set in motion a change process that resulted in the managers' defining and creating a plan that had a profound impact on the company's service and product Quality.

Another business leader expressed his vision in a three-page document, which managers then reviewed and discussed. In both cases, the expression of the leaders' visions stimulated significant change. The length of the expression of the leader's vision is not important; it's how clearly others understand and accept the vision.

2. Second Party Validation.   Merely expressing a leader's vision, however, is not enough to effect acceptance for change. A second person, someone who has credibility with the managers and employees, can validate the leader's vision. Although a select few charismatic leaders do not require this second party validation for acceptance of their vision, they are rare.

The purpose of validation is to reaffirm to employees, middle management, and supervisors that the pending change is needed and is in their best interests. This second party validation reinforces credibility for the leader's vision and stimulates acceptance and support for the proposed changes.

Who validates the leader's vision is critical. The second party must be seen as a trusted colleague who has wide acceptance within the organization. This person may be a manager, a trusted employee, or even a respected consultant.

3. A Clear Description of the Vision.   A messenger describes the elements of change to employees in a way that is clear and understandable. Ideally, the best messengers are the leader and the trusted person validating the need for change, but others may also be able to carry the message. In addition to explaining the step-by-step actions of the proposed changes, this messenger must outline:

- Why the change is taking place.
- The employees' role.
- The benefits to be derived from the changes.

This step is more than important. It is vital. It takes time and shouldn't be rushed.

Example.   These three key actions—expressing the leader's vision, second party validation, and describing the elements of change—were successfully applied by Chrysler Chairman Lee Iacocca in his restructuring of the company in the late 1970s.

- Iacocca had a vision for the company.

- Congress became the validator by endorsing his vision with billions of dollars in loan guarantees.

- The messengers were the news media reporting on Chrysler's changes. In addition, Iacocca delivered the message by appearing in television ads explaining his vision and what the company was doing to make that vision a reality.

The American public was sold. They believed that Iacocca's changes were necessary and, more importantly, that the changes would be successful. They expressed their belief by buying hundreds of thousands of Chrysler K-cars, Iacocca's "Quality" car.

Would Iacocca have been as successful if any one of the key change steps had not been applied? What if Congress had not validated his vision with the loan guarantees? What if the powerful messenger of television hadn't been successfully employed? It's highly unlikely that Iacocca would have been as effective in making the sweeping changes he implemented at Chrysler. Consciously or not, Mr. Iacocca knew and applied the three critical steps for visionary change.

Fast-Track Tip 12

Apply the three key actions for visionary change:

1. Establish the vision.
2. Have a trusted person validate the need for, and the value of, the change.
3. Have an articulate messenger describe the change so that everyone understands the process.

Comparing Vision- and Crisis-Driven Change

Organizational change for Quality improvement can certainly come from either a crisis or a leader's vision. As I stated earlier, crisis change is reactionary because the motivating force is external. Companies who implement Quality-advancing changes only in response to pressure from the competition—to survive—are reacting to an external force. They are allowing external events to force change on them. Unless carefully disciplined, such reactive, crisis-motivated change can cause questionable results.

By comparison, visionary change is more proactive because it comes from an internal source. Instead of reacting to a negative external force, visionary managers see a brighter future for their company. They want to improve Quality because they want to be the best in the industry. This kind of visionary-motivated Quality-advancing change is more easily controlled and holds greater promise for enabling the company to offer higher-Quality products and services long term.

Establishing an Effective "Change Process"

While defining and confirming the "why" of change is critical, it's not enough. Change can be planned and prepared for to ensure success.

Managers can deal with change in one of two ways: They can play "catch-up" after the fact, or they can proactively plan for change. It's easy enough to project the outcome of change and the post-change situation. It's more difficult to define and plan the change process—how the change will actually take place. Skilled managers carefully guide change through a planned process that avoids, as much as possible, negative and sometimes intense reactions from employees.

Years ago, as a high school principal, I was confronted with a difficult situation involving a poorly performing teacher. The faculty recognized the problem and waited for me to do something. Many of them approached me privately, expressing their support for terminating or transferring the teacher in question. However, being young and unfamiliar with how to deal with the process of change, I had no idea what lay ahead of me. Clearly change was needed, but how to implement it? I held numerous discussions with the superintendent and legal counsel to establish a plan to terminate the teacher. I followed every legal action required to the letter and successfully terminated the teacher without challenge. Everything had gone according to plan except one glaring problem— negative staff reaction. I learned the hard way that *negative reaction to change almost always directed to the process and not the outcome.*

Fast-Track Tip 13

No matter how much agreement there is on the need for change, in the end there will always be criticism of how the change took place.

Criticism of how change takes place can't be completely eliminated, but it can be tempered. You can take several key actions to make the change process easier and to produce less negative reaction:

1. Pace the Rate of Change

Do you want evolutionary or revolutionary change? The difference is in the pace of the change.

A good example of evolutionary change was how the National Geographic Society changed the cover of National Geographic magazine. From 1910 through 1964, the magazine cover sported a border of leaves around the photograph or illustration. The editors decided to delete the leaves and change the border to the plain yellow we're familiar with on today's magazine. Sensitive to reader reaction, they decided to go slowly in making the change. The following issue appeared with a portion of the leaf border missing. Readers didn't notice the change. Every few months over the next few years, a portion of the leaves was removed. Finally, after many years, a yellow border was all that remained. It was a slow process, but it worked and didn't prompt negative reaction from readers.

While evolutionary change is like climbing an oak tree by sitting on an acorn and letting it grow, revolutionary change involves radical, sweeping changes that often stimulate intense emotional reactions.

At some point in the change process, you must decide on the rate of change for the organization and particularly how fast the employees in the organization can move. While there's no hard and fast rule for the "right" rate of change—it's an important consideration to keep in mind.

2. Avoid Questionable Change Methods

For more than 40 years, management studies and management experts have supported using a series of key actions to effect organizational change:

1. Establish a clear "mission statement" for the organization, and communicate it to all managers and employees. Include it in annual reports, employee handbooks, etc. Everyone should know and understand the corporate mission.

2. Involve managers in group planning and off-site team building sessions to stimulate direction and commitment.

3. Establish reporting relationships, with accountability for the achievement of the mission.

4. Use the preparation of a strategic plan as a vehicle to realign corporate thinking and priorities.

5. Conduct training to develop new and unified leadership and management skills to affect the planned changes.

6. Institute new processes to reinforce and even reward new behaviors.

As the Director of Organizational Development for Kaiser Permanente for 10 years and for many years as an independent consultant, I successfully used these accepted methods for organizational change. Many managers wrote letters thanking me for my guidance in helping them effect change in their organizations.

However, a few years ago, I stopped and took stock of these accomplishments with a critical eye. How successful were these methods in establishing long-term change? Frankly, I realized something was missing, an element from the change model that was inhibiting dramatic organizational change.

The generally accepted model of organizational change is based on several assumptions that:

- Attitudes drive behavior.

- Combined behaviors create processes.

- Proper processes will yield the expected results.

Graphically, the model looks something like that in Fig. 4.2. It sounds good and looks logical, but something is missing. The six actions for change described earlier focus on changing behaviors. *The assumption is that employee attitudes and processes can be changed by changing employee behavior.* What if this assumption is wrong? What else might we focus on to implement change? Certainly other options exist. You could focus on changing attitudes, on processes, or on applying new criteria to the results.

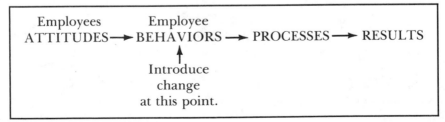

Figure 4.2. The traditional approach to change

Let's take a moment to examine these alternatives. Every manager knows how difficult it is to change attitudes. Changing attitudes about Quality is about as easy as changing long-held prejudices. Ask employees about Quality and they'll say, "We already do Quality work." They're insulted that you'd question their beliefs and performance supporting Quality. They become skeptical when you talk about taking action and making changes to improve Quality. At best, they'll see it as a "hot new program" that will be soon forgotten, much like Quality Circles, Management by Objective, and participative management.

As a high school principal in the late 1960s and early '70s, I was confronted with intense racial prejudice in a school with an evenly split biracial student body. Trying to educate students in this tense, inflammatory setting proved almost impossible. Although we tried everything to reduce the prejudice, the line was clearly drawn creating white and black sides of the school. The racial situation was so intense that basic education was nearly impossible. After two years of unsuccessful efforts to change prejudicial attitudes and behaviors, I tried a completely different approach. Teachers were instructed to stop talking about racial issues and instead to focus on the interactions between students in completing assignments in their areas of discipline. They were told to design projects and activities that would require the students to work together in groups or as a class. At each weekly staff meeting, the teachers reported on their projects and the results.

The test of our success took place in the cafeteria. For years, the cafeteria had a student-initiated black side and white side, with the middle isle acting as "neutral" territory. After several months, we began to see changes. First, a few black and white students would stand in the center isle and talk peacefully. By spring, they'd talk at tables, but always in the center of the room near the neutral zone.

What was different? I had unknowingly modified the change model to focus not on attitudes and behaviors, but on the *processes* of education. At the time, I called them "activities," but they were processes. I'd discovered an easy way to effect change that cost little to nothing and produced remarkable results.

Unfortunately, for the next 15 years, I believed the management professors and gurus about how change takes place in organizations. Like everyone else, I focused on changing behaviors. More recently, I "rediscovered" my more effective, Fast-Track change model and focused on process and not people. When I first started applying the Fast-Track change model (see Fig. 4.3), I stopped discussing skill development, new behaviors, catchy slogans, and mission statements to effect organizational change. Instead I emphasized processes. Now I encourage organizations

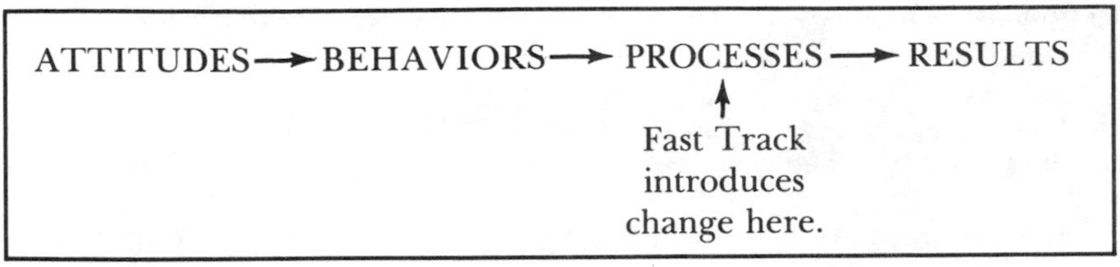

ATTITUDES ⟶ BEHAVIORS ⟶ PROCESSES ⟶ RESULTS
                                          ↑
                                    Fast Track
                                    introduces
                                    change here.

Figure 4.3. The model for Fast-Track change

to examine every process that affects results. Everything from management decision-making processes to key manufacturing processes comes under scrutiny.

Fast-Track Tip 14

To achieve dramatic, rapid organizational change, focus not on behaviors or attitudes, but on the processes that affect results. Change the processes, and you change the behavior and attitudes. Change the process, and you change the individual.

---

3. Use the Fast-Track Model for Change

The challenge in the Fast-Track organizational change model is to examine each process to see if it can be improved to better serve the organization. "What is best for the organization?" is a key question. By using the organization as leverage, no one takes the change personally and negative reactions can be minimized.

As you focus on changing the processes that affect results, changes in employee behaviors and attitudes automatically follow. As processes are improved to better serve the organizations, employee behaviors change to meet the challenge. Over time, as employees successfully apply new behaviors and skills to meet the requirements of process improvements, their attitudes change. Almost magically, employees become involved and even initiate Quality-enhancing changes to *processes*.

4. Use Process-Oriented Language

How does all this affect building a Quality-driven organization? It begins with changing the language you use to describe the process of advancing to Quality. The old way of describing Quality improvement might have sounded something like this:

> Over the next few years, our focus is going to be on improving the Quality of our products and services.

Here the focus is on *results*. Or it might be something like this:

> Quality is a function of everyone being the best at doing his or her job.

Here the focus is on *behavior*. Or how about this:

> Our goal is to strengthen everyone's commitment to Quality.

The obvious focus here is on *attitudes*.

By changing our language to focus on the *process* portion of the change model, manager and employee reactions will be much more positive than if the focus is placed elsewhere. Try these examples and see how you personally react to them:

> To advance the Quality of our products and services, we are going to examine each of the manufacturing processes.

> The highest priority to improve Quality of our products and services is to evaluate and streamline each of our manufacturing processes.

> Meeting our customers' expectations requires each process to be defect-free.

Notice the use of the words "process" or "processes" in each of the last three statements. The use of these words makes the issues clear and points to where the effort will be directed.

Implied in this language is an equally important shift away from personal performance to the systemic process that affects outcomes or results. Using the Fast-Track model for organizational change, the act of change actually becomes natural. Employees become actively involved in the change/improvement process. They recognize and take actions that improve not only the processes but also, ultimately, the Quality of your product or service. It is interesting to see how their behaviors and commitment change to support of the newly changed process they have helped create.

Fast Track at a Glance

✔ People are inherently afraid of change because they fear what they don't understand and can't control.

✔ If managers, supervisors, and employees know and understand the need for change and the process of change, they'll be less resistant and more accepting of it.

✔ Change is usually stimulated either by a business crisis or by a leader's vision of what an organization might become.

✔ Crisis change is external and less controllable. Visionary change is internal and planned.

✔ The three key actions to effectively convey a leader's vision to others include (1) a clear expression of the vision, (2) a second party validation of that vision, and (3) a clear explanation of the process of change and employee involvement.

✔ Effective organizational change requires a carefully planned process.

✔ To reduce negative reaction to change and to increase acceptance, (1) pace the change, (2) avoid questionable change methods, (3) focus on processes instead of on behavior, attitudes, or results, and (4) structure the language of the message to reflect the emphasis on process.

5
Understanding Your Customer

Managers embarking on Fast Track often ask, "Where should I begin?" A good place is with your external customer, the one who pays the bills and who is at the very heart of your success. As managers, supervisors, and employees come to understand and value external customers in the context of Quality, the efforts to make sure these customers are truly satisfied take on new meaning. Satisfied customers are particularly valuable because they express their enthusiasm and gratitude for exemplary products and service by telling others. People enjoy telling friends and loved ones about a wonderful product or a terrific service. When your customers' needs and expectations are met and exceeded, they'll go out of their way to tell others about your company and your company will succeed. Word of mouth is the best form of advertising for any business. Understanding your customers, their needs, and their expectations is a vital part of Fast Tracking.

Understand your customers by asking these five questions:

1. Who are your customers? While this may sound basic, it's amazing how few employees can identify customers by name.

2. What do you know about their needs and expectations?

3. How satisfied are they?

4. Can your organization become more responsive in servicing customers?

5. What actions are needed to improve customer satisfaction?

If you thoroughly answer each of these questions, you'll gain insight into your customers and how well you are meeting their needs and expectations. Asking these questions is an important exercise to use with your managers and employees. Most of them will say they know their customers, but their understanding is usually only cursory. It's much like an iceberg. You can see perhaps one-third of the iceberg above the surface, but two-thirds of it is hidden under water. On the surface, your staff may feel they know and serve their customers well. But if you challenge them with the preceding five questions, you'll find that they actually know very little about what their customers want and how to better meet and/or exceed their expectations.

Try a little experiment at your next staff meeting. Ask your staff the five questions about your customers. Go beyond the quick and easy surface answers. Encourage them to really explore and examine each question. When they think they have thoroughly answered the question, ask, "And what else?" The outcome of all your questioning will inevitably lead to their concluding, "We could do better," "We need to do more," or "We must improve the service to our customers." This is an important breakthrough with your staff. Ultimately, managers and employees must recalibrate their thinking in order to recognize that their products or services aren't as good as they ought to be or could be. They recognize that good can become better.

Fast-Track Tip 15

Be sure that you can answer these five critical questions:

1. Who are your customers?
2. What do you know about their needs and expectations?
3. How satisfied are they?
4. Can your organization become more responsive in servicing customers?
5. What actions are needed to improve customer satisfaction?

The final question becomes the power question, "What are we going to do about improving service to our customers?" The rest of this chapter can help you and your staff answer that all-important question.

Customer for Life

The owner of a large American automobile dealership in California once told me about his goal for each customer to become a "customer for life." He wanted every customer's experience with the products and service from his dealership to be so positive and so satisfying that each would return year after year to purchase a second, third, and fourth automobile. He wanted them to be so satisfied that they would not consider going to another dealership or buying a competitor's make of automobile. This manager was establishing an important value for guiding and building his organization into a true Quality company. "Customer for life" became a requirement to guide how he and his staff conducted business on a day-to-day basis.

I've since asked other managers about the concept of "customer for life." Test this challenging concept on yourself by taking the following measures.

- Ask yourself, "Would I be willing to work hard enough and make the changes in how business is conducted to create the kind of loyalty that would make customers for life?" If you could create lifelong customers, you could guarantee success regardless of your industry or product.

- Ask your staff, "What kind of service would it take for you personally to become a lifetime customer?" Use a chalkboard or chart pad to record their responses. Typical responses might include "courtesy," "good prices," "value for my money," "quality products," "easy return policy," and "personalized service." Push and encourage them to really think about this question. When they believe they've answered the question, keep asking, "And what else?" Remind them that they are talking about creating lifetime loyalty.

- Once they've created the list, ask, "How do we measure up on each item on the list?" Usually this question is first met with silence. Finally, someone will identify one or two areas in which your company or products can be improved. If you continue this discussion and really probe, your staff will uncover other areas that need improvement.

So what is the value of having these discussions with your managers and employees? For one thing, they help your staff begin to understand and value the concept of serving customers in creating lifelong customers. They also help clarify the action needed to build long-term relationships with customers. The results of these discussions can have a tremendous impact on your organization. If you can lead your staff to recognize the value and importance in creating customers for life, you'll have a guaranteed customer base. As any businessperson knows, it is easier to sell new products and services to established customers than it is to continually find new customers. In addition, your advertising costs will drop because advertising to a targeted audience is much less expensive and more effective than advertising to an undefined one.

Fast-Track Tip 16

Your service and products must be good enough to create customers for life.

Focus on Current Customers

Accept the challenge to understand everything you can about your customers—their background, expectations, how to meet their expectations, and what it would take to build their present level of satisfaction. Fortunately, for most organizations, getting to know the customer needs and expectations isn't an expensive proposition. Although, in a few instances you may need outside help, in most firms you can do it with your existing staff. While there are many ways to gain insight into your customer, the following four Fast-Track Key Actions are the most effective.

1. Mystery Shopper

Whether your product or service is distributed through a wholesaler or through retailers, mystery shoppers can become an important way to determine how your customers are being serviced. Usually, outside persons are hired to come into your company and act as if they were buying your product or service. They evaluate the level and courtesy of the service they receive based on criteria established beforehand. Afterward, the mystery shoppers prepare reports describing the results of their experience and rate it against the criteria.

Management in a large retail firm in the Dallas/Fort Worth area uses the mystery shopper technique on a regular basis. They hire professional mystery shoppers to travel from store to store, evaluating the service at each location. The mystery shopper reports are sent back to the store managers, who can then use the data to take appropriate action to improve service quality.

You can become a mystery shopper yourself via the telephone. The next time you call into your organization, listen critically and carefully. How was the phone answered? How courteous was the person on the other end of the line? If this had been the first time you'd called, would you want to do business with this organization again? One of the tragic mistakes many companies make is that they make the newly hired, least experienced employees the receptionists and expect them to meet customer needs and expectations.

2. Customer Questionnaires

At one time or another, most of us have had the opportunity to fill out a questionnaire regarding the service we've received. It's a common practice for restaurants in particular. Unfortunately, in many organizations, the customer questionnaire becomes so commonplace that the customers don't fill it out unless the service is extraordinarily good or poor.

The airline industry uses the customer questionnaire in a more focused manner. Instead of having questionnaires in all the seatbacks on every flight, they target particular flights, handing out questionnaires to each customer and asking them to evaluate the service. Airlines have the advantage that their "captive audience" has a considerable amount of time to mark a questionnaire. Most companies can benefit from a targeted questionnaire rather than a random approach to customer questioning.

One approach is to set aside a particular day or week to survey customers. The point is to have a focused time for customers to respond to questionnaires. In some companies, it's effective to mail questionnaires, and to have customers fill them out and return them. However, mailed questionnaires must compete with the other thousands of pieces of mail that people receive. It's often more effective if you can ask the customer directly to take the time to complete the questionnaire.

Whether direct or mailed, customer questionnaires can provide insight into your customers' expectations and how those expectations are being met. Determining customer expectations is covered in more detail in Chap. 10, "Quality Audits."

3. Customer Interviews

This technique is more time consuming, but it yields more information than questionnaires. Many customers are unwilling to take the time to write out answers to a questionnaire, but surprisingly they are often willing to be interviewed. Many customers are flattered by the personal nature of a face-to-face interview, and they will take the time to share their feelings and views about your service and products. These interviews can be on a random basis. When there are large numbers of customers, you can use sampling or enlist a research firm to collect data.

4. Focus Groups

This technique originated with marketing companies in an effort to bring customers and potential customers together to discuss their perceptions and expectations for new products. Based on information gathered in the focus groups, the company could then modify or change the product to better meet customer perceptions and expectations.

Focus groups can also be a valuable tool for assessing your present customer. Five to 10 customers come together for a joint, one- to four-hour discussion on a series of preplanned questions. Usually, you have to give the customers something in return for their time, such as a nice meal, a discounted service, or a free gift. Facilitating a focus group requires more than simple interviewing skills. The facilitator must be able to draw out ideas from the participants and record their ideas. He or she must keep the meeting from disintegrating into a "gripe session." The leader must balance the discussion between gaining insight into:

1. Customer needs and expectations.
2. How well the company is presently doing in meeting those needs and expectations.
3. Customer suggestions for improvement.

All of these four techniques—mystery shoppers, customer questionnaires, customer interviews, and focus groups—are valuable in gaining insight into your external customers. The real power comes from combining two, three, or all four techniques. At first you may think these assessment techniques are a waste of time. I assure you that they can provide meaningful information to improve Quality at all levels. Invest the time to get to know your customer with these tools, and you'll be sure of a high return on your invested time (ROIT).

Fast-Track Tip 17

The reward for spending the time getting to know and understand your customer is the ability to identify actions to take and increase customer satisfaction, heighten market share, and produce additional sales.

Understand Your Lost Customers

Anyone in business can tell you that finding new customers is expensive. Some experts contend that it is three to five times more costly to find new customers than it is to retain old ones. The four assessment techniques just described can be applied to understanding so-called "lost customers," people who typically don't complain but who simply disappear—taking their money with them. These customers are passive-aggressive. While they may leave passively, they're saying to themselves, "I'll fix you. I'll never come back."

In Fast-Track TQM, there are only two acceptable reasons that customers go away: They die, or they move away from the geographic area you serve. Even the second reason is questionable, since you can often continue serving customers in different locations. The absolutely worst reason they leave is dissatisfaction. If you use the four Fast-Track techniques to understand your customers, you will have the basis of planned change for improved Quality.

Any time customers buy less of your product or service, it is a signal that you need to make contact and find out what's causing the problem. Why are they buying less? Are they in some way dissatisfied with your product or service? It may be that they have found better source for the product or service. Their business strategies may have changed, or their market may have declined. But you need to find out. By determining what the problem is, you can often help resolve it either for them or with them. It's like becoming a business partner with your customers.

Fast-Track Tip 18

It costs many times more to gain new customers than it does to keep old ones.

Lip Service vs. Hard Service

It's easy to talk about commitment to Quality service and products. But it's much more difficult to demonstrate commitment on a day-to-day basis. This is the difference between lip servicing and "hard servicing" Quality. Most companies talk about Quality, service, and customer satisfaction, but how many actually deliver it day in and day out? One retailer uses television ads that talk about "friendly, helpful customer service." In reality, you can never find a clerk in their stores when you need one. "Friendly" and "helpful" are myths.

As you collect data about your customer and their levels of satisfaction, you will gain important insights into whether you are giving lip service or hard service to Quality advancement. Surveys, questionnaires, focus groups, and reports aside, the most satisfying service you can give your present and prospective customers for them to experience Quality service by your company. Ask yourself and your staff, "Do we provide lip service or hard service when it comes to Quality products and services?" Then take a long, critical look at the data you've received from the assessment tools. What is the data telling you?

Fast-Track Tip 19

Be honest in your assessment. Are you giving lip service or hard service when serving your customers?

Your Commitment to Customers

Your commitment to advancing Quality in your organization is directly related to the time and effort you're willing to take to understand your customer. Successful Fast Tracking isn't possible without a thorough understanding of your customer's needs and expectations, or without the insight into how well you are meeting those needs and expectations. Recognize that understanding your customer takes time and in some cases additional resources. Management's willingness to invest the time and resources to get to know and understand what your customer needs and expects is an indicator of commitment to Quality.

Fast Track at a Glance

✔ The most important customer is your external customer, the one who pays the bills. The internal customer's needs must also be met.

✔ Every effort in TQM must be focused on satisfying both your internal and external customers' needs and expectations.

✔ To truly service your customer, you must be able to answer these five questions: (1) Who are my customers? (2) What do I know about them? (3) How satisfied are they with my products and services? (4) Am I satisfied with the efforts my organization is making in serving my customers? (5) What actions does the organization need to take to better serve my customers?

✔ Most employees, supervisors, and managers believe they know and serve their customers with Quality, but few actually do.

✔ Your service and products should be good enough to create customers for life.

✔ You can assess your current customers' needs, expectations, and levels of satisfaction by using mystery shoppers, customer questionnaires, customer interviews, and focus groups.

✔ Lost customers rarely complain. They simply disappear.

✔ A change in a customer's buying habits may be a signal to reexamine Quality issues.

✔ Too often, companies talk about delivering Quality service, but miss out on providing consistent day-to-day Quality.

✔ Willingness to devote time and invest money in understanding your customer is evidence of commitment to the Quality process.

PART 2

The Fast-Track Paradigm

This second part of the book deals with the Fast-Track Paradigm, the sequence of events that makes the Fast-Track Method to Quality a success. Every process has critical key actions that make it a success, and so it is with the Fast-Track Method to Quality. I've combined these key actions into a paradigm to easily understand the Fast-Track process. In fact, more than 20 years of experience have gone into developing and testing the Fast-Track Paradigm. Over the years, each of the events has become refined and polished to the point that they can cost-effectively and efficiently advance any organization's Quality.

The paradigm method has been successfully used to advance Quality in numerous organizations (product and service) to full TQM status.

The diagram on page 62 lays out the Paradigm model. These are the events used in the Fast-Track Method to advance an organization to TQM status as fast and as efficiently as possible. The sequence of events in the Fast-Track Paradigm is important. In most organizations, it should be closely followed as described. Steps 1-3 are designed to assist executives in fully understanding the process of integrating TQM into their organization. Steps 1 and 2, in particular, develop the knowledge base and understanding that allow senior managers to make an informed decision regarding the involvement of their organization in TQM. However, it's unlikely that any group of managers who complete steps 1 and 2, and fully understand the benefits to be gained from TQM, would decide not to participate and continue the TQM process.

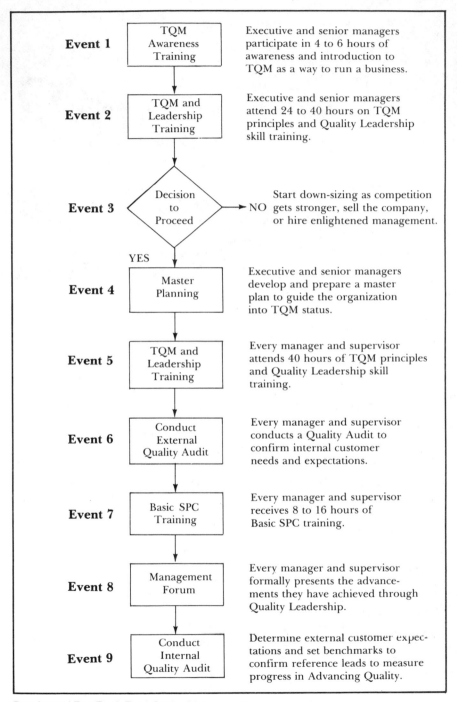

Event 1 — TQM Awareness Training — Executive and senior managers participate in 4 to 6 hours of awareness and introduction to TQM as a way to run a business.

Event 2 — TQM and Leadership Training — Executive and senior managers attend 24 to 40 hours on TQM principles and Quality Leadership skill training.

Event 3 — Decision to Proceed — NO — Start down-sizing as competition gets stronger, sell the company, or hire enlightened management.

YES

Event 4 — Master Planning — Executive and senior managers develop and prepare a master plan to guide the organization into TQM status.

Event 5 — TQM and Leadership Training — Every manager and supervisor attends 40 hours of TQM principles and Quality Leadership skill training.

Event 6 — Conduct External Quality Audit — Every manager and supervisor conducts a Quality Audit to confirm internal customer needs and expectations.

Event 7 — Basic SPC Training — Every manager and supervisor receives 8 to 16 hours of Basic SPC training.

Event 8 — Management Forum — Every manager and supervisor formally presents the advancements they have achieved through Quality Leadership.

Event 9 — Conduct Internal Quality Audit — Determine external customer expectations and set benchmarks to confirm reference leads to measure progress in Advancing Quality.

Paradigm of Fast-Track Total Quality Management

Events 4-8 are specifically designed to enhance and strengthen an organization's internal ability to deliver Quality products and service. The Fast-Track process is based on the critical premise that, before you discuss Quality advancement with external customers, you must make every effort to ensure that the *internal* delivery of Quality products and service is at its best. Too often, organizations have a bad experience with TQM because they catch the vision of the importance of understanding and meeting/exceeding customers' expectations, but the organization lacks the internal capability to provide improved Quality in products and services. They immediately define their customers as external only, and hold interviews and discussions with them to determine expectations for Quality services and products. However, asking customers to clarify their expectations actually raises their expectations. Customers now expect something to happen! If the organization can't deliver with improved Quality, customers become even less satisfied with the present level of products and service.

An important aspect of the Fast-Track Method to Quality is ensuring that the organization develops the capability to deliver consistent Quality service. Initially, the Quality improvements are internal and impact internal customers. Events 4-8 are designed to build organizational capability in a two-phase process:

1. By fostering commitment, knowledge, and understanding.
2. By developing a process for implementing and applying skills with accountability to ensure that those skills are consistently applied and Quality is improved.

Quality audits, event 9 in the Paradigm, should be undertaken only when an organization has demonstrated over several weeks or even months that they've developed the capability to provide consistent Quality products and services to the customer. Then and only then should inquiries be made with external customers to clarify as precisely as possible through a Quality audit:

- What they expect.
- How well the organization is currently meeting those expectations.
- What they can do to improve.

The chapters in this section of the book are designed to provide a clear understanding of each of the Fast-Track Paradigm's events and how they can be developed and conducted within an organization to maximize the commitment and understanding of the Fast-Track principles for TQM. Each chapter covers a Paradigm event. Each shows you how to take your organization through the beginning awareness phases to high levels of Quality improvement. As you go through this section, carefully examine the principles and concepts presented. Ask yourself, "How can I apply this in my organization?" Then use the chapters as a model—a blueprint, if you will—for how you can enhance and advance your organization to Quality improvement.

After reading this section, you should be able to describe:

1. The elements of the Fast-Track Paradigm.
2. The importance of training.
3. The value in involving everyone in the Quality advancement process.
4. How to develop positive attitudes toward TQM.
5. How to define a leader's role in TQM.
6. The 20 essential TQM principles.
7. How to apply the information to make an informed choice about whether Quality advancement is the right business decision for your organization.
8. How to prepare a Quality Master Plan.
9. How to conduct a Quality audit.
10. How to conduct a management forum.

6

Event 1: Fast-Track TQM Awareness Training

Virginia Satier once said, "Awareness is the basis of change." So it is with Fast-Track to Quality. Initial awareness training for senior and middle managers not only expands their understanding of Fast-Track to Quality, but actually *begins the process of change*. As managers gain insight and understanding into the value and benefits of being a Quality-driven organization, they begin to examine their own behaviors, question the present organizational processes, and critically look at how the organization conducts business. This self-examination process stimulates the willingness to consider alternative methods for advancing the organizational drive to TQM.

The whole Paradigm model begins with basic awareness training.

Ongoing processes of change continually evolve from small beginnings and, with a structured format, keep getting better and better as time passes. So it is with Fast-Track to Quality.

A Different Way to Lead an Organization

Critical to building management's awareness of TQM processes is the recognition that they require a different style of decision making. Under TQM, decisions are made in a collaborative way. Traditional autocratic decision making is replaced with consensus. In the consensus process, several managers are involved and share in making the decision. Although there may not be full agreement on taking an action, each manager agrees to support the decision that the group agrees on. Managers leave a consensus meeting feeling as though their viewpoint has been heard and considered. They agree that every action taken will support the success of the decision, even when they disagree with the ultimate decision.

In the consensus process, decision making often takes longer, but the time to implement the decision is shorter. In contrast, in an autocratic or democratic decision-making process, those who voted against the decision may be unwilling to support the majority decision. They may be so disenchanted they may take actions to sabotage success. Figure 6.1 shows the difference between a typical American company run by autocratic/democratic decision making and a consensus-run Fast-Track TQM company. An example of how the TQM consensus process impacts implementation time is the brief three and a half years Chrysler required under TQM to bring the Viper automobile from the decision-making stage into full production. Under the old autocratic system, it took them eight years to do the same with the Saturn.

Time savings are not the only benefit. In a Fast-Track Quality-driven organization, priorities are revised and resources are reallocated as the needs of the customer are more clearly defined and understood. Resources are allocated on a priority basis to directly improve the organization's ability to meet or exceed the customer's expectations. Managers and employees are more directly involved in making work assignments, and they participate in job rotation. Another important change is the unity created by having every manager and employee involved in the decisions and implementation process, their efforts focused on Quality improvement.

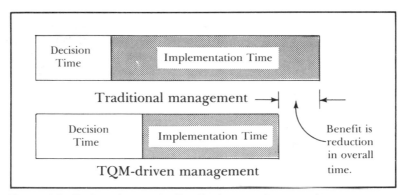

Figure 6.1. Traditional versus the Fast-Track way to decision making

Play "Employee Roulette"

You will have successfully implemented Fast-Track TQM when you can play "employee roulette." By randomly approaching any and every employee in your organization and receiving a positive response to the following three questions will demonstrate Quality breakthrough.

1. What is the value and importance of Quality in our organization?
2. What actions have you taken over the last 30 days to enhance and improve the Quality in your areas of responsibility?
3. What are you presently doing to improve the Quality of your current assignment?

A positive response to each question clearly demonstrates employees' understanding and support of TQM principles. Their actions demonstrate their involvement and participation to advance Quality at all levels. While it might take two to three years to get the "right answers" to all three questions from every employee, the effort is worth it.

Fast-Track Tip 20

Fast-Track TQM includes a different way of doing business, requiring consensus decision making. As more people are involved in the decision-making process, and implementation time is shortened. Increased employee influence on decision implementation builds team unity and team spirit.

Short- and Long-Term Results

It's the American way of business to produce immediate results. Company presidents want to show stockholders a handsome return on their investment—and quickly. Unfortunately, typical TQM processes are often directed only to long-term results available in three to five years. Yes, it takes time to advance and build a TQM-driven organization.

But Fast-Track TQM gives you both short- and long-term results, with measurable results in six to nine months. Ongoing advances continue to be made every quarter and every year, with successes measured in dollars.

The secret to the success factor in Fast Track is accountability (described in Chap. 12). Regardless of the TQM method you choose, building and developing a Quality-driven organization is a journey requiring the continual training and involvement of employees at all organizational levels.

Fast-Track Tip 21

Through accountability, measurable results can be achieved within six to nine months.

Develop Capable Leadership

In developing a Quality-driven organization, it's imperative that senior managers, and later managers and supervisors at all levels, receive the necessary training in leadership to enable them to advance an organization's Quality. Training can't be limited simply to TQM principles. The training must focus directly on developing leadership skills to lead employees to Quality advancement.

For many managers, learning to become a Quality-driven leader may be their greatest challenge. Being able to lead and inspire others to Quality improvement isn't easy. Some managers may have to make significant personal changes in order to integrate employee involvement and collaboration into their personal leadership styles. Specific leadership skills required for TQM success are discussed in Chap. 7.

Fast-Track Tip 22

To effectively lead for Quality, autocratic managers have to significantly alter their personal leadership style.

The Importance of Training Everyone

If you accept that doing it right the first time and every time is vitally critical for TQM success, then you're ready to examine what it takes to make it a reality within your organization. With the exception of unexpected equipment malfunction, failing to do it right the first time is caused from inadequacies in the capabilities of employees. Either they don't have the ability to perform, or they don't have the motivation to consistently achieve at the required levels. Typically, training is applied only to develop skills for performing tasks without considering the motivation to achieve accuracy.

Fact 1: Training can improve both skills and motivation to support continuous Quality improvement.

Fact 2: Regardless of the present level of Quality, training will improve the consistency of work performed.

I'm frequently asked, "After we've completed the initial Fast-Track TQM Training, what's next?" The answer is "plenty—more training!" The list of skill areas to improve performance is almost never-ending. Managers and employees benefit from training in project management, presentation skills, public speaking, problem identification, advanced statistical process controls, and time management, among many others. When doing it right the first and every time becomes the priority, training becomes a never-ending process of building and enhancing the necessary skills to make it happen.

Fast-Track Tip 23

Only continuous training can ensure that managers and employees have the skills and motivation for continuous Quality advancement.

Understanding the Internal Customer's Expectations First

As we well know by now, the critical challenge you must meet in Quality advancement involves identifying your customers and their needs and expectations. But which type of customer should be first? While the *external customer* is usually easily identified, usually only a small number of the organization's employees come into contact with external customers. On the other hand, entirely understanding your *internal customers'* needs and expectations is more important than focusing on the external customer.

In fact, more harm can be caused by discussing Quality expectations with external customers before doing so with the internal ones. Just talking about Quality with external customers raises their expectations for improved products and services. The danger comes in not having the internal capability to deliver on these expectations. The message is clear: Get your internal act together before advancing to external customers for Quality improvement.

Every employee and every manager serves multiple internal customers. It may be the department down the hall, the individual standing next to them on a manufacturing line, or a division located in another building. In a Fast-Track TQM-driven company, all managers, supervisors, and employees have the responsibility and the accountability to know their customers, understand their ever-changing expectations, and consistently perform to meet or exceed those expectations. Once this is achieved, the external customer becomes the next priority.

How Employees Are Involved in the Fast-Track TQM Process

Every employee in an organization should receive four to eight hours of initial training to understand TQM principles, their importance to the organization, and their role in advancing Quality. Employees must clearly recognize that they have a direct opportunity and responsibility to make a difference in enhancing the Quality of products and service. Figure 6.2 outlines four ways employees can directly impact Quality enhancement in their organization.

1. Employee Suggestion Program. Every employee has ideas about how to improve the organization. An important part of employee participation in Quality advancement is therefore an employee suggestion program, which allows the expression of those ideas in a low-risk setting. The process used by Alaska Railroad in Chap. 21 is an excellent example of an innovative approach to involve employees and to hear their ideas.

QUALITY-ADVANCING STRATEGIES FOR EMPLOYEES

1. Employee Suggestion Program
2. Taking Personal Initiative in Assigned Work
3. Participation in Work Team Meetings
4. Participation in Quality Improvement Teams (QIT)

Figure 6.2. How employees participate in Fast-Track

2. Taking Personal Initiative in Assigned Work. Personal initiative is at the heart of TQM. Employees who catch the vision of the importance and value of Quality improvement in their personal work areas will consistently take action on a daily basis to improve Quality. Error-free work the first and every time becomes a point of employee pride. Employees involved in Quality enhancement processes not only consistently produce error-free work, they continually make good work better. They offer ideas and suggest ways that their daily work can be improved.

3. Participation in Work Team Meetings. Frequent employee meetings also reinforce employee value to the organization. As groups of employees who work on a particular process meet regularly, they discuss process problems, make suggestions to directly improve processes, and find ways to make them even better. These meetings are usually led by the immediate supervisor. Occasionally, department heads may attend to confirm their understanding, show support to the process, and offer their insights and experience.

4. Participation in Quality Improvement Teams (QIT). An assigned group of employees and supervisors use a formal problem-solving process to review particular problems and come up with recommended solutions. These so-called Quality Improvement Teams (QITs) can make a direct and positive impact on Quality improvement. The QIT concept is discussed in more detail in Chap. 13.

Too often, organizations begin with a broad understanding of these four TQM employee involvement areas, and then seem to lose sight of their combined value. By not taking full advantage of employee suggestion programs, individual personal initiative, work team meetings, and Quality Improvement Teams, an organization's Quality enhancement efforts benefit only a select few managers and employees rather than everyone.

Many managers, looking for a quick fix to Quality improvement, seize on the idea that TQM consists only of Quality Improvement Teams. Their entire effort to improve Quality rests with building and developing QITs. What a mistake! They are missing out on applying the full capabilities and resources of their employees to improve Quality. Chapter 13 describes more than a dozen strategies to maximize Quality advancement.

Fast-Track Tip 24

For successful TQM, all employees must be directly involved in the Quality-enhancement process.

Fast Track at a Glance

✔ Awareness is the first step in making the change to Fast-Track TQM.

✔ Fast-Track TQM is not a program, but an ongoing process of constantly striving to be better and more competitive.

✔ Fast-Track TQM requires major changes in how decisions are made, how resources are allocated, and how employees are involved in the organization.

✔ While you should be able to see measurable results with Fast Track within six to nine months, Quality will continue every month.

✔ Fast-Track TQM reduces expenses and increases revenues.

✔ Managers must be taught how to lead for Quality enhancement.

✔ Continuous training at all levels is required for an organization to constantly enhance Quality by meeting and exceeding customer expectations.

✔ Successful Fast-Track TQM requires that every manager, supervisor, and employee have the responsibility and accountability to know, meet, and exceed his/her customers' needs and expectations.

✔ Employees can directly impact Quality improvement by (1) employee suggestion programs, (2) taking personal initiative in their work, (3) participating in work team meetings, and (4) working on Quality Improvement Teams.

7

Events 2 and 5: Fast-Track TQM Principles and Continuous Quality Leadership Training

Developing an effective TQM organization is a matter of supervisors, managers, and employees *accepting the basic Fast-Track principles* and having the *necessary leadership skills* to make it work. In the Fast-Track Paradigm, teaching the principles of TQM and developing leadership skills in managers and supervisors are the most time-consuming aspects of the process. To be effective, the training must be highly interactive, with numerous group exercises to allow participants to clarify the concepts and try out their newly acquired skills.

Over the years, I've conducted hundreds of training sessions with thousands of managers and supervisors. My experience has taught me that these training sessions have the greatest impact if they are spread out over time. The ideal scenario is 40 hours of training conducted in four- to eight-hour sessions over at least a five-week period. This provides an opportunity for the managers and supervisors to take the principles back to their employees and actually try them out. They can then return to training and receive feedback on their efforts.

The worst training schedule is the "marathon" style—five consecutive days of eight-hour training. While many consultants use this format, it doesn't allow participants the opportunity to experiment and test the principles in a real world setting. It doesn't allow them to build their experiences on information from the previous classes. Managers and supervisors coming out of such marathon sessions may take away a few principles or concepts—but they leave behind 80 to 90 percent of what was taught. At best, the marathon method is only entertaining and awareness building with modest skills development.

Some organizations find it difficult to schedule full-day training sessions, even when they're spread out over a five-week period. An effective alternative involves dividing the training into four-hour increments with two sessions per week. This allows the organization a little more flexibility in scheduling, and minimizes the interruption of daily work.

Fast-Track Tip 25

Schedule Fast-Track TQM skill training over several weeks to give participants the opportunity to try out new concepts and skills in a work setting, and then return to the training classroom for feedback and more skills.

Fast-Track TQM Awareness Training is designed to achieve four major goals:

1. Acceptance of Fast-Track and Quality principles.
2. Effective leadership skill development.
3. Problem-solving skill development.
4. Development of personal action plan.

Let's look at each of these in more detail, along with the activities involved in attaining each of these goals.

Goal 1: Acceptance of Fast-Track TQM Principles

Almost every manager, supervisor, and employee has heard about and knows something about TQM. Some have read about it in trade journals or books. Others have had friends who have been involved in a TQM process. These people usually come to Fast-Track TQM Awareness Training with a positive regard for TQM. They have caught the vision and are eager to learn more about developing TQM in their own organizations.

At the other end of the spectrum are people who bring a wide range of personal blocks to TQM. They're sure they know everything there is to know about it, and they don't want any part of it. These trainees are the most challenging to win over to TQM. Success with TQM training isn't a matter of age or years of experience, but simply a matter of being open and teachable.

In the middle are the majority of managers and supervisors who attend training. They know a little about TQM, but have some understanding about how it works. Fortunately, they usually have an open mind and are receptive.

People's beliefs are based on their personal experiences. Without acceptance and positive attitudes toward TQM on the part of managers and supervisors, an organization will have limited success advancing to Quality. The trainer's challenge is to add positive *experiences* during the training event. The trainees must be clearly shown how applying TQM principles benefits the work group, the organization, and them personally. As people begin to glimpse the potential value of Fast-Track TQM, their resistance and negative attitudes begin to fade. It's a matter of getting employees at all levels up on Quality and how they can make it happen.

Fast-Track Tip 26

Employees develop positive beliefs about TQM if you clearly demonstrate the personal benefits, the benefits to their immediate work group, and benefits for the organization as a whole.

Fundamental TQM Principles

Twenty basic principles are the driving force behind developing a Fast-Track TQM organization. These principles have been tested and applied successfully with thousands of managers and supervisors. My staff and I have thoroughly evaluated each of these statements in terms of their impact in driving and supporting the Fast-Track TQM process. Simply put, they work.

It's vital that managers and supervisors who lead the TQM process have a thorough understanding of each of these principles. Perhaps even more importantly, they must accept and believe that these principles will build TQM in their organizations. Personal blocks or resistance to any of the 20 basic principles will flaw an individual's attitude and seriously hamper his or her ability to advance Quality.

Examine each of the statements in Fig. 7.1. Test each of them from your personal experience. Can you validate that each of them is true? Any item that you question or challenge means that you need some additional explanation and understanding on how that principle supports and builds a manager's views and attitudes toward TQM.

FAST TRACK TO QUALITY TEST

T	F	
___	___	1. If it can't be measured, it can't be improved.
___	___	2. Work accomplished can be broken into subparts or process steps for review and analysis for advancement.
___	___	3. Teamwork is required.
___	___	4. A feedback system is needed to identify current status and the need for course corrections.
___	___	5. Establish habits for Quality advancement.
___	___	6. The emphasis is on Quality.
___	___	7. Expect results within six months to a year after implementation.
___	___	8. Establish a climate where Quality is first among equals of schedule and cost.
___	___	9. Direct efforts to eliminate systemic flaws during planning, implementation, and evaluation.
___	___	10. Error-free work is the most cost-effective way to advance Quality.
___	___	11. Executive commitment is mandatory in leading long-term support.
___	___	12. Train those working together at the same time, whenever possible.
___	___	13. Use charts and graphs to display achievement in Quality advancements.
___	___	14. Align Quality emphasis with key business goals.
___	___	15. Focus on improving operational processes and not individual performance.
___	___	16. Recognition for Quality performance is more successful than financial rewards.
___	___	17. It is better to measure a few important things, than many unimportant things.
___	___	18. No level of defect is acceptable.
___	___	19. A Quality advancement plan and approach must be custom-tailored to meet each organization's unique needs.
___	___	20. Clients define the standards for Quality measurement.

Figure 7.1. The 20 Fast-Track TQM principles

In Fast-Track TQM Awareness Training, each manager is given the same opportunity to question and challenge any of the principles. Their questions and concerns enable the trainer to clarify the principles and further explain how they fit into the TQM development process. It's interesting to watch even the most resistant managers and supervisors become enthusiastic about developing TQM as they gain more insight and understanding into the principles.

Try the exercise in Fig. 7.1. Have participating managers mark each of the statements "true" or "false" according to their own experience. When they've completed the test, ask if anyone marked any of the first five statements "false." Almost without exception, one or more of the managers will have. Here is an opportunity for the leader (or facilitator) and the group to discuss why the answers should have been true. For Quality-driven managers, all the answers on the test are true. Work down the list in this fashion, five questions at a time, discussing any false answers to ensure understanding they are "true" in a Quality-driven company.

Then ask the group, "What are the important values we hold in developing Quality products and services for our customers?"

As the managers offer values, write them down on a chart pad for all to see. Then ask, "How important is it for us to strive to meet or exceed our customers' expectations?" This question acts as a touchstone, stimulating the internal questioning, "Can I support that statement?" and "Does that fit for me?"

Note: When conducting training around the 20 principles, the facilitator should not try to convince managers and supervisors of the value of any of the principles. Instead, they should allow the class to challenge and question, and then let other participants respond to those challenges. Without exception, someone in the class will see value in each of the principles, and will rise to defend it, explaining its value and purpose to others. With the trainer acting as a facilitator, the participants themselves become the trainers, helping one another gain insight and understanding into these all-important principles.

Fast-Track Tip 27

Managers must be allowed to question and challenge of the 20 Fast-Track TQM principles. Only when they have resolved all their questions and concerns, and have accepted the principles, are they ready to proceed with TQM.

Understanding the Competition

An important aspect of developing a positive attitude toward TQM is understanding your competitors—who they are, their strengths and weaknesses. Managers and supervisors are almost always surprised to find their competitor a formidable foe, someone who is able to claim a substantial portion of the market share.

The following eight areas can be use in a systematic examination of an organization, and its comparison with the competition:

1. Image

2. Reputation

3. Cost competitiveness

4. Availability

5. Repeat business

6. Growth rate

7. Defect free

8. Support service

During this stage of the training, try playing "what if?" with managers. "What would happen to competitor A if you did x?" We play out various scenarios and their possible outcomes based on strategies they might adopt and strategies the competition might adopt. Invariably, managers feel alarmed by the possibilities, and often make statements such as "They're better than we are" or "We've got to do something different."

Competitor analysis is always an eye-opener for managers. As they examine the competition and compare their own products and services in the eight areas, the room often becomes very quiet. When the trainees realize that the competition is very likely sitting in a similar classroom examining their own organization and planning strategies to become even more competitive, they realize that, no matter what, they need to become even better. The training participants begin to see that TQM does in fact have a real and necessary place in their organization, and they start becoming active participants to make that goal a reality.

Fast-Track Tip 28

Know your customer's strengths and weaknesses—and how you compare.

TQM Language

To communicate effectively, people need a common language with mutually agreed-upon definitions. An important part of developing a positive TQM attitude is developing this common language. Being able to talk about TQM not only helps managers, it also acts to unify them as a team.

The first step in building this common TQM language is to put together a glossary. In training, the glossary is usually developed on a wall chart. As words are used that seem unusual or extraordinary, they are added to the chart with an explanation or definition. The glossary charts should be displayed and continually expanded throughout the training.

As training progresses, participants become increasingly comfortable with this new language. They begin to use it easily and often. An outsider listening in might think the group members were actually speaking a foreign language because of the unique words and word patterns used. As participants practice their new facility with the TQM language, it's almost magically building new and positive TQM attitudes.

Fast-Track Tip 29

A shared TQM language enables managers to talk about Quality enhancement, and acts to solidify groups into effective teams.

Defining a Leader's Role in TQM

As managers and supervisors examine TQM principles and how they are applied, inevitable questions arise:

How do I lead for TQM?

What's my role as a manager in the TQM process?

How should I perform to get employees to advance Quality in the organization?

These questions reveal a breakthrough moment in the training process and in shaping positive TQM attitudes. This breakthrough occurs after managers and supervisors have accepted the concept of TQM and its principles. Now they want to know how to get on with it, how to become part of it, how to make it work effectively in their organization.

At this point, I lead managers through a process of specifically defining their roles and their authority in developing TQM. In a "what if?" process, they identify actions and behaviors they can apply as a successful TQM leader. Managers typically come up with 15 or 20 specific actions they might utilize to advance Quality in their organization. Usually we list them on a large newsprint chart, and then discuss the statements and further refine them.

On a second sheet of paper, we define the manager's present "role and style model," how leadership is currently being applied in the organization, specifically present managers' actions/behaviors. The value in this exercise is in comparing the present processes of leadership with the TQM way.

As they compare the two sheets (the manager's current role model against TQM leadership actions/behaviors), they quickly recognize the need for change. While there is usually some congruence between the two charts, there are also some glaring differences. It rapidly becomes apparent that leadership under TQM must be applied in a different way to advance Quality.

Fast-Track Tip 30

To understand how to lead for Quality enhancement, managers must define the specific behaviors and actions that they can apply to advance Quality in their own organization.

Once managers have identified their TQM leadership roles through specific behaviors, they are ready to define and establish the necessary levels of authority. Inevitably, someone in the room says, "Yes, I have the responsibility, but I don't have the authority." Managers' authority must match their responsibility. If not, you'll only have increased frustration and maybe even anger on the part of managers.

Managers in most organizations use language that does not clearly define levels of authority. In Fast-Track TQM Awareness Training, I give them a simple set of words to define authority levels in carrying out their responsibilities in their role as leaders for TQM. This set of words allows everyone to have a common understanding about authority. The following are the four levels of authority:

1. **Complete:** The manager does not have to answer to anyone. He or she can take action and proceed.

2. **Act and report:** The intent is to take action, but the action taken must be reported to the boss to avoid surprises.

3. **Act after discussion and agreement:** Through collaboration with others, all parties agree on the decision and the manager takes action.

4. **Provide input:** The manager provides input, but someone else makes the decision.

As managers' roles are identified, the related levels of authorities are assigned so that everyone knows what is expected. After completing this process, every manager should be able to say, "I have the responsibility, and the authority."

Fast-Track Tip 31

If managers have the responsibility, they must have the authority to act, or at least a clear understanding of their level of authority.

Case Study

At this point, I lead participants through a specially prepared case study that examines an organization having difficulty being successful in the marketplace. The exercise allows participants to apply many of the 20 Fast Track TQM leadership principles and enables them to turn the company around. The process becomes a confirmation for them that Quality does indeed have a place in their organization and that Quality can be used to advance it to even greater success.

Shaping and forming new, positive TQM attitudes takes time. It doesn't occur after only a few hours of training. By spreading the training out over several weeks, participants can test their own personal views and re-examine their own leadership values. Often highly skeptical managers leave awareness training with the attitude, "I am still skeptical, but I'm willing to give it a try." This is training success! If you can develop willingness in people to try, test, and experiment with Fast-Track TQM Principles, their subsequent success will lead them to become stronger and stronger proponents in leading for TQM.

Goal 2: Effective Leadership Skill Development

One of the benefits of developing effective TQM leadership skills is the fact that these same skills can be effectively applied in other parts of life. The leadership skills used to create success in an organization have equal success when they're applied in a home, in a church, or in a service club setting. Many of the examples I use in Fast-Track TQM Awareness Training to develop workplace leadership skills come from applying the skills with family members, friends, and other associates. It not only helps managers relate to the concepts, but also helps them make the skill transfer to the other areas of their lives.

These leadership skills are different from management skills. We manage projects, things, events, time, and resources, but we lead people. Consider yourself. Would you rather be managed or led? Of course, you'd rather be led.

In Fast-Track TQM, developing leadership skills, not management skills, is the issue. To develop continuous Quality leadership, you have to identify the leadership principles that will support and advance an organization to Quality. Instead of calling it Total Quality Management, perhaps it should be called Total Quality Leadership. It's certainly a more accurate description. The U.S. Navy has recognized the critical leadership role in TQM, calling their Quality processes Total Quality Leadership.

The following sections describe the critical elements in training managers to Quality Leadership.

Fast-Track Tip 32

Improving a manager's group and one-on-one presentation skills directly influences his or her effectiveness in leading for Fast-Track TQM.

Goal 3: Problem-Solving Skill Development

Ninety percent of all the TQM training courses available make problem-solving skill development the centerpiece of their training effort. What they leave out is the development of positive attitudes and leadership skills. The Fast-Track Method of TQM includes all three, which in my opinion are critical to your Quality-advancement success.

Since there is so much already written about problem-solving skills and how they apply to TQM, let's concentrate on just the four problem-solving areas essential to Quality improvement and how they fit into the Fast-Track Method.

1. Solve the right problem.
2. Track progress.
3. Set performance standards.
4. Involve everyone.

Solve the Right Problem

In organizations with an established course of Quality improvement, it's common to see managers and employees actively involved in problem solving. While problem solving is unquestionably a valuable part of TQM, it's frustrating to see so much time and energy wasted on problems of little consequence.

Think about tossing a rock into a pond. The rock causes a big splash and smaller ripples. Too often, organizations become involved with the small ripples while ignoring the big splash. In Fast-Track TQM, problem-solving efforts focus on big splash problems. Because the splash problems create the ripples, the smaller problems are resolved along the way too.

You've undoubtedly heard about Pareto's 80/20 rule: Eighty percent of your problems are caused by 20 percent of the situations. This holds true in problem solving for Quality advancement. If you carefully examine your problems, you'd likely find that only a handful—about 20 percent— are real, "big splash" problems.

Anytime a workgroup focuses on a problem to solve in Fast-Track TQM, I have them ask, "Why did we select this problem over others?" The group must go through the process of understanding how and why they chose to devote their time and resources to a particular problem. Invariably the groups' answers during this process are revealing and often lead them to focusing on other more important problems.

Fast Track 33

Don't waste your time and resources solving problems that have questionable value to improving your organization's product/service Quality.

Track Progress

A common TQM principle says "you can't improve what you can't measure." If you're going to measure something, you first have to establish a benchmark, a point from which to measure your progress. Most organizations have plenty of data about their product or service. Unfortunately, the data is often of little or no use. Perhaps the format is unsuitable, or the data is not the kind that can help advance the organization to TQM. Or the organization tracks data in so many areas that it becomes overwhelming and confusing.

Recently, in working with a group of managers who report to a big city mayor, one of them wanted to show how capable they were in tracking their success. He produced a stack of computer-generated graphs four inches thick. I asked him, "Who reviews and uses this material?" He didn't know. He said it was distributed throughout the organization, but he couldn't say how or whether it was used. I challenged him to omit the reports for two months and see if anyone missed them. He did and received calls from only two calls from managers.

It's critical in the Fast-Track process to collect only the data that people in the organization find valuable, data they can actually use to improve their performance. Don't waste valuable resources collecting data and preparing charts and reports that have little or no value in improving the Quality of your organization's products or services. Each manager will have greater success advancing Quality by limiting data tracking to three or four areas—maximum.

Also, use your resources and time to track only the items over which you have direct control. If you collect data on items you can't control, it may be interesting, but it won't advance the Quality of your products or services.

Fast-Track Tip 34

- Keep data collection formats simple and usable.
- Limit data collection to only three or four areas.
- Gather data only in areas over which you have direct control.

Set Performance Standards

Performance standards pose a Catch 22 situation: It's important to have a target for people to work toward and accomplish. However, as people achieve those standards, by definition, the standard becomes a defined level of mediocrity. If everyone is doing it, it becomes mediocre performance.

The usual outcome is that performance standards are constantly raised. Of course, you know the common employee response when they are told that the performance standard has been raised 5 percent or 10 percent. "They want us to work harder—again!"

If instead you change your language slightly and refer to the current performance standard as the "minimum," the whole picture changes. Then you ask, "If these are our minimum performance standards, how much better are we?" The employees together, not management, set ever changing performance standards. Adding the word "minimum" changes the focus of the standards set by work groups. As members of the group become more skilled and capable, they keep raising the standard. By asking, "How much better are we?" the group continually raises the standards and works to meet those new standards.

Note that the group determines the standard. This is a critical difference. The manager or supervisor and the employees must meet jointly to define and set the standards for performance. It cannot be something imposed on them.

Not long ago, a manager told me how thrilled he was that the departments in his organization had been meeting the performance standard for several weeks running. I asked him what his next step might be. He said he was working on new standards. I asked, "How do you think your employees will respond if every time they meet a standard, you raise it?" He got the point. We then discussed the concept of minimum standard and letting the work groups challenge themselves beyond the minimum. At last check, his work group had reset and achieved new minimum performance standards three times and were continuing to improve.

Fast-Track Tip 35

Utilize the minimum performance standard in setting standards, and let employee work groups set the standards for their areas. Avoid imposing management-generated performance standards.

Involve Everyone

In the beginning, it's easy for organizations and their managers and employees to become excited about Quality improvement and even to make some major improvements in their products or services. But it's all too easy to let the initial excitement wane and relegate the job of Quality advancement only to Quality Improvement Teams (QITs) or similar units. As we've seen, however, Fast-Track TQM is much more than QITs or Quality circles. *Fast-Track Quality improvement requires the involvement of everyone in the organization on a day-to-day basis.* Only when everyone is working and problem-solving to enhance and improve the Quality of service and products in their area of responsibility can a company see consistent and significant improvement in Quality and realize the full benefits of Fast-Track TQM.

The problem-solving process used must be so simple and effective that all employees can use it anytime in any situation to improve Quality (see Fig. 7.2). In the Fast-Track TQM, we problem-solve using Fast-Track acronym PACE:

Plan to make a difference.

Act to understand the problem.

Check for causes and solutions.

Excel in improving Quality.

Goal 4: Develop a Personal Action Plan

Developing managers' skills and abilities to advance Quality is only half the solution. Each manager must have a personal action plan for applying the proper skills before they leave training.

I always ask managers in our training seminars, "How many of you have told your employees where you are today?" The majority of employees know their manager is attending training of some sort, even if they don't know the topic. As a manager returns from Fast-Track TQM Awareness Training, most employees are curious, even eager to know what the manager learned.

This is your *window of opportunity*. People are most teachable when they're curious. This teaching window may be open for only a few hours. So it's vital that managers use it to bring their employees together and talk about the principles of Quality and their value to the organization. Many managers opt for conducting minitraining sessions with their staffs on the principles and applications in their areas. This is one of the advantages of spreading the manager's TQM skill training over several weeks. It enables the managers to schedule a minitraining session with their employees almost immediately after each session.

Too often, managers return from training and miss the critical window of employee teachability. After all, they've already been pulled away from their duties for hours or days for the training sessions. Believing they have "too many things to do," they put off meeting with their employees and passing on the key points and benefits of TQM. What a pity! They've missed a golden opportunity to readily involve all their employees in Quality advancement at a time when they are most teachable. If managers can keep in mind they get paid to produce results, not perform duties,

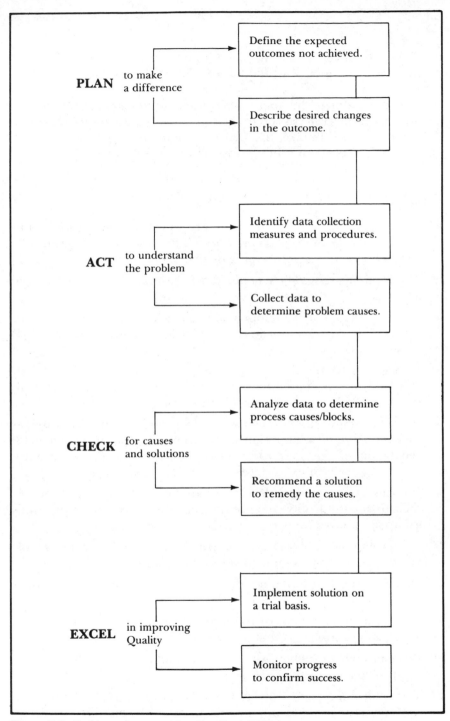

Figure 7.2. Problem-solving model to Fast-Track TQM

they'll be more likely to see the value in immediately meeting with employees and getting on with the business of advancing Quality in their area.

At the conclusion of the final TQM training session, managers prepare a plan in what they will pass on to their employees and how it can best be delivered. This usually takes the form of an outline that managers can use and follow in their minitraining sessions with their employees.

Fast Track at a Glance

✔ Employees, supervisors, and managers must possess the right attitudes and skills to make TQM work. Attitudes toward TQM can be changed as they learn the value of Quality improvement.

✔ TQM training should be scheduled over several weeks rather than all at once.

✔ Training should achieve four major goals: (1) a positive TQM attitude, (2) effective leadership skills, (3) problem-solving skills, and (4) an action plan.

✔ Managers need to challenge, question, and finally accept the 20 Fast-Track TQM Principles if they are to have the right attitude and skills to effectively lead for Quality advancement.

✔ It's vital to understand the competition's strengths and weaknesses, as well as how your organization stacks up in the areas of (1) image, (2) reputation, (3) cost competitiveness, (4) availability, (5) repeat business, (6) growth rate, (7) defect free, and (8) support service.

✔ It's critical that managers develop a common TQM language to enable them to discuss Quality enhancement and develop the unity of a work group as an effective team.

✔ To develop the necessary skills in leading for TQM, managers must apply specific leadership behaviors and actions.

✔ Managers need to define not only their responsibility, but also their level of authority.

✔ Too often, organizations focus on problems of little consequence and ignore larger problems that affect Quality performance.

✔ When tackling a problem, work groups should ask, "Why did we select this problem over others?"

✔ You can't improve Quality unless you can measure it. Track and collect data only (1) in three or four areas, (2) that directly affects Quality enhancement, and (3) that you have direct control over.

✔ Use the minimum performance standard concept to continually encourage work groups to establish and meet higher performance standards.

✔ Managers must use the window of opportunity when they return from a training session, when employees are most teachable to train them in TQM principles.

8

Event 3: Making the Critical Decisions

In making the all-important decision whether to proceed with the Fast-Track TQM process, you've got to be clear on several critical issues. Since a commitment to TQM can require major changes in how your organization is managed, as well as a reallocation of its resources, it's vital that you take the time to make the TQM decision intelligently and logically, avoiding getting caught up in the "Quality hype" so pervasive in trade journals and news magazines.

Over the years in working with managers, CEOs, and presidents of organizations, I have used the following series of questions to assist this important decision-making process. The questions form a "decision tree." A "yes" answer to a question automatically leads you to the next critical question. A "no" answer anywhere along the process halts forward progress and moves you out of the matrix and away from TQM. By examining Fig. 8.1, it's easy to see the flow of questions and how they lead to the critical decision, "Should we become a TQM organization?"

Rather than make this decision by yourself, I encourage you to meet with your managing staff to review and discuss these questions. While the ultimate decision rests with you as the organization's leader, other managers' insights can prove useful. And if you decide to proceed with Fast-Track TQM, you'll already have "buy-in" by your senior staff.

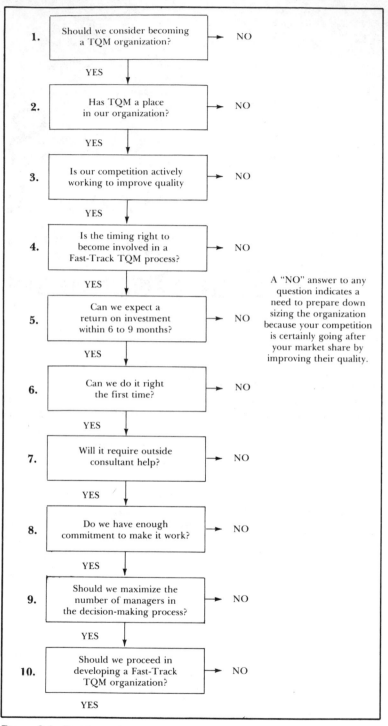

Figure 8.1. Decision-making tree to advance to TQM

Question 1: Should We Examine and Consider Becoming a TQM Organization?

A "yes" response to this question is a win-win situation. You have virtually nothing to lose by examining in more detail what Fast-Track TQM can do for your organization. It's absolutely imperative that managers understand that, at this stage, it is an examination process—no decision has been made. In all correspondence, discussions, and meetings, this fact should be made clear. The decision to proceed with TQM must be based on clear facts and data. Encourage your managers to examine the question objectively and resist the temptation to get caught up in the emotional pressure that "everyone should support Quality no matter what." Quality has value only if your staff and customers see it as valuable and only if it benefits your organization.

Question 2: Does TQM Have a Place in Our Organization

An important part of deciding whether TQM has a place in your organization involves identifying specific units within the organization in which Quality improvement might have value. Fast-Track TQM can operate very effectively within a single department or division in a company without having the entire organization realigned to Quality. Of course, an organization can achieve greater benefit by having total involvement in TQM, by having every manager and every employee committed to Quality advancement. However, Fast-Track TQM can still have profound effects when applied on a more limited basis.

Ask yourself and your management staff, "In which areas, units, or divisions might TQM create value for our organization?" Create a chart on a piece of newsprint identifying the divisions or departments, along with specifically what benefits each might derive from Quality improvement.

As managers go through this methodical process of identifying the benefits and the value that Quality advancement can bring to individual departments or divisions, they gain insight into how Quality might benefit their own areas, as well as commitment and the willingness to proceed.

Question 3: Is Our Competition Working to Improve Their Quality?

The real question, of course, is, "Should we proceed with Fast-Track TQM *at this time?*" It's not a question of whether the organization should become Quality-driven, but whether you'll do it now or later. As I've told many managers, *please be aware that your competitors are planning for Quality advancement.* At this moment, your competitors may be sitting in Quality planning meetings. For many companies, the decision to become Quality-driven becomes a matter of survival. Competing successfully may depend on how effective you are in developing a Quality improvement process for your products/services. Ask yourself and your management staff, "How is the Quality issue affecting our competition?"

Unfortunately, some managers blindly believe that their company will be around for a hundred years without any change. But change is the nature of successful business. One client, the manager of a large engineering firm who had caught the vision of Fast-Track TQM and who understood the importance of Quality in competing successfully, told his staff, "If we aren't successful in becoming a Quality-driven organization, we are not going to be in business five years from now."

Question 4: Is the Timing Right for Our Organization to Get Involved in a Fast-Track TQM Process?

You can certainly build a rational argument for a "yes" or "no" response to this question. On one hand, you might say, "Regardless of what activities are going on in this organization at this time, TQM is something that we have to proceed with." Or you might say, "TQM is important, but this is not the right time."

Let me say that there is never a "perfect time" for becoming involved in TQM. It may not be the best sales or manufacturing cycle. Perhaps some new products are being introduced. The reasons for not becoming involved in Quality advancement are endless. The truth is, in most companies, the timing may not be right, but there will never be a time when the timing is perfect.

Managers who catch the Fast-Track TQM vision, who recognize the potential of its power, feel an urgency to get on with becoming a TQM organization. You and your managers must examine, "Why isn't this a good time to advance Quality?" and "Why is this the best time to advance Quality?"

"Is the timing right for TQM and your organization?" A "yes" answer means that, regardless of the activities going on right now, this is as good a time as any.

Fast-Track Tip 36

Waiting for the "perfect time" to initiate Quality improvement is a mistake. That time will likely never come.

Question 5: Can We Expect a Return on Our Investment Within Six to Nine Months?

In order to decide to proceed with TQM, the answer must be an absolute "yes." The president of a medium-sized company that had been involved with Quality improvement for nearly 18 months enthusiastically described the activities their company was involved with in developing and strengthening Quality products and service. I asked the bottomline question, "What evidence do you have to show that your Quality improvement process has caused a return on your investment?" He told me that over the next few months, his company would be conducting evaluations to confirm his belief of success.

This president's blind faith is both typical and disturbing. Many otherwise very effective leaders of organizations are willing to spend thousands, even millions of dollars on Quality advancement processes without being able to demonstrate quantitatively that the process has made a difference. *An effective process to advance Quality must be able to demonstrate performance improvements within six to nine months.* If it is not demonstrating measurable improvements, the Quality improvement process must be reevaluated and redesigned.

"Doing it right the first time" doesn't apply just to developing a product or service. It applies equally to becoming and developing a TQM organization. The plan for developing a TQM organization must incorporate points of accountability to measure performance improvements for each of the managers participating in the process. Every manager and supervisor involved must be able to demonstrate the effect of his or her leadership in applying the principles of TQM and in advancing the organization.

Managers and supervisors achieve what they are held accountable for. If there is no accountability in the Quality-advancement process, there is questionable progress. If there is no measurement, how do you know your managers and company are advancing?

Fast-Track Tip 37

An effective TQM design should be able to demonstrate measurable performance improvements in six to nine months.

Question 6: Can We Do It Right the First Time?

Too often, companies needlessly waste time and money in Quality-improvement processes that don't work the first time and have to be substantially revised. The Fast-Track Method of improving Quality is a proven method to advancing an organization to TQM. *Fast-Track does it right the first time.* It can provide demonstrated short-term improvement in six to nine months and continued long-term improvement for years to come.

One of the most common causes of TQM failure is thinking that it consists only of statistical process controls (SPC). Fast-Track TQM isn't simply about numbers. It's about leadership, about organizational change. It's about managing and leading organizations in a different way. Statistical process control is merely one of the tools along the way to TQM.

A basic principal of Fast-Track TQM says, "First, improve the Quality of management, and second improve the management of Quality." It's a fundamental principle in learning to do it right the first time. A later chapter will provide a couple of case studies that will outline the events that lead to doing it right the first time.

Fast-Track Tip 38

To improve Quality, first improve the Quality of management. Then improve the management of Quality.

Question 7: Will It Require
Outside Consultant Help?

It probably will. Even if an organization has a capable training department and a handful of managers who have attended a variety of TQM
seminars, the organization is not necessarily capable of developing a
successful TQM organization. Outside expertise is most valuable during
the early stages of initial management training. An outside consultant has
a unique "arm's length" view and can ask the penetrating and often
difficult questions that may be awkward or impossible for internal personnel.

Outside consultants also have experience in working with other organizations. They can bring that experience to the discussion, steering the
process and helping the organization avoid costly mistakes that others
have made.

In organizations that have 350-400 employees or more, it's usually most
cost effective to have the outside consultant train in-house trainers. The
in-house personnel can, in turn, train middle managers, supervisors, and
employees.

Regardless of the organization's size, it's imperative that senior management receive their training from a qualified, outside consultant.

Fast-Track Tip 39

Use the experience of an outside Quality consultant in the planning
and training of senior managers.

Question 8: Do We Have
Enough Commitment from
Our Managers to Make It
Work?

A common question is, "How many managers and employees have to be
committed to the Quality process for it to work?" I wish there were a
simple answer like 50 or 75 percent. Years ago, I used to talk about a
"critical mass," between 30 and 40 percent of the managers and employees committed to Quality. However, over the years, I've found that
it's not the absolute numbers that count, but which managers are committed and which managers are stumbling blocks. It's the "who" rather than
the "how many" that makes a difference.

In every organization, some managers have more influence than others. It's these influential managers who become critical in terms of how much commitment is needed for Quality advancement. Since the success of Fast-Track TQM is based on leadership, when deciding whether to proceed with Quality advancement you must ask, "What level of commitment do we have from the influential managers, particularly senior managers?" While the ideal is commitment from senior staff on down through the supervisory level, the most critical commitment comes from the senior managers. Chapter 14 offers details in how to develop management commitment.

The agreement sheet in Fig. 8.2 is a document used with many of our clients to help them confirm their understanding of and commitment to Fast-Track TQM. It is modified to fit each client's unique language and needs. Once managers have received some awareness and skill training on Quality advancement, they are ready to make a personal decision about whether to commit to TQM. To help them make that decision, managers need to know what's ahead. What does it mean to their individual jobs and to their area if they support TQM? They also need to know the kind of help and support they'll receive in training their employees, supervisors, and managers for TQM. *Managers will support and commit to TQM if they know it will benefit them, their department, and the organization, and that they'll be supported in their efforts.*

The first part of the agreement in Fig. 8.2 outlines what the senior managers—the president, vice presidents, and senior staff—are willing to do to support other managers in advancing the TQM process.

The second portion of the agreement outlines what individual managers and supervisors are willing to do and what they'll be expected to do to advance TQM. As already mentioned, it's important that these staff members receive some introductory TQM training before they are asked to sign such a document and commit to TQM. Often presidents and senior managers make the mistake of asking managers and supervisors to sign on before they know what will be expected. They feel coerced and pressured into agreeing to something they know nothing or very little about. They end up resenting the process and are unable to really commit to it.

Each manager receives two copies of the agreement. The upper portion is signed by the company CEO, the president, and/or the vice president in charge of their particular area or division. Managers sign both copies and return one. One is on parchment paper (8½ × 11 in. format) and framed to hang in their offices. The agreement becomes a kind of contract between senior management and managers and supervisors.

Many managers and supervisors proudly display their agreements on their office walls. They take pride in showing the agreements to others. It

---

JOHANNA DAIRIES COMMITMENT TO QUALITY

Johanna Dairies intends to become the "Best Dairy" in America within five years and be recognized as such by producers, suppliers, employees, regulatory bodies, customers, and consumers. To accomplish this goal we must adopt a customer driven focus of serving *every* customer, internal and external, beyond their expectations *every* time.

—We fully endorse this goal and make the following commitment:

—We will ensure that all managers and employees are fully trained in the principles and methods of total Quality management.

—We will consistently support all managers and supervisors as they involve employees in the process to improve product Quality and service beyond the expectations of their respective customers.

—We will specifically encourage and support (a) full empowerment of employees, (b) increased tolerance of risk taking and failure, and (c) public recognition of all contributions to Quality efforts.

_____Dated: _____

Signed by the President

I fully endorse the goal of Johanna Dairies becoming the Best Dairy in America by serving *every* customer beyond their expectations *every* time.

Accordingly, I make the following commitment:

—I will understand my customer's changing expectations, and document progress in exceeding those expectations.

—I will encourage a generation of ideas which significantly improve product Quality and service with a goal of serving every customer beyond their expectations.

—I will champion the empowerment of all employees to aggressively pursue continuous improvement in product Quality and service through education, training, and a day-to-day working environment supporting our Quality goal.

_____Dated: _____

Signed by the Participating Manager

Figure 8.2. Agreement

is their "badge of honor," their written proof that they are participating in Quality enhancement for their company and that they have the full support of senior management to do it.

Clearly, managers are willing to make a commitment when they know their role and responsibilities in Quality advancement and they have commitment from senior management. If the Quality-enhancement pro-the proper training, recognition, and opportunities for managers to demonstrate Quality improvement. The written agreement helps confirm that support is available and gives managers a sense of comfort as they advance Quality applying Fast-Track principles.

Fast-Track Tip 40

Managers will support what benefits them personally or what benefits their department, division, or company. It's imperative that managers understand their role and the support that they will receive in actively participating in Fast-Track TQM.

Question 9: Should We Maximize the Number of Managers in the Decision Process?

The quick answer is yes. But who should be involved? Certainly the president and vice presidents. It addition midlevel managers must be directly involved. Extending the decision-making process beyond the vice president level has the advantage of helping midlevel managers "buy into" the process early, avoiding a hard sell later. Managers who feel they are part of the decision to make the organization Quality-driven are much more likely to do the work needed to make that decision a reality.

Question 10: Should We Proceed in Developing a Fast-Track TQM Organization?

This question should not be taken lightly or answered too quickly. A "yes" response can be given only when the president, vice presidents, and midlevel managers are fully committed to advance the organization to TQM. To become Quality-driven, senior management must be willing to incorporate a different style of leadership, involve a different process for making decisions, allocate resources differently, and involve managers and employees in the day-to-day operations. It's a big step. Is it the best step for your organization?

Even if it is the best step for your organization, are you willing to provide the leadership to steer your organization in the Quality direction? One president who was near retirement clearly understood the value and importance of advancing his company into Quality improvement. He foresaw the commitment and involvement that would be needed from him to make the necessary changes to become Quality-driven. We sat in his office late one night and agreed that the decision to proceed with TQM would make it necessary for him to defer his retirement for at least two years. A change in leadership early on in the TQM advancement process would have been too difficult for the company to ensure TQM success. In the end, he decided to defer the process for several months while he searched for a new president. As it turned out, the new president was selected from within the company and within 90 days began the journey with Fast-Track TQM began.

Can You Make These Bold Statements?

If you and your organization are ready for Fast-Track TQM, you should be able to make the following bold statements without hesitation:

1. We've fully examined the process of becoming a TQM organization.

2. TQM has a definite place in our organization.

3. We cannot change adequately without becoming a TQM-driven organization.

4. The timing is right for us to get involved in the TQM process.

5. We can expect a return on our investment in TQM within six to nine months.

6. We can establish the right Quality processes for our organization the first time.

7. We are committed to getting the necessary outside help to make the TQM process work.

8. We have plenty of commitment from our management to make TQM work.

9. We're willing to maximize the number of managers involved in the TQM decision-making and planning process.

10. We're ready to proceed with developing a TQM organization.

Fast Track at a Glance

✔ The decision to become a Quality-driven organization must be made logically, not emotionally.

✔ Nine critical questions must be answered with a "yes" before making the final decision to become a TQM organization.

✔ TQM may prove to have value in one or two areas or divisions without involving the entire organization.

✔ Staying competitive may be the driving force behind the decision to develop TQM.

✔ There is no "perfect time" to launch TQM.

✔ An effective TQM process should demonstrate a return on investment within six to nine months.

✔ The Fast-Track Method of TQM focuses first on improving the Quality of management and second on improving the management of Quality.

✔ At minimum, senior managers and in-house trainers should be trained by a qualified Quality consultant.

✔ It's not the number of managers who are committed to TQM that's important, but the number of influential managers who are committed.

✔ Written agreements outline senior management commitments and support, as well as manager and supervisor commitment and accountabilities.

✔ Involving key managers below the vice president level in the TQM decision-making process helps them become committed to the Quality process.

9

Event 4: Preparing a Quality Master Plan

I firmly believe, "Success occurs because it is planned and prepared for." Preparing a Fast-Track Master Plan for Quality advancement is imperative in developing a TQM-driven organization. It is a three-year planning map for moving the company to TQM success.

Preparing a Master Plan is much like developing a small-scale strategic plan with a very specific focus on Quality. Unlike strategic planning, which usually involves only a key group of five to ten senior managers, Fast-Track Master Planning involves midlevel management with as many as 20 to 100 managers participating.

Why so many managers? Wouldn't it be easier to plan with a smaller group of top managers? Of course it would. But keep in mind that establishing a Fast-Track TQM organization is not simply a "program" that is introduced and soon forgotten. Rather it's a different way of managing, a different way of providing leadership to advance the organization. By involving a greater number of managers in the planning process, more of them will "buy in" to Fast-Track TQM, and they will do so sooner. Instead of just a few managers catching the vision of the power, impact, and benefits of Fast-Track TQM and then having to sell the others on the concepts, you'll have early acceptance by the majority of the greatest challenge group—midlevel managers. Involving these managers in the planning process helps them own the process and accept the idea that TQM is important to the success of the company. Managers who feel ownership in TQM have a greater stake in making it a success.

Managers at a Master Planning session must believe that they are there to examine the TQM process, and that they will define a plan and schedule events to improve Quality. Ultimately, they must be part of the decision-making process. In fact, the majority of the time in Fast-Track Master Planning is spent defining how managers will provide leadership in the organization, how they will work together, and what their organization's model of leadership will look like. A company is more likely to have success with TQM if managers understand the concept of TQM, what it brings to the organization, establish cooperative relationships, and develop a common language to talk about Quality as it evolves in their organization.

Fast-Track Master Planning is much like a team-building session with senior and midlevel managers. It helps define how managers will lead the organization in ways that will consistently improve the Quality of products and services. This doesn't mean that the management styles and methods used in many companies are ineffective. On the contrary, most organizations already have effective leadership in place. But TQM will likely require some major leadership changes. It may require changes in how resources are allocated. It may involve changes in how problems are identified and resolved. It causes an examination of how the organization deals with internal conflicts. It surely involves a different way of involving midlevel managers and employees in making the organization a success.

Fast-Track Tip 41

The process of Fast-Track Master Planning is important in creating unity and common understanding among managers. It is a process of involvement.

Why Bother with a Master Plan?

Some managers might be tempted to skip the Master Planning process altogether in favor of getting on with the tasks of improving Quality. Resist the temptation! The Fast-Track Master Plan will become your map for success. It will guide your organization in the how's and why's of Quality improvement. And this is just one of several benefits of having a Master Plan.

1. The most important benefit is that it will establish a clear organizational direction. Having spoken over the years with thousands of managers and supervisors, I find that the one thing they express frustration with is the lack of clarity about the direction their organization is going. What's

missing is a leader with the strength to take a stand and point the direction.

Organizations with clearly established direction function with more unity. Their managers and employees are better able to collaborate and share information. Instead of confusion and complaints about lack of communication, there is a sense of mission. When senior managers clearly declare the direction of the company is to enhance and build Quality, managers and supervisors are better able to follow the lead. And what better direction to establish than Quality improvement? Who can argue with its merits?

2. A second benefit of Fast-Track Master Planning is that it helps create and build team unity. Anytime people try to function in groups without a focal point, chaos and confusion reign. A moblike mentality takes over, and little, if anything, gets accomplished. Over the years, I've facilitated hundreds of team-building planning retreats with managers of both large and small organizations. *Building a team always involves creating a common goal on which everyone can focus.* When management makes Quality the focus, managers, supervisors, and employees are able to rally to that cause. TQM becomes the binding force, the unity of purpose that causes people to link arms and work diligently to accomplish the shared goal of Quality improvement. This common direction and Quality focus help people share information, collaborate more effectively, and communicate more openly. In short, Quality focus creates strong teams.

3. Your company will also realize that Fast-Track Quality Master Planning creates a step-by-step process with which people can identify. Master Planning creates a series of events designed to advance the organization. Once identifiable events are created, then schedules, timelines, and accountabilities can be established to make the planned events a reality.

Outcomes of the Planning Process

The Fast-Track Master Planning process should yield five important outcomes for your organization:

1. A corporate mission statement to advance Quality

2. Organizational value statements regarding the importance of Quality

3. Relationship agreements to work as a management team

4. A TQM code of behavior

5. Events, responsibilities, and timelines to build TQM success

(Chapter 13 describes the flow of these outcomes as a part of a year-long process in building management commitment to Fast-Track TQM.) Let's examine each of these outcomes in more detail.

Corporate Mission Statement to Advance Quality

Most companies have mission statements that outline the purpose and direction of the organization. However, as Quality becomes a priority in both products and service, it's necessary to review and recast the mission statement to reflect the new emphasis.

Some managers doubt the value of mission statements. In the November-December 1991 issue of *Harvard Business Review*, Dr. Mike Beers, a professor in organizational behavior, describes how mission statements can have limited impact on advancing the organization. Too often, employees and managers don't understand, and can't relate to, corporate mission statements. The words are cast on posters, manuals, and annual reports, but they don't really influence the organization's direction without belief and action.

In working with hundreds of corporations, I've concluded that perhaps the greatest benefit of a mission statement is in the process of preparing it. The discussions, the challenges, the questions that managers wrestle with as they hammer out a mission statement creates a common understanding of where the organization is going. It forces managers to define why they're doing what they're doing and how they go about doing it. It's an invaluable process that helps managers develop a common vision for the organization.

Whether or not your organization has a mission statement, *it's essential to write one with Quality as a priority.* Even if your company's mission statement was recently prepared or revised, revisiting it and challenging it with TQM principles is imperative to becoming a successful Quality-driven organization.

Your mission statement should incorporate four important factors:

1. Who the organization serves

2. How the service or product will be provided

3. The commitment the organization has in serving its customers

4. What the organization is willing to do to serve its customers

Maximize the number of managers participating in preparing a statement. Every manager who works on the process will have a clear understanding of the value and importance of Quality as it relates to the company's mission. The statement preparation requires several hours of discussions, questions, and challenges before it finally evolves into the one simple sentence. Although it becomes a clear statement of direction, its real value is that the process of preparing it created a unity of purpose, direction, and commitment among the company's managers.

Mission statements that managers and employees can personally relate to, and in which they find guidance and direction, are the most effective. In most cases, simpler is better. Portions of a mission statement can evolve to becoming a company motto. Take, for example, the Ford Motor Company's motto: "Quality is Job One." The benefit of this statement is that every employee in the organization, as well as buying customers, can relate to this statement. The number one priority in the company is clearly Quality in its products and service.

Many Quality consultants advise avoiding slogans or simple mottos. While it is important to stay away from the "motto-of-the-month" syndrome, missions statements that are simple and catchy can be effective. If the mission statement is something everyone can quickly grasp and understand, it will be more meaningful and clearly state what the organization is about.

Fast-Track Tip 42

Create a simple, relevant mission statement that all managers and employees can understand, relate to, and support.

Organizational Value Statements Regarding Quality

Every individual has values, behaviors, and ideals they think are important. Likewise every employee and every manager in an organization has a viewpoint and opinions about what should be important in the company and how it should operate—what its values are about. Fast-Track Master Planning can help you establish and clarify your organization's values.

Ask the questions:

What do we value in the concepts of TQM?

What can TQM bring to our organization?

The answers will unfold the key values your staff holds. You'll find that Fast-Track TQM can be advanced in your company more quickly when the values adopted by the organization are the same ones commonly held by many people, such as honesty, integrity, hard work, and doing a day's work for a day's pay.

As with mission statements, it's the *process* of establishing organizational values that's really important. It will help managers share their understanding of what's important to the company. The value statements will act as a framework for discussions about how to improve Quality. Once the statements are formulated, they will help in future decision making and in the allocation of resources. When faced with difficult decisions, managers can ask themselves, "Is this decision in line with the company's values? Does this decision violate any of the company's value statements?" By having managers come to a common agreement about organizational values, you've taken a big step toward making your company Quality-driven. In many organizations the value statements are converted to Quality Requirements. Every decision or action is measured against the requirements (values).

Figure 9.1 represents the value statements used to guide leadership actions for years to come.

You might question these statements because they smack of motherhood and apple pie. Nevertheless, they're values that most employees and managers readily accept. There is nothing in Western Growers Association's value statements that their staff would reject. The statements are supported by the managers and employees, and they will act as guidelines in how to lead and work within the organization. Like with the mission

---

WESTERN GROWERS ASSOCIATION "QUALITY" VALUES

1. Reliable/timely response and solutions to meet customer needs and expectations.

2. Defect-free products and service to all customers.

3. Professional delivery and promotion of Quality services.

4. Determination of customer expectations and the goal of meeting or exceeding them.

5. Providing proactive surprising service.

Figure 9.1. Sample value statement by Western Growers Association

---

Fast-Track Tip 43

Establish organizational values that all employees and managers can support.

---

statement process, the process of creating value statements is as valuable as the outcome itself.

Relationship Agreements

An important part of the Fast-Track Master Planning Process is establishing an understanding and ultimately a written set of agreements about how managers intend to work together in leading the organization. This includes issues such as the recognition of conflict and how it can be resolved. It serves as a structured guideline in how the management group will work together one-on-one and in management meetings.

Perhaps more importantly, individual managers take the outcome of the agreement-setting process into their own work areas and establish the same type of guidelines with their employees in how they will work together. The process begins by asking the question, "How can we best work together?"

Take a moment to review the sets of agreements in Fig. 9.2. These were established by two companies, Alaska Railroad Corporation (ARRC) and Western Growers Association (WGA). What similarities do you see in the two sets of agreements? What differences? Each set of agreements was created by a group of managers who said, "This is what is important for our company, and this is how we want to apply leadership in working together."

Fast Tracking Tip 44

Managers strengthen their unity and their leadership effectiveness as they clarify how they will work together.

Fast Tracking TQM Code of Behavior

A manager can operate from any one of four management lifestyles as they lead to advance their organization:

WGA MANAGEMENT AGREEMENTS

1. Be accountable for performance agreements.
2. No hidden agendas.
3. Constructive confrontations.
4. Decisions by consensus.
5. Share ideas/views openly.
6. Support each other in the achievement of personal and department goals.
7. Involve affected departments in our department's business.
8. Treat each other with courtesy and respect.
9. Consistently know and meet/exceed both internal and external customer expectations.

ARRC MANAGEMENT AGREEMENTS

1. Cooperation to achieve a goal.
2. Full and fair disclosure (willing to trust).
3. Backing (supporting) decisions.
4. Take time to share and listen, discuss issues—interdepartmental issues.
5. Take responsibility for your own decisions.
6. Understand, accept, appraise, and support the functional roles within the organization.
7. Continue to be good corporate citizens.
8. Operate on a basis of mutual respect.
9. Commit to cooperative effort.
10. FOCUS on the positive.

Figure 9.2. Sample relationship agreements

1. Win-lose
2. Lose-win
3. Lose-lose
4. Win-win

1. In win-win, the manager says, "I'm going to do everything to win and am taking action to support and ensure that everyone else I interact with in the organization also wins." Everyone is on the same track to win, helping one another achieve mutual goals. This may sound a little unrealistic. It is certainly counter to the more competitive, win-lose orientation most of us grew up with and different from the dog-eat-dog reality of most American businesses.

2. In the win-lose style, the manager's mindset is, "I'm going to win, you are going to lose." This is a common management style in North America, perhaps fostered by our love for athletic competition. There is clearly one winner and everyone else loses.

3. Lose-win is a less common orientation than win-lose. Here the manager may, on occasion, get into a position in which he or she says, "It's better to sacrifice for the good of the organization or for the good of someone else." This style quickly leads an organization or work group into achieving less than their best. The losers are receiving or giving less than full value. Consequently, the sum of the total efforts is diminished.

4. Lose-lose is destructive for everyone, including individuals, departments, and the entire organization. An example of a lose-lose situation might be frustrated or angry employees who are involved in behaviors damaging to the organization such as theft, sabotage, or giving away trade secrets to competitors.

It's also the orientation needed for real TQM success. Win-win means that everyone, both the individuals and the entire organization, benefits from advancing Quality. It means that all the individuals in the organization have a clear understanding of what they can do to support and contribute to building not only their own success, but also that of the organization.

You can build senior management support for the win-win style with the following great activity. In the first couple of hours together with your senior staff, describe the four work styles—win-win, win-lose, lose-win, and lose-lose. Give examples of each from within your industry. Then ask the group to create a master list of what win-win would mean for the organization. Begin by asking the group, "What does win-win mean for our organization in building Quality products or services?" In a larger group, it may be necessary to break into smaller groups and brainstorm win-win lists before getting back together to create a master list. Chart the answers on newsprint for all to see. The list should contain 10 to 25 key actions.

The real power in the win-win process comes at the end. Once your group has drafted their list, challenge the group by asking, "Are you committed and will you take every action listed to support our win-win requirements?" After receiving a verbal "yes," ask each manager to come to the chart and sign his or her name, indicating support in building a Quality-driven organization through the win-win requirements as defined.

At this stage in the senior management process, the group begins to establish expectations and accountabilities. The managers are beginning to define the "how" of building Quality. The group should schedule another meeting in 60-90 days to reinforce their commitment to win-win actions. At this meeting, each win-win item should be reviewed to confirm conformance and support. Situations/actions in which win-win isn't working well should be reviewed and reworked. The outcome of such a review is usually a rededication to making win-win work. The review process, which should be held every three to four months in the first few years of TQM as a maintenance process for the group to strengthen and reinforce their working relationships.

Figure 9.3 contains a sample list of win-win statements established and adopted by 350 managers and supervisors stating how they can work cooperatively together for a common win-win purpose.

Events, Responsibilities, and Timelines

The final step in the Fast-Track Master Planning Process is what managers originally thought they were meeting for: planning events that will advance the organization in TQM. The event plan should include a schedule—what's going to happen when—as well as responsibilities and accountabilities—who's going to do what and how it will be evaluated. Figure 9.4 is a typical example of a Quality event and its time schedule.

Facilitating the Planning Process

I've discussed the events of the Fast-Track Master Planning Process, but how exactly do you facilitate the process? As mentioned earlier, the planning process should involve senior and the next level of managers. *All members of the senior management staff must be present during the entire process.* It's easy for senior managers to feel they have "too much to do" to attend a two- or three-day planning meeting. Yet no senior manager should be excused—not to answer phone calls, not to attend a special

EXAMPLES OF WIN-WIN

1. Commit time to listen and communicate.

2. Achieve realization, sensitivity, and respect for the roles and responsibility of others.

3. Share resources, including experiences, and avoid waste and duplication.

4. Everyone realizes stimulation, satisfaction, and enjoyment from his or her work.

5. Act in the best interests of the company, and trust others to do the same.

6. Encourage and support full empowerment of employees to aggressively pursue continuous improvement in product and service Quality.

7. Encourage and support increased tolerance of risk taking and failure.

8. Ensure the integrity of JDI long-term objectives of becoming "Best Dairy."

9. Achieve financial objectives.

10. Establish and operate in a TQM Culture.

11. Recognize and reward contributions to the Quality process.

12. Customer and industry recognize we are the best in our industry.

13. Establish milestones and formally celebrate.

14. Promote mentoring through levels and across organization.

15. Break old traditions.

16. Consistently exceed customer expectations.

17. All employees know how to perform their jobs.

18. Eliminate barriers that foster anything other than win-win.

19. Processes established for continual feedback at all levels.

20. Consistently seek feedback from our customers.

Figure 9.3. Example of win-win statement at JDI

meeting, and not to complete a project that must get done. Having senior managers in attendance will not only make sure they are up to speed with the TQM process, but it will also confirm manager commitment to TQM.

In most cases, the planning process must be led by an experienced facilitator. Regardless of who facilitates, it's imperative that he or she have a clear understanding of the five outcomes: establishing a mission statement; creating organizational value statements; determining outcome agreements; establishing a TQM code of behavior; and planning Quality

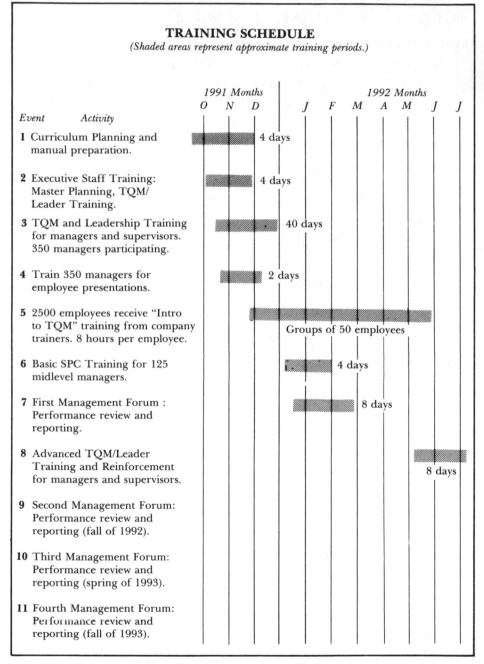

Figure 9.4. Schedule of events

enhancement events, responsibilities, and timelines. If the facilitator is clear on these desired outcomes, rapid progress can be made. While many managers will be anxious to move quickly to the final step (establishing events, schedules, and responsibilities), avoid moving too quickly through the first four steps. *These steps are the most important in establishing a thorough and common understanding of TQM and in helping managers build a sense of teamwork and commitment to the Quality process.* The entire process should take approximately 16 to 24 hours, preferably at an off-site location where there won't be any interruptions.

A facilitator's success is based on his/her ability to *ask questions,* not to tell others what to do. Asking provocative questions stimulates thought and discussion; it allows people to test their ideas with others and finally reach understanding and agreement about how to proceed in advancing Quality in the organization. Each step in the planning process should be centered around a set of questions. The facilitator asks questions and records participants' responses on large newsprint. As the newsprint pages fill, they can be posted around the room. Recording participants' verbatim responses not only validates their participation, it also lets others see and evaluate the answers for further thought and discussion.

Fast-Track Tip 45

Master Planning facilitators need special skills and abilities to ask penetrating questions.

The Steps in Facilitating

The following areas need to be examined and discussed in the planning process. Each area is accompanied by the key questions the facilitator can use to stimulate dialogue.

Step 1: Examine the Present Leadership's Effectiveness

1. What is it about our leadership that we want to keep doing as we advance toward TQM? (Be sure to chart the responses to all questions.)

2. What is it about our leadership that perhaps we should start doing to support and advance the organization to TQM?

3. What is it about our leadership that we should stop doing as we advance toward TQM?

Step 2: Clarify the Organization's Quality Mission Statement

1. Where does the issue of Quality fit into the mission of our organization?

2. In defining our mission, who is the ultimate customer that we are striving to serve?

3. What actions can be taken in serving our customer?

Step 3: Establish Organizational Value Statements Toward TQM

1. What is there about our personal values that we want included in our leading the organization to TQM?

2. Of the values listed on the chart, which top five or six should be finalized into a polished document?

3. Can you support these values as evidenced by your daily example?

Step 4: Establish a Set of Agreements on Working Together as a Leadership Team in Advancing to TQM

1. As a management team, how do we want to work together to be effective in providing leadership to the organization?

2. Can we honor and keep the agreements that we have identified?

3. Are you committed enough to quit if you consistently violate one or more of the agreements that we've established?

Step 5: Establish a TQM Code of Behavior

1. List on a piece of paper, the standards, guidelines, or rules that you hope every employee and manager would operate by in supporting TQM in the organization.

2. Identify five or six of those listed that you feel are critical for inclusion in the standards of behavior for TQM.

3. Can you support by your own behavior the standards that are identified here?

Step 6: Establish a Schedule of Events, Assignments, and Time Frames for TQM Advancement (Fig. 9.4)

1. What major events are necessary to advance the organization to TQM status over the next two years?

2. Who is going to be responsible for the completion of each of the events?

3. What are the time frames required for each event and the sequence of the events and timing?

Fast Track at a Glance

✔ The Fast-Track Planning Process should involve 20-30 senior and upper-level managers.

✔ A Fast-Track Master Plan will establish organizational direction, create and strengthen team unity, and develop a step-by-step process for TQM.

✔ Master Planning establishes (1) a corporate mission statement, (2) organizational value statements, (3) a set of management agreements on how to work together, (4) a code of TQM behavior, and (5) a schedule of events and responsibilities for achieving TQM.

10
Events 6 and 9: Conducting a Quality Audit

Fundamental to Fast-Track to Quality is having a clear understanding of your customers' needs and expectations. As mentioned in Chap. 2, this insight rests on knowing who your customers are—both *internal customers* (within your organization) and *external customers*. Generally, if you meet customers' needs and exceed their expectations, you'll have customer *satisfaction*. Customer satisfaction, in turn, yields repeat and new business, increased profits, and greater market share.

It's critical to know your customers, their needs, and their expectations.

Large corporations spend thousands, even millions of dollars conducting market surveys and Quality audits to arrive at this information. They know that, if they can have accurate enough information and can create a product or service that fits those needs and expectations, they will have a highly salable product.

You can do the same thing—*with only a modest investment*—using a Fast-Track Quality Audit, which is a formal process employed to:

- Confirm and understand your customers' requirements for satisfaction.
- Determine how well you're meeting those needs and expectations.

A Fast-Track Quality Audit offers other benefits beyond making your product or service more salable and therefore more valuable to your customers. It can provide direction for all employees in working to truly satisfy customer needs and expectations. Whether we're talking about a manager, a mail clerk, a custodian, or a secretary, everyone in the company has customers. Managers and employees who are clear about their customers' needs and expectations become more effective in performing their job tasks and using resources wisely because they know what they're working toward—customer satisfaction.

The Never-Ending Need for Quality Audits

A Quality audit isn't something you do once and for all. You must conduct Quality audits on a regular basis because customer needs and expectations are continually changing. When automaker Henry Ford produced the first model Ts, customers could get one in any color they wanted, as long as it was black. As long as cars were available only in one color, customers expected only one color; they were satisfied with black. But as soon as automakers began painting cars in other colors, expectations changed; customers were no longer satisfied with only black cars.

The same is true of your customers. As your company gets better at meeting and exceeding customers' needs and expectations, it automatically "recalibrates" customer expectation upward. Now customers expect more. At that point, you have a new target, a new level of expectation to work toward.

A reasonable and inevitable question at this point is, "If customer expectations keep increasing, when does it ever end?" The answer is probably never. It's one of the things that keeps business exciting. And if you're not willing to meet and exceed your customers' ever-changing needs and expectations, you can be sure your competition will be. They're probably discussing Quality and how better to serve customers—your customers. As soon as they prove themselves better able to meet your customers' needs and expectations, they'll be the ones enjoying increased profitability and greater market share.

The Focus of a Fast-Track Quality Audit

A Quality audit should focus on three areas:

1. **Customer expectations:** Beyond his/her basic needs, what does your customer expect from your product or service?

2. **Present fit:** How well is your product or service doing at meeting those expectations? What is the present "fit" between customer expectations

and your product or service? If we were to design a report card of expectations from the customers, how would your company score?

3. **Suggestions for improvement:** How do your customers think your product or service can be improved? While customers don't know all the intricacies or activities that go on within your organization, they have a unique vantage point. Their view can provide a new perspective on how better to meet their expectations.

Fast-Track Tip 46

Regularly reevaluate your customers' ever changing needs and expectations.

How the Fast-Track Quality Audit Is Structured

Assessing Internal Customer Needs

A successful Fast-Track Quality Audit is a methodical, carefully planned process of understanding the needs and expectations of your customers. Internally, it might be understanding the needs and expectations of a department or of a work group and all the departments they interact with. Some departments, such as human resources, may need to assess their customers in every department in the organization.

The first step in conducting a Fast-Track Internal Audit is for the manager (foreman, department head, etc.) to list all of his/her area's internal customers. With whom does the department interface on an on-going basis? The list should include the individuals' names, titles, locations, phone numbers, and who they interface with.

An easy way to visualize these interrelationships and determine who should participate in the audit is to draw a small circle at the center of a sheet of paper. Have the manager put his/her name and department in this circle. Then, around the perimeter, draw circles to represent the departments they interface with. Label each circle, and draw an arrow from the center of the departmental circle to each individual within the other circles, identifying the number of times someone in the central department interacts with the departments on the periphery. (See Fig. 10.1.)

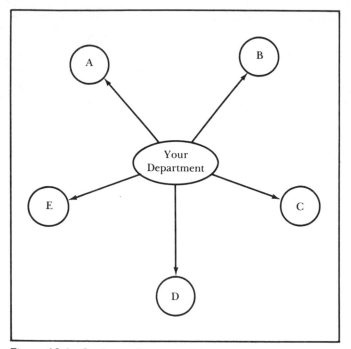

Figure 10.1. Confirming frequency of department interactions

Then keep a log of these interactions for a few weeks. This creates a clear picture of priorities—which departments or individuals the department interacts with most frequently and least frequently.

Once managers or supervisors identify their internal customers, they need to schedule meetings with the heads of those departments and key employees. They can use the interrelationship graphic (in Fig. 10.1) to determine who to meet with first. Number one on the schedule for meetings should be departments they interact with most, their most important internal customers. The purpose of the meetings is to determine customer needs and expectations: What exactly does each department need and expect from your department?

Caution: Identifying and clarifying needs and expectations are supervisory and management responsibilities, not the employees'. It's important that you don't create a situation in which employees are wasting time and disrupting work flow asking their internal customers about needs and expectations. The department heads *and* select employees should meet to discuss mutual needs and expectations with the department being audited. Once there is clarity and agreement on expectations, fit, and actions for improvement, all employees are brought together to review the findings and create an action plan. (Precisely how to conduct a Quality Audit is explained later in this chapter.)

Fast-Track Tip 47

Managers and select employees are directly involved in identifying and clarifying customer needs and expectations.

Assessing External Customer Needs

It would be a mistake for every employee or manager to contact external customers and ask about their needs and expectations. The process would become disjointed and can do more harm than good. External customers will see the company as well-meaning, but disorganized. A structured, well-planned process will yield both good data and stronger relationships with customers.

The place to start is with the manager making a list of external customers and the individuals who make direct contact with your department/company. Some customers will come in contact with more than one department within your organization (e.g., sales, shipping, customer service, etc.). To ensure a clear understanding of your customers' needs and expectations and how your company is meeting those needs and expectations, you'll have to be sure that each "contact point" between your customer and your company is assessed. Have the manager and perhaps one or two employees meet with the customers to conduct the audit.

Pitfalls in Conducting a Quality Audit

Knowing what to do—and what not to do—brings balance and understanding in planning and conducting a Quality audit with either internal or external customers. Here are some of the most common pitfalls to avoid:

Creating False Expectations.   Too often, when managers and employees catch the vision of Fast-Track TQM, they rush out—notepad in hand—to discuss needs and expectations with their customers. While the enthusiasm is commendable, the approach can create havoc. Conducting a Quality audit is a serious process that requires careful planning. Merely asking your customers about their needs and expectations automatically creates raised expectations. They're immediately convinced that something is going to change in the level of service they're currently receiving. If, after a couple of weeks or months they see no change, they'll be disappointed, and they'll value your current level of service even less. If you're not prepared to actually improve service to your customer, do not conduct a Quality audit. Only conduct an audit when you have the delivery capability to make internal improvements.

Asking Nonspecific, Unclear Questions.   The most commonly asked (and least effective question) asked in a Quality audit is, "What are your expectations of the service and products from our department?" Most customers aren't sophisticated enough to know what that question means. The usual response is vague, something like, "Well, gee, you're doing okay, I guess." The questioning process must be very precise and focused in order to guide customers through a thorough examination of defined needs and expectations.

Using Nonobjective Data.   Collecting data only in written statements or narrative format is a mistake. While such statements can provide interesting insights, they make it very difficult to compare customers' changing needs and expectations from one month or quarter to the next. Your data collection must include some numerical ratings to enable you to compare and reach objective conclusions.

Recording Data Haphazardly.   Some managers try to conduct customer Quality audit interviews "by the seat of their pants." They ask whatever questions seem to fit at the time. This is a big mistake. It's important to have a set of prepared questions or a formal questionnaire, and to record the information in a prescribed format. Not only will this make the data more consistent and reliable, it will convey an important message to your customers—you're organized. If you are serious about the Quality audit and recording the information, your customers will view it as a valuable process and that you are sincerely interested in receiving their input. The more effort you put into preparation, the more thoroughly your customers will respond, and the more you'll both gain in affecting product and service delivery.

Fast-Track Tip 48

Conduct a Fast-Track Quality audit only if you are truly serious about improving Quality to customers.

Defining the Quality Audit Process

Exactly how is a Fast-Track Quality Audit conducted? Clarity and precision are critical factors in producing accurate, usable data to improve your company's ability to meet your customers' needs and expectations. You can achieve clarity and precision by using a carefully prepared set of questions throughout the interview process.

Aim for face-to-face interaction whenever possible. Ideally, the interview should be done one-on-one, with interviewer and interviewee sitting together discussing the questions. Under these conditions, the interviewer can be ensured that the customer understands each question. When face-to-face interviews aren't possible, the next best solution is a telephone interview. The least effective alternative, although certainly possible, is an interview through written correspondence via the mail or fax.

When there are several customers, perhaps two or three of them can discuss their expectations as a group. However, in situations where unique factors vary widely from customer to customer, it's best to conduct the interview on an individual basis. It is absolutely critical that the people you interview are customers who actually receive the product/service, evaluate it, and sign off on its Quality.

In addition to interviewing the receiver of your products/services, it's also vital that you interview the decision makers, people from the customer company who make the decisions about buying your products or services. While people at lower levels in the customer organization may be satisfied with your products or services, the person who ultimately must be pleased is the decision maker, the person who determines whether or not to continue purchasing your product or service and how much to buy.

Seven Universal Areas for Conducting a Quality Audit

Both internal and external customer audits can be applied to collect data in seven universal areas. The areas are called "universal" because they apply equally well in any situation for any department or organization regardless of industry, service or product.

1. Timeliness of response
2. Accuracy of paperwork
3. Condition of product/service
4. Availability of product/service
5. Courtesy of service
6. Keeping promises (agreements)
7. Cost of operation

Figure 10.2. Seven universal areas for Quality auditing

Preparing the Interview Questionnaire

In preparing the questions for your customer Quality audit, keep the purposes of the audit in mind:

1. To determine your customers' needs and expectations
2. To assess how well you're meeting those needs and expectations
3. To gather suggestions for improvement

You can divide the interview questions into these three areas. Part 1 of the interview confirms your customers' expectations. Figure 10.3 applies each of the seven universal areas in collecting data about your customers' expectations. Note how each question includes one of the universal areas. (Leave plenty of space for your customers to record their responses.)

Part 2 of the questionnaire addresses "fit," how well your product or service meets or fits with the customers' expectations. (See Fig. 10.4.) It's your company's "report card" from your customer. You'll use the same seven universal questions used in Part 1, but phrased slightly differently. In addition, you should use a scoring scale of 1-10, with 10 being "we are totally meeting our customers' expectations all the time" and 1 being "we are never meeting our customers' expectations." Leave room below each question for narrative answers.

FAST-TRACK QUALITY AUDIT—PART 1

1. With regard to timeliness of response from our unit or department, what are your expectations?

2. With regard to accuracy of paperwork from our unit or department, what are your expectations?

3. With regard to condition of our product or service from our unit or department, what are your expectations?

4. With regard to the availability of our product or service from our unit or department, what are your expectations?

5. With regard to the courtesy of service from our unit or department, what are your expectations?

6. With regard to the keeping of promises (agreements) from our unit or department, what are your expectations?

7. With regard to the cost of operation from our unit or department, what are your expectations?

Figure 10.3. Confirming customer expectations

FAST-TRACK QUALITY AUDIT—PART 2

8. On a scale of 1-10, how would you rate our unit or department in meeting your expectations in regards to timeliness of response?

9. On a scale of 1-10, how would you rate our unit or department in meeting your expectations in regards to accuracy of paperwork?

10. On a scale of 1-10, how would you rate our unit or department in meeting your expectations in regards to the condition of our products/service?

11. On a scale of 1-10, how would you rate our unit or department in meeting your expectations in regards to the availability of our product/service?

12. On a scale of 1-10, how would you rate our unit or department in meeting your expectations in regards to the courtesy of our service?

13. On a scale of 1-10, how would you rate our unit or department in meeting your expectations in regards to keeping promises (agreements)?

14. On a scale of 1-10, how would you rate our unit or department in meeting your expectations in regards to cost of operation?

Figure 10.4. A report card in meeting expectations

Ask the customer to give a numerical rating and specific examples of situations where the company failed to meet his/her expectations. The narrative responses will provide some valuable insights and give the customer a reference gauge for their numerical responses.

Part 3 of the questionnaire elicits suggestions from customers about how you can improve your product or service. (See Fig. 10.5.)

To simplify recording and later analyzing the data, you might want to break the questionnaire into three pages, with one part per page. It's vital that customers be given plenty of space in the narrative and suggestion sections for plenty of detail.

Fast-Track Tip 49

Request specific examples of areas in which your product or service is not meeting customer needs or expectations.

FAST-TRACK QUALITY AUDIT—PART 3

15. What specific suggestions do you have for improving our timeliness of response?

16. What specific suggestions do you have for improving the accuracy of our paperwork?

17. What specific suggestions do you have for improving the condition of our product/service?

18. What specific suggestions do you have for improving the availability of our product/service?

19. What specific suggestions do you have for improving the courtesy of our service?

20. What specific suggestions do you have for improving our ability to keep promises (agreements) with you?

21. What specific suggestions do you have for reducing the cost of operation?

Figure 10.5. Suggestions to better meet their expectations

Conducting Customer Interviews

Figure 10.6 is a list of eight key actions in conducting a Quality Audit interview with either internal or external customers.

The interview itself should be conducted in as private a setting as possible, preferably at the customer's location or facility. Going to customers' offices or plants to ask them about their expectations and discuss how you can better serve them delivers a strong, positive message. It lets the customer know that you are sincere and serious about TQM and about serving them better.

Note: Conducting a successful Fast-Track Quality Audit interview isn't easy. At first, most managers feel awkward and uncomfortable because it isn't a typical business conversation. It's not easy to have a customer tell you that you aren't giving them everything they want. But after conducting a couple of these interviews, most interviewers feel more comfortable with the process and are better able to focus on what the customer is telling them. The key is to convey to customers that you sincerely want to understand and meet their expectations and that the company is willing to work toward improving service.

Throughout the interview, confirm your understanding of what the

---

QUALITY AUDIT PROCESS

Step 1: Identify customer(s) by department (organization) and by name.

Step 2: Bring common customer group together as appropriate. Explain purpose of meeting.

Step 3: Ask the questions from Figs. 10.3-10.5 to confirm customer expectations. Record responses verbatim with two- or three-word summaries.

Step 4: Repeat the seven questions in Fig. 10.3 to confirm "fit" based on a scale of 0-10.

Step 5: Confirm suggested actions to improve service/product by asking the seven questions in Fig. 10.3.

Step 6: Confirm customers' comments by summarizing, "What I heard you saying was..."

Step 7: Declare action/process to apply to improve service/product delivery.

Step 8: Thanks for taking the time to....

Figure 10.6. Steps in conducting a Quality audit

customer is saying. "What I hear you saying is...." Parrot what customers say to ensure you fully understand their comments.

Once customers recognize that you are willing to listen to them and want to take action to meet their needs and expectations, you'll gain a partner in Fast-Track to Quality. You'll find that they will be willing to work with you to improve Quality. As customers recognize you are willing to be assertive in understanding and meeting their needs and expectations, they will begin to take the initiative to provide continual feedback about what you're doing right and the areas that need improvement. This informal but continuous customer feedback will become an important part of your success in TQM, and will help you reach your goal of meeting/exceeding the needs and expectations of every customer, every time.

Fast-Track Tip 50

Whenever possible, conduct customer Quality audit interviews face-to-face in a private setting.

Preliminary Analysis of Customer Expectations

Whenever possible, have the employees who actually serve customers analyze the customer questionnaire data. It sends employees the message that customers are intimately involved in the formulation of an action plan to better serve them. It also helps the employee "buy into" both the problems and the solutions involved in TQM.

Analyze the data from three perspectives:

1. Your ability and your competitor's ability to meet expectations.

2. Your customer's expectation "fit" and how it impacts your reputation.

3. The impact on your image. Satisfaction with how you are perceived (company image).

Let's take a closer look at each of these areas:

1. Are you exceeding your competition's ability to meet customer expectations? You must gauge each of your customer's expectations against whether your competitors are meeting or exceeding those expectations. No matter how good your competition, you have to be better in your ability to serve your customers. It may not be possible, in a short period of time, to extend your service delivery to meet or exceed all of your customers' expectations. It will take some time to develop the service delivery capability to perform at that level. But the goal must be able to provide better service than your immediate competition.

2. What is your present level of meeting customer expectations and how is it affecting your reputation? Reputation is what customers say about you to others. It's vital that what people say about your company and about its products/services is positive. Even if customers can presently say only that the delivery of service is improving, that's a positive statement. Examine each of your customers' expectations in relationship to your reputation in the universal seven areas:

- Timeliness of response
- Accuracy of paperwork
- Condition of product/service
- Availability of product or service
- Courtesy of service
- Keeping promises
- Cost of operation

3. How is your delivery of service to your customers affecting your image? Image is how people view your company, it's your "look." It involves factors like packaging, timeliness, fit-for-use, and the appearance of your employees. Reexamine customer expectations with regard to the seven universal areas, and see how they affect how your customer perceives your service/product delivery.

Usually, a preliminary examination by a few employees of the data gathered in a Quality audit will stimulate responses such as, "We could do better" and "We need to do better."

Action to Meet/Exceed Customer Expectations

With the data collected, it's time to meet with your employees, confirm their understanding of your customers' expectations, and create an action plan to meet and/or exceed those expectations.

The meetings should include any employees who are involved in providing the product/service to your customer. Ideally, the meetings are relatively brief—30 to 45 minutes—and held once or twice a week. Several shorter meetings are more effective than marathon meetings. In short meetings, it's relatively easy to generate and maintain enthusiasm. These brief meetings also enable employees to discuss the information during the work week, reach conclusions, and formulate ideas for the next meeting.

Some managers might be tempted to "run" these joint meetings, giving employees little space to offer their input or ideas. Fast-Track success depends on participation and input from all employees. The concept works only if employees and management work as a team. If you set a participatory tone in the meetings, employees will feel freer to share their insights and ideas. Including all members in these meetings and encouraging their participation will strengthen the team feeling. It will help them not only focus on their common goal of improving Quality, but also build the unity needed to work as a team.

Fast-Track Tip 51

Fast-Track TQM succeeds only when management and employees work as a team. Involve all your employees in Quality improvement planning and in the necessary changes to processes.

Sometimes it's difficult for people to express themselves in a large group. It may be an advantage to divide a larger group into subgroups of two or three. Assign specific problems or customer expectations to work on, and then have each group report on their ideas. To stimulate creative solutions, try brainstorming (see Fig. 10.7). For five minutes or so, have everyone throw out ideas without evaluating them. Encourage outrageous ideas. Use large newsprint charts to write down everyone's suggestions. Later you can go back and evaluate the best ideas.

The outcome of these meetings will be a Fast-Track TQM action plan for Quality improvement in serving each customer. The Quality action plan jointly prepared by managers and employees should be specific in terms of individual processes and assignments—who is going to do what and by when. Whenever possible, prepare a schedule of the various changes that will take place.

You've moved from a vague idea of what "Quality" means to a clear description from your customers, and further to specific actions for improvement. Now you progress from the concept of improving Quality for your customer to specific actions that work groups or individual

---

BRAINSTORMING TIPS

The idea in brainstorming is to come up with a large number of ideas. The adage, "If you want good ideas, come up with many ideas," holds true for brainstorming. Creative, usable ideas come from a large number of ideas. You want to encourage the generation of many ideas in a short period of time. To maximize your effectiveness with brainstorming, try these suggestions:

1. Set a time limit. Usually five minutes is about right.
2. Defer judgment. No criticism or judgment should be allowed during the idea-generation phase.
3. Encourage the wildest ideas participants can come up with. It's easier to "tame" wild ideas later than to "punch up" lukewarm ideas.
4. Stress the quantity, not the Quality, of ideas. The more ideas participants produce, the better ideas they'll produce.
5. Encourage "hitchhiking," i.e., building on one another's ideas.
6. Have one member of the group act as a recorder and write down the ideas where others can see them.

Figure 10.7. Brainstorming tips

employees can take. Think of it as a funneling process, from larger to smaller, from the larger picture to individual acts.

As mentioned earlier in this chapter, simply broaching the question of customer expectations automatically raises customer expectations. Now that you've conducted a Fast-Track Quality Audit, customers will expect improvement in the service they've been receiving. As you work through the planning process and develop your Quality action plan, you must keep your customers informed of your progress. Customers may expect service improvement within a week or two. In reality, it may be several months before the necessary adjustments can be made internally to improve service. It's important that you keep your customers informed so that they know that their expectations have been heard and understood and that you're taking action to meet those expectations.

Continuous Customer Follow-up

In addition to keeping customers informed about your Fast-Track TQM action plans, it's critical that the Fast-Track Quality Audit process be repeated on a regular basis. As customer needs and expectations constantly change, and as customers encounter other suppliers, their expectations change and expand. As their own business needs change with new market trends, their expectations change. It's up to you to keep your company's products and services meeting those ever changing customer expectations.

A Quality audit should be repeated every few months. It helps "recalibrate" your understanding of their expectations. It also continually lets your customers know that their expectations are your number one priority. Since you already have a numerical rating of your present fit with your customers' expectations, repeat audits can serve as a comparison. Over a period of time, you'll be able to graph your progress and demonstrate the impact of your efforts to improve Quality and meet your customers' expectations.

Fast Track at a Glance

✔ A Fast-Track Quality Audit is a formal process of getting to know and understand your customer's needs and expectations and determining how well you're meeting those needs and expectations.

✔ Customer needs and expectations constantly change; Fast-Track Quality Audits must be repeated on a regular basis.

✔ A Fast-Track Quality Audit should examine (1) customer expectations, (2) how well you're currently meeting expectations, and (3) customer suggestions for improvement.

✔ Identifying and clarifying customer needs and expectations is a management, not an employee, responsibility.

✔ In conducting a Fast-Track Quality Audit avoid (1) creating false expectations, (2) asking nonspecific questions, (3) using nonobjective data, and (4) recording data haphazardly.

✔ Be certain that the people who participate in the Quality Audit are decision-making customers, people who evaluate the product/service Quality and make decisions about purchasing it.

✔ Interview questions should assess seven universal areas: (1) timeliness of response, (2) accuracy of paperwork, (3) condition of product/service, (4) availability of product/service, (5) courtesy of service, (6) keeping promises (agreements), and (7) cost of operation.

✔ Whenever possible, conduct Quality audit interviews face-to-face in a private setting, preferably at the customer's location.

✔ Analyze data from customer interviews in terms of (1) your ability and your competitors' ability to meet expectations, (2) customer expectation "fit" and how it impacts your reputation, (3) your image, and (4) your return on investment.

✔ Keep customers informed about your progress in TQM.

11

Event 7: Statistical Process Controls

Applying Statistical Process Controls (SPCs) to improve the Quality of manufacturing was first used by Bell Labs. During the 1920s, SPCs were used extensively to improve the Quality of products produced later in the war effort. Talk with people who worked in many of those defense plants, and they'll tell you how applied statistics and measurements were used to ensure defect-free products. They even use the phrase "defect-free."

Today techniques have been refined to enable managers to use statistics to analyze and even predict the occurrence of defects in the manufacturing process. At the heart of SPC is determining a standard deviation. Many of us remember this term from our days in statistics classes. It required a complicated mathematical formula. Fortunately, it has become a simplified process that every employee or manager in the organization can understand and use. All that's needed is an inexpensive, handheld calculator and a little training.

Most managers readily acknowledge the usefulness of SPC in the manufacturing process, but they question its application in service industries. Don't be blindsided by this kind of limited thinking. Any process or activity that is repetitive, such as invoices or the number of customer contracts required to make a sale, can benefit from the application of SPC. The principles of SPC can be as valuable to service industries as it is to manufacturers.

While managers, supervisors, and employees need only modest training to understand and apply the basic principles of SPC, there's danger in introducing SPC too early in the TQM process. Before this tool can be effectively used, an organizational culture that supports Quality must be firmly established and in place. Leadership must be adequately developed.

It's common for some managers to become confused and think SPC is the same as Total Quality Management. In reality it's but one of several tools. It is clearly not the place to start TQM. Only when all these factors are in place will the introduction of SPC have any meaning and benefit to employees and the organization.

The details and processes of SPC are readily available in statistics and industrial books for the reader's further inquiry.

Fast-Track Tip 52

Don't be fooled by the value of statistical process controls (SPCs). They are only one of many tools in your TQM toolbox. With only a small investment in training, employees at all levels can successfully utilize SPCs.

12

Event 8: Conducting a Management Forum

A Management Forum is the most powerful part of the Fast-Track process. It is the driving force that sustains TQM in the organization. It builds focus, creates accountability, and develops TQM identity. It provides an opportunity for employees to receive that all-important recognition for their work. And, perhaps most importantly, it lets managers and supervisors show in a very visual way the good job they are doing. As one manager said, "It's a chance to show off my good stuff."

In the Fast-Track Paradigm, the Management Forum is carefully structured to follow all the basic training on TQM principles and Quality leadership. Following the final training session on basic Fast-Track TQM principles, organizations are encouraged to take a 60- to 90-day "application" period that furnishes managers and supervisors with an opportunity to apply the skills and principles with their staffs. At the last training session, trainees are told that on a specific date within 60 to 90 days, "We'll come back together and share experiences. Each manager is expected to give a five- to eight-minute presentation to other members of the training class describing their success in applying Fast-Track TQM principles and skills." They are also told that senior managers, including the president and vice presidents, will be attending the meeting to receive their presentations.

During these presentations, managers are instructed to follow a structured agenda with a six-step presentation format, as shown in Fig. 12.1. The last step in the figure is what the Management Forum is all about. It provides an opportunity for each manager and supervisor to show the actions they've taken with their staff in applying the skills they've learned in Fast-Track TQM and in Quality Leadership Training. It enables them to demonstrate how they've led their work group to improve Quality in their area and the results.

Step 1: Staff identification. Managers/supervisors identify who on their staff has participated in achieving the Quality improvements being presented.

Step 2: Problem statement. This step provides a clear statement of the problem they have been working to resolve.

Step 3: Confirm problem. Managers must demonstrate evidence to confirm a problem existed and its impact.

Step 4: Option description. Managers share the solution options that they and their staff considered in resolving the problem.

Step 5: Action identification. Managers describe the specific course of action they and their staff took to alleviate or reduce the problem's effects.

Step 6: Confirm improvement. Managers confirm the performance improvements achieved through their efforts. To the extent possible, these performance improvements are expressed in terms of dollars.

Figure 12.1. Presenting at a management forum

Fast-Track Tip 53

It's vital to the success of Quality Advancement that Management Forums be held 60 to 90 days following Fast-Tract TQM and leadership training. This ensures accountability and the opportunity to recognize exemplary achievements.

When managers are asked to confirm and define performance improvement, it does not mean cost savings. As soon as you define performance improvement as cost savings, managers interrupt this with, "I've got to cut somewhere in my department." The issue is not to make cuts for cost savings, but to make actual performance improvements. Improving performance may mean being able to shorten the time it takes to complete a task, removing a persistent cause of defects, or directly improving the service to customers to better meet their needs and expectations.

As managers give their presentations, the forum leader or facilitator divides a sheet of large newsprint into three columns and posts them for all to see. For each presentation, the manager's name is written on the chart in the first column, a brief synopsis of the action taken in the second column, and in the third column actual dollars effected by the performance improvement. By translating performance improvement into actual dollars, you create a methodology for measuring the progress and advancement of TQM in the organization.

During the managers' presentations, an overhead projector is made available to display data. Each manager is expected to illustrate the situation with handouts, graphs, and charts on cards taped to the front wall. They deliver their presentations according to the structured outline (Fig. 12.1).

The presenters' immediate reward is a round of applause. Since a group of 30 managers usually takes about a half-day to make all their presentations, the managers can be served a lunch following their presentations. The day becomes one of celebration, recognizing individual and group achievements. After lunch, managers spend the remainder of the day receiving additional reinforcement and training on TQM skills and principles.

Fast-Track Tip 54

Management Forums not only create accountability; they sustain excitement and interest in advancing Quality. They become times of celebration and congratulations.

Each presentation not only serves to let the management know what their staffs are doing to improve Quality, but it also enables the group to validate and confirm the contribution of individual managers to the organization's Quality advancement. I recently completed a series of Fast-Track Management Forums with 120 managers presenting over a four-day period. Each day, 30 managers made their presentations. The company president and vice president attended each morning session for the presentations and stayed through lunch. At least one senior manager attended each of the supplemental afternoon training sessions over the four-day period. If I could have altered anything in these Management Forums, it would have been for every manager to be able to hear all 120 presentations, not just the 30 in their training group. But this company directly serves the public, and a portion of their managers had to be on the job providing leadership and direction back at the office.

How did the president of the company feel about the Management

Forums? He said, "I had no idea of the achievements being made in Quality improvement in our organization." He continued, "I've heard of many examples over the last few months where a situation was impacted by TQM, but I had no idea about the depth and scope that its impact was actually having on our organization."

Accountability—the Secret of Fast-Track Success

Accountability is what a Management Forum is all about. Management Forums certainly provide opportunities for managers' leading and directing for Fast-Track TQM success to "toot their own horns" by presenting their accomplishments. But they do much more. They create a focal point for managers. They know that they will be expected at a specific time and place to demonstrate the actions they've taken to improve Quality. This is accountability.

Most managers and supervisors at lower levels have never been given the opportunity to give a group presentation to management. It's fascinating to watch them come in with new shirts, new ties, new suits. For some, it is the first time in a long while that they've worn a suit. Others come in and present in their daily work attire whether it's jeans or slacks and an open shirt. What's really important is not what they choose to wear, but that they are given the opportunity to show their accomplishments and be accountable in front of other managers and in front of the company president. Of course, when managers first participate in a Forum, the presentations are understandably a little rough. The presenters are awkward. But they improve each time they do a presentation.

Another important aspect of the Management Forum presentation is in the preceding week or two, managers work with their staffs organizing, planning, and preparing their presentation. Because a Management Forum is an organization-wide event, enthusiasm and excitement run high. Both managers and employees want their department or unit presentation to be good. They want to be accountable for improving Quality in their area.

More than establishing accountability, Management Forums create "positive" accountability. Forums are not seen as a threat or a punishment. Every presentation is viewed as beneficial. Every manager is seen as a valuable contributor to the TQM process in the organization. Management Forums keep both managers and staffs working to advance and improve the Quality within their areas of responsibility and to meet and exceed their internal and external customers' needs and expectations.

Building a Company-Wide Management Team

I previously talked about the process and importance of work groups' having a common goal, a common focus for their efforts. Management Forums become just such a focal point for managers and employees. They become the occasion for looking at where you've been and for sharing ideas and actions that have taken place to advance Quality. Management Forums provide a common purpose for Quality-enhancing actions. They enable both managers and employees to see how their efforts have not only benefited the customer, but also how they have benefited their work unit and their organization. Management Forums provide the glue that keeps the company-wide management team cohesive.

Over many years of working with organizations facilitating Management Forums, I have never seen a manager or a supervisor come to any of these sessions unprepared. All of them have worked diligently with their immediate staffs to effect Quality improvements within their assigned areas, and they can demonstrate their success. While some of them may have felt nervous and anxious about the Quality of their presentations, they are eager to show that the Quality improvement in their area was a direct result of their leadership.

Learning from One Another

It's enjoyable to watch a Management Forum take place. Often as managers make their presentations, other managers pull out pads and take notes. The Forum becomes a pooling of ideas. Managers get ideas from one another on how to collect data, how to take action to improve Quality, how to motivate and build staff commitment and motivation. As they watch and listen to other managers, they receive ideas about how to make a better presentation and how to effectively use handouts, graphs, and charts. Often, at the end of a presentation, managers in the audience will ask questions about how the presenting managers gathered their data or how they developed their presentation material. Rather than a competitive atmosphere, Management Forums foster a cooperative climate where managers help one another.

Over time, presentations at Management Forums get better and better. Organizations in their second, third, or fourth round of Forums see more polished presentations, and the presenters are more sophisticated in their ability to demonstrate and display their accomplishments. Presenting at Management Forums allows managers to reexamine how they are solving problems, how they are gathering data, how they are focusing on Quality improvement in their areas. Management Forums make sure the learning process is ongoing and that Quality advancement continues at higher and higher levels.

Fast-Track Tip 55

Management Forums should be structured to encourage questions from the audience and the sharing of ideas. A cooperative rather than competitive atmosphere must be established.

Providing Recognition

Everyone has the desire to be valued and recognized. Before an organization's president and vice presidents attend a Management Forum and receive presentations from their staffs, they are coached in how to confirm and validate each manager's or supervisor's contribution by asking clarifying questions and avoiding any criticism.

Because recognition is vital to Fast-Track TQM success and to the advancement of Quality in the organization, the Management Forum is structured to ensure individual and group recognition. First, the group offers a round of applause at the conclusion of each presentation to show their respect and their acceptance of the presentation. Second, graphs and charts used in each presentation are displayed so that others can examine them during the break or lunch, and ask questions. It's fun to see how much pride the managers show in talking about their accomplishments and sharing them with others. They know they are part of something that is making a real difference in the organization.

And finally, soon after the presentations, each presenting manager receives a personal letter from the company president, thanking them and acknowledging their important contribution in advancing Quality.

A Time to Celebrate

At the conclusion of the presentations, we bring out a large sheet cake. It's time for the group to celebrate the success they've achieved together. Usually, the inscription on the cake is something like, "We Are Making a Difference Together." The president offers a few remarks to the group about their success and cuts the cake. There's another round of applause— the group congratulating themselves for their success.

At an organization's very first Management Forum, we make an even bigger fuss around the celebration cake. Before the cake is cut, the group, including the president and vice president(s), huddle around the cake and have their picture taken. Copies of the group photograph are made and signed by the president and presented to each group member. Usually, the president writes a little inscription or note like, "You are a valuable part of our TQM team," "You are helping us make a difference," or "Thanks for being part of our TQM team." It's interesting to see how employees value these photographs. Often they mount them in frames and display them in their work areas. Some even ask if they can have an extra copy to display at home. All these little pieces of the celebration act to reinforce Quality performance and build value in working together to make a positive difference to advance Quality in serving each customer.

Improving Communication Skills

During the weeks prior to Management Forum presentations, work group discussion and collaboration increase markedly. An esprit de corps is established by people working together. The target of an upcoming Management Forum moves the cooperation to higher levels of positive interaction. Management Forums create a reason for employees to sit together and discuss the principles of Quality improvement and how they are being applied within their work unit. It stimulates communication between departments as they share information and solutions to common problems. As one manager put it, "Management Forums provide a new purpose for our Quality improvement process."

Of course, ultimately, the purpose of Quality improvement isn't to present accomplishments at meetings, but rather to improve service to the customer and further the success of the organization. Management Forums become a Fast-Track tool to accomplish both improving communication on the job and service to customers.

Measuring Fast-Track TQM Success

One of the greatest weaknesses of advancing an organization to TQM is the difficulty in measuring the progress of Quality improvement. Management Forums become an easy solution to this problem. As managers give their presentations and translate their actions into performance improvement dollars, determining the progress and value to the organization of Quality improvement is easier. Keep in mind that the performance improvement dollars aren't necessarily cost savings. I often hear managers say, "Performance improvement is nice, but we need cost savings to have a more efficient operation." The need is clear for reducing the expense side in making your operation more efficient. *But if you have consistent enough improvement in performance, it will translate into more efficiency and reduced expenses.* The focus must be kept on performance improvement to better serve the needs and expectations of your customers. *The better you become at serving your customers, the more efficient your organization becomes and the more cost effective your managers' actions become.*

To measure progress, at the end of each Management Forum, the dollars from the performance improvement columns are added together and totaled. Using Fast-Track TQM, it's not unusual for performance improvements in a single Management Forum to equal millions of dollars. One of my clients had 230 managers participate in the Forum. Eight different groups presented their successes for a total of more than $14 million! Understandably, the company's president was in awe at the impact of their Quality improvements and how better service to the customer yielded a more cost-effective organization.

Fast-Track Tip 56

The performance dollar figures generated during the presentations enable management to easily determine the return on TQM investment.

Efficiency vs. Quality Management

During the first Forum (60 to 90 days after the initial TQM training), managers and supervisors usually focus on problems of improving efficiency in their work areas. Their vision of Quality at this point is centered on being more efficient on a day-to-day basis. As they prepare for their second Management Forum (six months later) and their third Forum (another six months later), their focus shifts to customer expectations. They begin to talk more about understanding their internal and external customer and exceeding specific customer expectations.

How does this subtle, but important customer-oriented shift take place?

As managers and supervisors gain a better understanding of their customers' needs and expectations and begin to have some success in meeting those needs and expectations, they become aware of this whole new area on which to focus their Quality-improvement efforts. Instead of simply improving efficiency, the customer becomes the focus. Their question becomes, "How can we improve Quality to better serve the customer?" They've caught the greater vision of improving Quality and finally see what TQM is really all about.

As mentioned earlier in this chapter, the organization's president and vice presidents are coached before the Management Forum on what to expect and how to best receive the presentations from their employees. I confirm that the majority of presentations during the first and sometimes the second Forums will be efficiency-focused. This isn't a problem. It's part of the natural evolution of Fast-Track TQM. In fact, the more rapidly internal efficiencies are improved, the faster the energy can be applied toward better serving the customer. I also tell them to expect the customer-oriented shift to occur in the second or third Forum, 8 to 12 months after the initial TQM awareness training. This gives senior management a vision of where the Management Forum process is going, and enables them to calibrate their managers' and supervisors' expectations of the process.

Senior Management Support

Six to eight weeks before the first Management Forum, the organization's president sends a letter to each of the managers making presentations. The letter outlines the process, giving them some guidance and counsel on how to prepare for the presentations and what will be expected by senior management. Figure 12.2 is typical of this type of letter. The important and underlying message of the president's letter is that senior management values and supports them in their efforts to advance Quality in the organization.

In addition to formal Management Forums, many presidents and vice presidents take the time to meet more informally with their managers to discuss ideas and actions being taken to advance Quality. These "miniforums" offer the added benefit of being very personal.

Presidents should be encouraged to regularly write notes and letters to their managers, supervisors, and employees. These written reminders to staff confirm that senior management values their efforts to improve Quality. It lets them know that senior management supports them and is leading the way toward TQM.

Dear Management Team [or, if possible, have individual names computer generated],

Several weeks have passed since we completed the training to advance Western Growers Association into Fast-Track Total Quality Management. In October, we'll be having follow-up meetings to give every manager an opportunity to describe the progress he/she has made in advancing the principles of TQM.

Our meeting will truly be a forum, a "Management Forum," a place to share ideas and openly express your views on how to advance Western Growers to Quality improvements. This will become our ongoing way of working together. I am personally looking forward to our meeting as a time of sharing and a time of celebrating our successes together.

I encourage you to take advantage of the time remaining before our first Forum to work together with your staffs to develop graphs, charts, and handouts to demonstrate your success. In your presentation, please be sure to include ways in which your unit worked cooperatively with others and how others have worked with you. Each manager will have approximately five minutes. Please follow these five steps in making your presentation:

1. Describe your target area(s) to improve Quality by your unit.
2. Demonstrate (with graphs, if possible) the impact of the defect you're working on.
3. Describe the action taken by your group to remove or moderate the defect's effect.
4. Show the resulting Quality improvement (graph) in serving your customer.
5. Translate the effect of your Quality improvement into dollars.

We are encouraged and look forward to hearing about and celebrating your successes.

Sincerely,

Name
President

Figure 12.2. President's letter to managers

Sustaining TQM Success

Most organizational TQM efforts generate excitement and enthusiasm in the first 6 to 12 months. After that, things can fizzle. It seems that no one is really interested or concerned about Quality enhancement, and it becomes yet another "program" whose life has come to an end. It's a tragic waste of money, time, and energy, not to mention all of the lost opportunities and benefits that TQM can bring to an organization.

In Fast-Track to Quality, the Management Forum process sustains and builds continuing focus on Quality improvement in the organization. CEOs and presidents who want to be successful with TQM adopt Management Forums as part of their ongoing leadership of the organization. *It is not only through accountabilities that Quality can be consistently advanced. It is also the excitement, enthusiasm, discussions, and idea sharing generated during Management Forums that create a sustained emphasis and focus on Quality.* When every manager, supervisor, and employees is concerned about and engaged in Quality enhancement, Quality becomes an institutionalized part of the way your organization does business. The Management Forum sustains this process.

Sometimes companies experience difficult times, and the president or CEO might be tempted to forego a scheduled Forum. This is a mistake! It gives the message to everyone in the organization that Quality improvement has become less important, less of a priority.

When new managers are hired into the organization, it's vital that they receive the training to understand the TQM principles and develop Quality leadership skills. If a new president is brought into the organization, he or she must understand the success TQM is having in the organization and the importance of Management Forums in sustaining that success. For some new presidents, it's difficult to wholeheartedly embrace the Fast-Track TQM process when it is already in place and operating and doesn't have their "fingerprints" on it. A new president's support, however, can add even greater value to the process of improving Quality.

Fast Track at a Glance

✔ Management Forums should be scheduled within 60 to 90 days following Fast-Track TQM Awareness Training, and then every six months thereafter.

✔ Managers and supervisors should follow this structure when making presentations: (1) identify staff who participated, (2) state the problem, (3) demonstrate that the problem actually existed, (4) show solution options considered, (5) identify the action taken to resolve/moderate problem, and (6) confirm that improvement has been made.

✔ Performance improvement does not necessarily mean cost savings.

✔ Performance improvement, translated into dollars, provides a way for senior management to calculate return on investment with TQM.

✔ Management Forums create "positive" accountability.

✔ The Management Forum process builds company-wide unity, and encourages managers and supervisors to share ideas and learn from one another.

✔ Recognition is a major part of keeping people motivated. The Forums provide an opportunity for managers and supervisors to receive much needed recognition from senior management.

✔ An atmosphere of celebration should be established at Management Forums.

✔ As Management Forums progress into their second and third cycles, senior management will see managers and supervisors shifting their Quality-enhancement efforts from an efficiency emphasis to an emphasis on customer needs/expectations.

✔ Management Forums become the major tool in sustaining Fast-Track TQM success over time.

PART 3

Fine-Tuning and Putting the Fast-Track Paradigm to Work

Part 3 contains the "secrets" of Fast Track, the elements that make the process truly magical. Anyone can give you a recipe, a listing of ingredients, but without an adequate description of the "how-to's," the dish will likely be a failure. So it is with the Fast Track to TQM.

After reading this section, you will be able to describe:

1. Fifteen strategies for advancing Quality.
2. How to build management commitment to the Quality-advancement process.
3. The seven key leadership skills for Quality leadership.
4. The six key actions to guarantee TQM results.
5. How to improve employee performance.

6. The four steps to empowering your employees to meet and exceed your customers' expectations.

7. The seven communication channels essential for involving your employees in the Quality process.

8. The ten rules for Fast-Track success.

13

Fifteen Strategies to Fast Tracking

Total Quality Management can take many directions in an organization. But which Quality-advancing strategies are best for your organization? And when should they be implemented? To be able to answer these questions, you need a clear and thorough understanding of the options. Without such an understanding, you're much like a boat builder trying to construct a ship without complete and accurate plans.

All the Quality strategies described in this chapter should ultimately be applied to Fast-Track TQM organizations over a four- or five-year period. The danger comes in tackling too many at once. Some of the strategies are more relevant in the early months of developing TQM, while others are more sophisticated and better suited to later stages.

All the Quality strategies focus on achieving two primary goals: (1) customer satisfaction and (2) defect reduction.

1. Achieving customer satisfaction means consistently exceeding the expectations of customers. Occasionally, it is necessary to pleasantly surprise customers with extraordinary service. The intent is to create a level of satisfaction high enough to ensure that customers will readily tell others about your Quality goods and services. Ultimately, this increased reputation should yield repeat business, increased market share, and bigger profits.

2. Achieving a high level of customer satisfaction is directly related to reducing defects. The intent is to apply Quality strategies that will consistently reduce defects in both products and service, and ensure consistently improved customer satisfaction.

Fast-Track Tip 57

All your TQM strategies should be directed toward achieving two goals:

1. Customer satisfaction
2. Defect-free products and services

The Fast-Track Strategies for Quality

Examine each of the following strategies to gain a thorough understanding of its value and importance in the Quality process. Examine and determine how each strategy might be implemented in your own organization. The key is to understand the strategy and introduce it in a planned and purposeful manner. While timing is critical, only you can determine the correct timing for implementing each strategy in your organization. Read through each description carefully. The timing and implementation of each strategy are unique to each organization. The strategies are not listed in any order of importance. Use the checklist in Fig. 13.1 to establish your own priorities and timeline for each of the

---

Strategy 1: Employee empowerment
Strategy 2: Self-managed work teams
Strategy 3: Quality improvement teams (QITs)
Strategy 4: Statistical process controls (SPCs)
Strategy 5: Competitive benchmarking
Strategy 6: Supplier partnership
Strategy 7: Skill training
Strategy 8: Setting organizational direction
Strategy 9: Conducting Quality audits
Strategy 10: Customer scorecard
Strategy 11: Graphing achievements
Strategy 12: Design Quality into the product/service
Strategy 13: Instructional manual-driven
Strategy 14: Employee suggestion programs
Strategy 15: Activity-based cost (ABC) management

Figure 13.1. Checklist of Fast-Track Quality strategies

strategies. Determine specific dates, and outline the methods you'll use to implement each Quality strategy.

Fast-Track Tip 58

While Quality consultants can offer Quality-advancing strategies, only you can decide when to apply those strategies for your organization.

Fast-Track Quality Strategy 1: Employee Empowerment

Fast Tracking means that every employee is empowered with the right and the responsibility to take daily and consistent action to enhance and improve the Quality of products and service provided. "Every employee" means just that—everyone from the newest hire to the oldest veteran, from management to employees. The idea is that all employees will take the personal initiative to consistently examine their own work to ensure that it is being produced or provided defect free on a regular basis.

Empowering employees—whether it's managers or employees, 1 or 10,000—requires the same steps. First, employees must be encouraged to speak up, to contribute their ideas, suggestions, and concerns. It's natural for employees to be fearful about speaking up. Most organizations discourage employee input. In a Fast-Track TQM organization, employees quickly learn that it's safe to speak up and share ideas. It's clearly evident that they won't be punished, but rather rewarded for taking personal initiative. As more and more employees experience this reaction, they take initiative to become involved and contribute their talents, skills, insights, and ideas. Before long, everyone in the organization has caught the "me too" spirit and is actively participating in Quality advancement. Chapter 17 provides a detailed description of how to empower employees.

Fast-Track Tip 59

Success with Fast-Track TQM is predicated on employee involvement and appropriate risk taking at all levels.

Fast-Track Quality Strategy 2: Self-Managed Work Teams

In self-managed work teams, employees meet jointly with their immediate supervisor to examine and discuss the outcomes required and expected of their work group. The work group members collaborate to determine the best methods, best strategies, and best actions their group can take to accomplish desired outcomes. In Fast-Track self-managed work teams, every member openly shares his or her input to advance and improve the processes used by the group.

One of the earliest and most successful applications of self-managed work groups occurred nearly 30 years ago at a Volvo manufacturing plant in Sweden. A new plant was being built, and the company brought together employees at each point in the fabrication process to determine how the work could best be accomplished within their assigned areas. The employees themselves determined the process, the number of employees to be involved, specific actions needed to accomplish the desired outcomes, and a schedule for achieving those outcomes.

The result was not only a wonderfully efficient plant, but a work team process that was cost effective and self-monitoring. It created teams that were able to complete tasks in shorter time periods, often with fewer employees. The employees also initiated a self-evaluation process that enabled them to continually scrutinize the processes and identify ways to make them more efficient and cost effective on an ongoing basis.

An important and unexpected outcome of the Volvo experiment was the increased level of employee satisfaction. The groups restructured jobs to ensure that they weren't overly repetitive, and provided cross-training so that employees could move from workstation to workstation. When the groups were able to accomplish tasks with fewer employees, they decided together who would move to other work teams or onto other tasks. Senior management assured employees that no one would be laid off due to increases in efficiencies by the work groups. The Volvo model of work teams proved that self-management by employees can not only improve Quality, it can create a motivated, satisfied workforce.

Self-managed work teams meet on company time and are usually led by an immediate supervisor. Participating supervisors need special training to enable them to facilitate the process effectively and help guide the teams to work collaboratively.

Some senior managers are highly resistant to the idea of self-managed work teams. But you don't have to convert your entire workforce in one giant step to self-managed teams. They can be effective started in selected areas of the organization. As these teams become effective, other groups can be converted on a planned schedule.

Fast-Track Tip 60

Self-managed work teams collaborate to determine outcomes, along with the best methods, strategies, and actions to best achieve those outcomes.

Fast-Track Quality Strategy 3: Quality Improvement Teams

Quality improvement teams (QITs) are specialized self-managed work teams. Employees come together and collaboratively identify solutions to particular problems that have already been identified for them. The QIT, in turn, recommends solutions to middle or senior management. To be effective, QIT employees must have thorough training in problem-solving techniques. They need to be able to have the necessary skills to work through the difficult and often potentially charged process of "this is how it has always been done." The ultimate goal is to reveal a solution to a vexing problem.

Quality improvement teams are generally led by a manager, usually someone at the midmanagement level. While QITs bear similarities to Quality Circles popular some years ago, they are distinctly different in the required involvement of middle management. Quality Circles were often led by professional facilitators. Their Achilles Heel was that they were never fully supported by midlevel managers—and TQM cannot succeed without the support and involvement of midlevel managers. In contrast to Quality Circles, midlevel managers become active participants and supporters of QITs. This management involvement ensures that the solutions offered represent the combined efforts of both employees and management. The support of midlevel management reinforces the opportunities to implement recommendations.

In most cases, QITs are assigned a problem, and their task is to come up with the most effective and efficient solution. A senior manager, and in some cases a midlevel manager, bring a group together to solve a predetermined problem. The assigning manager becomes the group's sponsor and gives them the authority not only to act, but also to leave their normal work tasks to work as a special team on specific problems. With the assigned manager acting as the QIT facilitator, the group works collaboratively on a solution, and then formally presents their recommendations to the sponsoring senior manager. Often, groups come up with more than one solution but with their preferences clearly established. The QIT sponsor (a senior manager) then reviews the proposed solution(s), to determine whether to implement it or bring it to a senior management group for further review. If several senior managers are to be involved in making the decision for implementation, they should be invited to the session in which the QIT members present their solution(s).

Fast-Track Tip 61

Quality improvement teams (QITs) must have the direct involvement and support of midlevel managers to guide the problem-solving process.

Fast-Track Quality Strategy 4: Statistical Process Controls (SPCs)

A more detailed description of SPC is included in Chap. 11. It is important to recognize SPC as only one of many tools to advance Quality.

Fast-Track Quality Strategy 5: Competitive Benchmarking

As we now know, "You can't improve it until you can measure it." Competitive benchmarking is a process by which a level of performance is determined as the "the best" in the industry and the target to achieve. It doesn't matter whether the best level is in the same industry or not. It may simply be the best, such as on-time delivery, cleanliness, or defect free. Virtually any industry and company can be set as the target level of Quality. You'll learn the most if you look at a variety of organizations and a number of competitive benchmarks. Pick the best in any area of Quality critical to your TQM advancement.

Competitive benchmarking is a way to keep your organization continually improving. When I talk about competitive benchmarking, I often use the phrase "world class." Not only do you want to be the best in your industry, you want to advance to the elite level of world class. If someone else is doing it, so can your company. If someone else is providing a world class level of service in a particular area, your company can too.

Don't get caught up in looking at only your immediate competitors and comparing your organization to them. The specifications defined by your industry may be mediocre at best. If everyone in the industry is meeting the same specs, they are in fact mediocre. Your intent is to become better, to excel on a world class level. Figure 13.2 describes a five-step process to establish benchmarks for comparing the progress of your organization's Quality advancement.

Work your action plan and repeat the rating process on an annual or semiannual basis to confirm progress.

Fast-Track Tip 62

By competitive benchmarking, you set your sights on others who are "the best" in what they do. If they can be the best, why can't you? The target is to become world class in your industry.

Fast-Track Quality Strategy 6: Supplier Partnership

To have world class Quality, you must have defect-free material and equipment from your suppliers. As your organization progresses through the TQM process, you'll find your suppliers willing to become collaborative partners in your success. In successful Fast-Track TQM organizations, suppliers are invited into the organization, not just limited

---

1. Select internal target areas to measure the advancement of your organization.
2. Identify world class organizations who excel in your target areas.
3. Set the scale for each target area. "The best" target organizations should be rated at 100.
4. Have the managers, supervisors, employees, and even some customers evaluate and rate your organization's performance in each category with a numerical rating such as 0 to 100.
5. Once you've rated your targeted areas, begin identifying specific actions to take in each category to advance the organization to world class status.

Figure 13.2. Five steps to benchmarking world class

to the purchasing department. Managers, suppliers, and customers frequently hold joint meetings to talk about how they can improve products and services.

As lines of communication are increasingly opened and understanding between the organization and suppliers increases, the relationships deepen. Often the number of suppliers decrease to a select few. It's much like the difference between having many casual acquaintances and having a few good friends who would do anything for you. It's not uncommon for companies with 100 or more suppliers to reduce the number to 50 or less under TQM. Some successful TQM organizations require their suppliers have a TQM process in place that continually improves the Quality of the goods and services they supply to the company. Sometimes suppliers and TQM companies even become jointly involved in Quality training sessions, sharing costs and facilities.

TQM establishes a different relationship between suppliers and the organization, one that goes beyond the usual we-buy/you-sell constraints. Suppliers who become involved in the TQM process with their customer companies become committed to meeting and exceeding your expectations. The result is that you and your company consistently receive high-Quality products and materials from your suppliers.

Fast-Track Tip 63

In TQM, suppliers become business partners, actively involved in the advancement of the Quality of your products and services.

Fast-Track Quality Strategy 7: Skill Training

To advance Quality in your organization, your employees require the skills to do their assigned tasks and to continually improve. No matter how good they may be presently, they have to be given the opportunity to get better if they are to produce world class Quality. Use the following three important techniques to increase employee skills and capabilities:

1. **Offer cross-training:** When employees can perform two or three jobs, they are better able to understand and support one another in advancing Quality.

2. **Provide practice:** It sounds so simple and yet it's practice that builds confidence and capability. The issue is not to become perfect, but to get better and better.

3. **Utilize team training:** Building effective teams creates unity and a support system in which to focus employee energies for best results.

In the service industry, the flow of paper is often a measure of Quality and efficiency. Barring mechanical failures, defects in the flow of paperwork can be attributed to human error. Service employees must have the skill and ability to move paper from one station to the next defect free. To achieve defect-free status, service industry employees need on-the-job (OJT) and classroom training. In many cases, OJT isn't enough to bring employees to the defect-free level, and additional classroom training must be used to ensure that level.

While some organizations may be reluctant to invest their resources in employee training, they'll find their investment is returned many times over in Quality products and services, satisfied customers, increased sales, and additional profits.

Fast-Track Tip 64

Continuous skill training for managers, supervisors, and employees is needed if you're to have ongoing Quality improvement.

Fast-Track Quality Strategy 8: Setting Organizational Direction

During the course of interviews with thousands of managers, supervisors, and employees, the most common complaint of all is that the staff does not understand the direction of their organization. The CEO or president may clearly understand the organization's direction, but somehow that vision doesn't trickle down throughout the organization.

In successful TQM organizations, the executive officer not only establishes the organization's direction, but also makes sure that every person in the organization clearly understands that direction. This vision is usually stated in two to three simple, easily understood statements. In organizations implementing Quality improvements, the company direction could be established by declaring,

The XYZ Company is committed to:
1. Producing defect-free products and services.
2. Minimizing the costs of defects.
3. Increasing the return on assets.

Not long ago, I spoke at the Marriott Camelback resort in Arizona. It was clear that every employee in the organization understood the company's direction in terms of Quality advancement. In addition to a name tag, each employee wore a small ribbon with the initials TAGS, which stood for "Total Associate and Guest Service." To employees it meant that their target was to enhance and improve services to their associates and guests by consistently meeting and exceeding their expectations. The acronym TAGS was simply a way to keep the organization's direction clearly focused in each employee's mind. And it worked. The resort's employees provided some of the best and most courteous service I've ever received. Truly world class.

Once employees have a clear idea of the organization's direction, they have a clear target to direct their energy and their actions. While the techniques and methods to advance Quality may change and evolve over time, the company target—its direction—remains consistently in place.

Fast-Track Tip 65

Consistent organizational direction, communicated clearly and frequently to employees, helps them know how and where to invest their time and energy most effectively.

Fast-Track Quality Strategy 9: Conducting Quality Audits

Clearly, understanding your internal and external customers' needs and expectations is at the foundation of TQM. Conducting Quality Audits helps to define those expectations and enables managers to quantify them. And, of course, once you can measure something, you can improve on it.

Internal and external customer Quality audits can be conducted in a variety of ways. Customer questionnaires can be sent randomly or in some cases to every customer. Focus groups, in which several customers are jointly interviewed, offer a more personalized aspect to the data-gathering process and can often provide more information about customer expectations and satisfaction than written questionnaires. Reply cards are another way to monitor customer satisfaction. Typically, they are filled out by the customer on the spot and dropped into collection boxes or returned by mail.

Regardless of the techniques used to gather information about customer's expectations and levels of satisfaction, it's important to gather information in specific areas. The Fast-Track Method identifies seven critical areas for assessment. (See Chap. 10, which is devoted to Quality Audits, and Chap. 5, "Understanding Your Customer.")

Fast-Track Quality Strategy 10: Customer Scorecard

Can you imagine attending a professional basketball game where the scoreboard is broken and no one knows the scores or game statistics? Players are dashing back and forth, working hard to make baskets, but neither the players nor the spectators know who has the most points. After a while, everyone would lose interest in the game because the baskets being made wouldn't matter; they'd have no meaning. The players would stop working hard to make points, and the spectators would stop watching the game. It's the same in a business setting. If the employees don't know the score—how they're doing—they'll lose interest and even stop working to improve Quality.

Every organization needs a customer scorecard to know how they're performing in enhancing Quality and serving customers. Without it, Quality-advancing efforts become casual and meaningless. Keeping a scorecard of customer satisfaction is a combination of two strategies already discussed: customer Quality audits and benchmarking. Quality audits can confirm your understanding of customer satisfaction given points on a regular basis. Benchmarking gives you a reference point from which to confirm and measure progress. Information should be gathered from both sources and transferred to a Quality scorecard.

I encourage you to actually create a scorecard. Use heavy 8½ × 11-in. paper with the heading "Quality Scorecard." Along one side, write in the seven categories assessed in Quality audits:

1. Timeliness of response

2. Accuracy of paperwork

3. Condition of product or service

4. Availability of product or service

5. Courtesy of service

6. Keeping promises (agreements)

7. Cost of operation

Using the 1-100 scoring system established for benchmarking and Quality audits, keep score on each category. Scorecards can be established for individual departments, divisions, or the entire organization.

People in sales areas should maintain individual scorecards on each of their major customers. As any salesperson knows, the 80/20 rule applies in sales: 80 percent of sales come from 20 percent of customers. How are you serving those important 20 percent customers? How are you serving the other 80 percent? Scorecards will enable each employee, each "player," to know exactly the progress being made in advancing Quality and serving customers.

Fast-Track Tip 66

Don't play the Quality game unless you're willing to keep score of your efforts. Without scorecards, people cannot know how well they're doing, and they soon lose interest.

Fast-Track Quality Strategy 11: Graphing Achievements

"Defect-free" is a cry commonly heard in Quality-driven organizations. But how do you know if you're even coming close to that goal if you don't keep track of your progress? Much like customer scorecards that monitor customer satisfaction, levels of defects should be tracked using graphs. They provide an instant visual of defects produced in products or in service. They let management and employees know where the problems are, the progress they've made, and how far they have yet to go to achieve defect-free status.

There's a pitfall in graphing, into which many managers stumble. They monitor and chart the production of their employees, how "hard" they work, rather than the actual Quality of work being produced at every stage. Frankly, who cares how hard people are working—how fast or how much effort they're putting into it—if the product or service they're producing is full of defects? Managers need to monitor and graph the Quality of work actually being produced. Only by charting the work produced can employees receive the kind of consistent feedback and validation they need to achieve defect-free status. A graph provides a powerful feedback tool that is quickly and easily interpreted by everyone.

A strategy to make graphs even more effective is to actively involve employees both in the collection of data and in the charting process itself. Expanding employee involvement in the process makes the data real and believable to them.

Keep one important rule in mind when you chart progress: Graph only what you have control over. If you get "graph-happy" and create graphs using data you can't do anything about, the graphs will quickly become meaningless for your staff. In contrast, if you graph only what you have direct control over, employees will see the advancements made through their efforts. This, in turn, points out the organizational direction, creating excitement and enthusiasm for the process of advancing Quality.

Fast-Track Tip 67

Graphs provide an immediate visual image of progress in becoming defect free.

Fast-Track Quality Strategy 12: Design Quality into the Product/Service

It seems so simple: Design and build Quality into the processes that deliver the product or service. Many organizations often have ineffective procedures and policies that negatively affect the product as it is being prepared or served to the customer. A food product, for example, that is poorly delivered with faulty service execution is doomed to failure.

Anytime a new product or service is designed, every consideration must be made to ensure that Quality is built into the processes and the product or service itself. It's far easier to provide a Quality product or service when it is designed with Quality as the number one consideration. It's costly to analyze products or services for the level of defects, figure out remedies, and then have to modify the process or products. It underscores the importance of the TQM principle "do it right the first time and every time."

But Quality isn't an accident; it's something that is carefully planned and prepared for. An important tool in planning for Quality is the flowchart of events. A flowchart process enables designers and planners to have a clear understanding of the activities and how they relate to one another, the sequence of events, and how each event affects the next. The more visual the planning process becomes, the easier it is to understand and to recognize how value is added through Quality improvements.

Fast-Track Tip 68

It's easier and less costly to design Quality into processes, products, and services than it is to rework for Quality improvement.

Fast-Track Quality Strategy 13: Instruction Manual-Driven

This strategy is so simple, it's often overlooked. Animation genius and theme park creator Walt Disney clearly understood the power and importance of having employees who understood and produced Quality in all of their actions and how instruction manuals could facilitate that process. In all the Disney theme parks—Anaheim, California, Orlando, Florida, or Tokyo, Japan—employees receive the same training, through carefully prepared instruction manuals, in how to best provide Quality service and products to their customers.

In the early days at his first theme park in Anaheim, Walt Disney was frustrated by the lack of consistency of service he saw given to park visitors. Employees not only gave inconsistent service, they sometimes gave guests misinformation. He knew he had a problem, and so he ordered a case of 3x5 file cards. He walked through the park and gave each employee 20-30 of the cards. He told them to write one commonly asked question on each card. At the end of the day, he collected the cards. They were sorted by job description and by type of question. Of course, he found plenty of duplication in the questions, but that was just the point. He realized that each position received 20-30 of the same questions. It was imperative that employees in those positions be able to answer these most commonly asked questions. He had sets of cards printed for each employee with the questions on one side and the correct answers on the reverse side. The employees, in turn, were asked to memorize the questions and the answers flashcard-style.

Simple? Absolutely. But it's taught millions of children their multiplication tables and it worked for Disney's employees. In only a few days, he was able to transform the delivery of service to his customers into consistent, Quality service.

Quality comes when every employee knows and understands how best to meet the needs and expectations of his or her customers. For Walt Disney, flash cards became his training manual. Today, the Disney company uses carefully prepared instruction manuals in classroom settings. Whether the instruction process is on the job or in the classroom, instruction manuals give a consistent message and ensure that employees understand what it takes to deliver Quality service to their customers every time.

Fast-Track Tip 69

Carefully prepared instruction manuals give employees consistent and specific direction in how to serve customers.

Fast-Track Quality Strategy 14: Employee Suggestion Programs

No matter what the job classification, every employee in an organization has ideas and insights to share on how to better serve customers. Certainly not all those ideas will be good ones, but as Albert Einstein said, "You need many ideas for a few good ones." To that end, you need to establish a process to encourage ideas and gather them together.

Enter the employee suggestion program.

Sometime ago, I was talking about employee suggestion programs with a group of managers when one of them said, "This is 1927 technology." Granted, employee suggestion programs certainly aren't new, but then neither is the wheel and it's still a great idea. The problem with employee suggestion programs is that they've been misused by most organizations. Many companies mistakenly believe they must give their employees monetary rewards to encourage them to share their insights and ideas. This isn't encouragement, it's bribery! Far more powerful than money is validating employees and giving them the recognition that says, "You're a value to this organization. We recognize and value your contributions. You make a difference." There are many ways to encourage and recognize employees. Chapter 15 describes specific techniques for building self-esteem and employee commitment. The intent is to change "I have to" attitudes into "I want to."

Many employee suggestion programs provide an almost immediate response to employee ideas and suggestions. In some organizations, management responds to employee suggestions within 12 to 24 hours. One of my clients, who has experienced phenomenal success with his employee suggestion program, has an unbreakable management rule that says all employee suggestions receive a written response within 48 hours.

This kind of almost immediate feedback creates excitement and satisfaction among employees. You don't believe it? Think about yourself for a moment. How do you feel when people really listen to your ideas, consider them seriously, and give you an almost immediate response about whether or not your idea can be implemented? If you're like most people, it makes you feel great, and you're more than willing to keep offering ideas and suggestions.

There are a variety of ways to retrieve employee suggestions. A common method is an employee suggestion box; employees fill out a simple form and insert it into the box. Another method is to report suggestions to the immediate supervisor. Still another, very efficient method, is to have a local or 800 number that employees can use to record their comments on a phone machine. (Alaska Railroad's successful use of a "hotline" number is described in more detail in Chap. 21.) When the idea is more complicated and requires drawings or charts, the suggestion box or reporting to the immediate supervisor works best.

There are three keys to making an employee suggestion work:

1. Feedback must be immediate and frequent.

2. Suggestions must be acted upon quickly.

3. Employees must receive personal recognition for their input efforts.

Fast-Track Tip 70

Properly structured employee suggestion programs can involve and encourage employees to actively participate in Quality improvement.

Fast-Track Quality Strategy 15: Activity-Based Cost Management

Activity-based cost (ABC) management is a process in which every action in an organization is monitored to confirm its actual cost in contributing value to the product or service. As a product advances through the manufacturing process, each stage of the process is broken down, monitored, and analyzed to determine cost and value. When managers can actually see the costs in end processes, they can begin to question those costs. What's driving the costs? How can they be minimized?

ABC management carries the secondary benefit of enabling managers to understand all the processes that go into preparing and providing a product or service to customers. It's a form of "hands on" management that gives managers the insight and understanding to be more efficient and effective in adding value to products and services and in advancing the Quality of those products and services.

Fast Track at a Glance

✔ You must understand all the Quality-enhancing strategies available to be able to choose the ones that will work best for your organization.

✔ Don't try to implement too many Quality strategies too quickly.

✔ All Quality-advancing actions should work to achieve two goals: (1) customer satisfaction and (2) defect-free products and services.

✔ Employee involvement at all levels is integral to the success of TQM.

✔ Self-managed work teams determine desired outcomes and then plan the best methods, strategies, and actions to achieve those outcomes.

✔ For self-managed work teams and TQM to work, employees must never be penalized by layoffs for increasing efficiency or reducing workload.

✔ Self-managed work teams can be effective throughout an organization or only in selected areas.

✔ Quality improvement teams (QITs) are specialized work teams that focus on particular Quality problems. To be effective, they should be led by a midlevel manager.

✔ Statistical process controls (SPCs) work equally well in manufacturing or service industry environments.

✔ With only a modest amount of training, employees at any level can effectively use statistical process controls.

✔ Competitive benchmarking asks the question, "Who's the best in the industry?" Those competitors then become goals to strive for, models to emulate.

✔ In successful TQM, suppliers become partners in your Quality-advancing success. They may even share the costs of Quality training.

✔ Skill training on an ongoing basis is necessary to achieve continuous Quality improvement.

✔ Cross-training is an effective way to improve employee skills while improving Quality.

✔ It's management's responsibility to set the organization's direction. Employees who are clear about the firm's direction and priorities can better serve their customers.

✔ Quality audits provide valuable data about customer needs, expectations, and satisfaction levels. They also serve as a progress report on your Quality-advancing activities.

✔ Customer scorecards let employees see how well they're doing on the seven key items in customer satisfaction. It is an effective way to monitor progress and give employees constant feedback.

✔ Graphs provide an instant "picture" of where defects occur and how Quality is effecting change.

✔ It's much less expensive to design Quality into your processes, products, and services than it is to rework for Quality later.

✔ Carefully prepared instruction manuals can solve the problem of inconsistent customer service. They ensure that employees get the same information about how to serve customers.

✔ Employee suggestion programs can be very successful in eliciting good ideas and involving employees, particularly when (1) feedback is immediate and frequent, (2) suggestions are quickly acted upon, and (3) employees receive personal recognition for their input.

✔ Activity-based cost management enables managers to analyze every action to determine its cost in adding value to a product or service at end processes along the way.

14
Building Management Commitment

Since Fast-Track TQM is management-driven, the single greatest challenge in developing a TQM organization is to establish management commitment. The success or failure of the TQM process depends on the extent of commitment of managers at all levels. Most organizations have a three-tiered management consisting of:

1. The executive staff with the president and vice president(s).

2. Middle managers reporting to the vice president level.

3. Supervisors, who direct the work of employees.

Of the three levels of management, middle managers are the most difficult group to bring into acceptance, understanding, and commitment to TQM. Failure of TQM can almost always be attributed to lack of commitment and involvement by middle managers.

Why do middle managers so often block TQM? Why are they so resistant to developing and advancing TQM? This question has been posed both to organizations that have difficulty establishing TQM and to ones that have great success with it. Together we've identified four characteristics of middle managers as a group that cause them to work against the TQM process. Note that these generalizations may not hold true for every individual midlevel manager, but they're consistent with the characteristics of most.

1. **Highly competitive:** Individuals who advance to midlevel management tend to be highly competitive. They have worked hard to set themselves apart from their peers as they've advanced up the organi-

zational ladder. Most middle managers aspire to join the senior ranks. Because of this drive, they're competitive and want to show their ability to achieve results for the organization. Since TQM involves a collaborative and cooperative process, it's harder for one person to claim all the glory.

2. **"Me"-centered:** Most middle managers want personal recognition that they have made a special contribution in the organization. Many organizations upgrade the perks significantly when one advances from supervisor to middle manager. Midlevel managers may receive automobiles, special offices, nicer furniture, personal secretaries, and executive keys that allow them into limited-access areas in the company. When managers do not receive such recognition, it's not uncommon for them to leave and find other organizations that will more readily recognize their efforts. The team-oriented approach to TQM does not set well with many "me-"centered managers.

3. **Power-oriented:** Many midlevel managers enjoy having power. It affects their dress, their language, even their gait. For some middle managers, a little power and authority inhibits their openness and willingness to exchange information with others.

As organizations embark on the TQM process, it doesn't take most midlevel managers long to understand and use the jargon associated with TQM. They talk about support and commitment without any real, internal commitment to Quality advancement or to TQM. Their words lack substance and are nothing more than glitter. Yet, for TQM to succeed, you have to pay special attention to the middle management level in order to build intrinsic Quality commitment.

Fast-Track Tip 71

Midlevel managers are the most resistant to buying into TQM. What makes them achieve midlevel management status is often what makes them fail with TQM. Without midlevel management support, however, TQM success is questionable.

Building a Foundation to Commitment

The following process was used with a company with 1800 employees to build TQM understanding and commitment from ground zero. About 40 managers, or 20 percent of the total manager staff, heard me give a two-hour presentation on Fast-Track TQM. I gave them a definition of Total Quality Management, and shared many examples of other organizations who had successfully applied the principles. I described the process most organizations use to develop and apply the principles. The initial response to my presentation was positive. Many of the managers asked questions or requested I clarify or expand on different points.

Of course, their awareness at this point was only in the beginning stages. But I'd at least piqued their interest, and we'd established a common language we could use to talk about TQM together. They understood more clearly who their customers were, both internal and external, and that Quality is determined by *customer* perceptions, not on their perceptions. Over the next few months, I held three TQM awareness meetings with managers from three plants to expand their awareness and begin the commitment-building process.

Fast-Track Tip 72

Building midlevel managemer commitment to TQM requires a clear understanding of the benefits they can realize.

To continue the TQM learning process, the company president established a schedule of quarterly meetings with 120 managers to enhance and build their awareness of the benefits of TQM to the company. This large group was divided into five groups, with each group's meeting limited to four hours. The president personally attended each of those meetings.

Two significant events happened at each meeting: a financial review and a book review. The president provided managers with a description of the performance and accomplishments of each plant and of the company as a whole. This served as both feedback and reinforcement for the managers.

The managers also participated in a book review at each session. A few weeks before each review meeting, managers were given a book on Quality advancement. They were instructed to read it and come to the meeting ready to discuss the principles and how they related to their personal experiences. This was an educationally diverse group, with some participants having graduate degrees while others were without high school diplomas. For some, it was the first time they'd read a book in years.

No one was really sure how this book review tactic would work. But when they attended the first review session, it was apparent that everyone had read the assigned book and were ready to discuss the principles. The discussions lasted two hours at each location.

While the first book review was a success, the subsequent reviews got even better. During the first session, managers seemed a little nervous with the process. This was new to them, and they weren't sure how to participate or exactly what was expected. Over the next quarterly sessions, however, they really got into the swing of things and everyone eagerly participated. They became more focused in their comments, more willing to share their ideas and views. It doesn't matter which books were used during these reviews (they were current TQM books describing TQM applications in a variety of businesses and industries). What was significant was the process of the book reviews—the discussions, the sharing of ideas and viewpoints.

By the third quarterly book review session, something interesting had happened. Managers weren't just reading the assigned books. They were seeking out other books and articles on Quality improvement on their own. They began describing TQM examples they'd read in magazines, newspapers, or other books. Now they were hooked. They wanted to know more and more about Quality enhancement.

Senior Management Involvement

Why were these sessions so successful? First, and perhaps foremost, is the fact that the president attended each of the meetings. He didn't just drop in. He stayed the entire four hours. Although the discussions were facilitated by a senior manager, the president actively participated in the discussions. It allowed managers to hear some of the president's ideas and views. And it enabled them to share their ideas and thoughts with him. This president-manager exchange gave managers a new level of comfort with the senior managers. It enabled them to discuss sometimes difficult issues in a safe environment. The president's attendance and involvement at these meetings gave managers a clear message about his commitment and his willingness to work with them. It gave them an invitation to directly and regularly provide him with input. It established a two-way communication between upper and middle managers that is key to TQM success.

Another reason for the success of the review sessions is the fact that the meetings were held in a relaxed atmosphere. They were held over lunch or dinner. Whenever possible, seats were arranged in a U-shape to allow free and open exchange of ideas from everyone.

Fast-Track Tip 73

Having senior management—the president and vice president(s)—directly involved with the sharing process with middle managers conveys the important message of commitment.

The Vision Statement

At the third quarterly review session, the president presented a TQM vision statement to the group for discussion. The statement had been prepared by senior managers at a weekly meeting. Each managers group from every plant was given an opportunity to review and discuss the vision statement and offer their opinions, insights, and ideas. Most of the managers found the original statement quite complete and well-written. Chapter 9 describes the developmental processes of developing a vision statement. Figure 14.1 shows the final version of the statement. Notice that the statement is purposely short, concise, and directly focused on the principles of TQM.

VISION STATEMENT

XYZ Company intends to become "The Best" in our industry within five years and to be recognized as such by producers, suppliers, employees, regulatory bodies, customers, and consumers.

Figure 14.1. Sample vision statement

Confirming and Declaring Midmanagement Commitment

The fourth quarterly meeting was the turning point. It was here that the managers would decide the critical question: Should the organization proceed with TQM? The managers had to decide whether they wanted to proceed from discussion to action with TQM. In the previous quarterly meetings, the president had made it clear to the managers that the ultimate decision to proceed with TQM was theirs—the decision wouldn't be made by the president or vice presidents. All 120 managers would vote on whether or not they wanted to adopt Fast-Track TQM. The managers had been reviewing and examining TQM principles for nine months. They had a clear picture of what TQM could do for the organization and the kinds of changes its adoption requires. Many of the managers had already approached the president privately and asked if they could proceed with TQM in their area. Although some managers were reluctant and still skeptical, there was clearly a movement among midlevel managers to move ahead with TQM.

The final vote meeting was carefully planned. Several weeks prior to this session, plant managers were instructed to meet with their managers and discuss the pros and cons of becoming a TQM organization. At the plant level, numerous meetings were held to get presentations ready. Managers were asked to identify five to eight pro and con items and come prepared to discuss each at the quarterly meeting.

Fast-Track Tip 74

Giving midlevel managers a vote in the decision to pursue TQM gives them "influence" in the organization, one of the proven keys to building commitment.

When the meeting was finally held, each management group gave their presentations and discussed the pros and cons. From the range of ideas expressed, it became clear there wasn't agreement on several of the items discussed.

A second item on the meeting's agenda involved reviewing data from a Quality Audit that had been conducted with both internal and external customers to determine success in meeting customer expectations. The company had used an outside research firm to conduct focus groups who met with internal customers and external customers to gather data. At the fourth quarterly meeting, the groups spent approximately two hours reviewing the Quality Audit results. The data indicated that while the organization was already producing Quality products and services, there was clearly room for improvement. Unfortunately, the data was not broken down by individual plants, and each plant management group was certain that any Quality problems described "weren't at our plant." But the data did show problems existed.

During this decision meeting, the managers' discussions eventually focused on a single theme, which was voiced in various ways:

What do we have to do?

What would we be expected to do?

What would we be held accountable for?

How would we have to change?

As each question was broached, the president responded with a clear description, outlining what midlevel managers could expect. He also confirmed and reconfirmed his commitment to the TQM process.

Executive Level Commitment Declared

At this point in the meeting, the chief financial officer, the director of human resources, and the operations manager made presentations on how they would support and become involved in the TQM process. The financial officer discussed how funds would be made available for training and for special needs to advance Quality. Managers were reassured that if they decided to proceed with TQM, the money would be made available and not diverted to "more important" areas. The human resources director gave a short presentation on how his office would support TQM and the management staff in their efforts. The vice president of operations for each plant's region talked about his or her personal commitment and support for the TQM journey. Finally, the president ended the management presentations with a personal message of his commitment to advancing TQM and supporting the midlevel managers in that process.

Reviewing the Contract

The real turning point in the meeting and in the managers' decision to wholeheartedly support TQM came with the distribution of the contract shown in Fig. 8.2 (Chap. 8). More than any verbal statement senior management could make to midlevel managers, the Commitment to Quality, as they called the document, clearly outlined what senior management was prepared to do in support of TQM and what managers would be expected to do to advance Quality.

The impact of the Commitment to Quality statement was further strengthened by the signature of the president and senior operating manager for each plant. There was also a signature space for each manager who was committed to and willing to participate in TQM. Signed statements were not kept by senior management, but returned to midlevel managers encased in a metal frame.

One might say, "Yes, but this is just a piece of paper. What's the big deal?" Interestingly enough, when managers sign their names to a document like this, it's significant, it's serious, it's real. When the president handed out the agreement sheets, at this point signed only by senior management, it was an amazingly intense and serious occasion. As each manager received the document, he or she would invariably stare at it, reading the words carefully. The most common statement made by the midlevel managers during this time was, "Finally, I know what management is willing to do and what I have to do to participate in the TQM process." While senior management had talked about their commitment and support in other sessions prior to this meeting, putting the commitment and the accountabilities in writing somehow "made it real" to the managers.

Fast-Track Tip 75

Agreement statements between senior and midlevel managers outline the commitment of senior managers to Quality enhancement and the responsibilities of middle managers in advancing Quality.

The groups talked about the Commitment to Quality statements for 30-40 minutes, clarifying and confirming their understanding of each item listed. At this point, the president purposely didn't ask managers to sign the documents. For now, the document would serve only to clarify what senior and middle management would have to do to make their company "The Best" in the industry.

The Vote of Support

Finally, it was time to take the vote, to decide on whether to proceed with the Fact-Track TQM process. Simple "yes/no" ballots were prepared and passed out to each meeting participant. The question was simple: "Should we apply and advance the organization by applying Fast-Track TQM principles?" Managers marked their ballots, folded them over, and passed them on to one of their colleagues. Senior management was purposely not involved in collecting or counting the ballots. A chart easel in the front of the room held newsprint divided into "yes" and "no" columns. As the ballots were read aloud, a tick mark was made in the appropriate column. Astoundingly, the managers voted unanimously—100 percent—to support and go forward with Fast-Track TQM.

Following the vote tallying, managers gave the decision and themselves a strong round of applause. At one meeting, the managers gave their decision a standing ovation for several minutes. Middle managers were ready to advance Quality with excitement and enthusiasm for the process.

Signing the Contract

Now the managers were asked to sign their Commitment to Quality statements. And they did so readily. Each one later hung the framed statements in his or her office.

It took 10 months to prepare midlevel managers for their decision to wholeheartedly support and commit to TQM. But the effort was well worth it. To launch TQM without middle management's support would have doomed it to failure. To apply Fast-Track TQM with the kind of excitement and enthusiasm that the managers demonstrated almost guarantees success.

Not only were the midlevel managers given the time they needed to make a personal commitment to TQM, they were given information. The Fast-Track Awareness training and book review sessions gave them the kind of data they needed to make an informed choice. Upper management made their support clear and specific; they told managers what their commitment to TQM was and how they would help midlevel managers advance Quality. And, finally, no one made the decision for middle managers. No one said, "We're going to become TQM-driven and you have to participate." Instead, upper management let the midlevel managers have influence, one of the key elements for building commitment. They let them decide for themselves whether to advance Quality in their organization. With adequate time, knowledge, and support, these managers made the best choice for themselves and for their company.

You may be asking, "Could I apply this model to my organization?" Absolutely. It's proven to be a most effective model for building and strengthening midlevel management commitment to TQM. Does it have to take 10 months to accomplish? Probably not. You could probably condense the timeframe to four to six months, and still achieve the same positive results. While it takes time to build middle management commitment, you'll find it's time well spent.

Fast Track at a Glance

✔ The characteristics that help individuals achieve midmanagement level are the same characteristics that are incompatible with TQM.

✔ Without midmanagement support, TQM success is questionable.

✔ Many middle managers speak the TQM language, but have no intrinsic commitment to the process.

✔ It takes time—at least four to six months and possibly more—to achieve intrinsic commitment for TQM in middle managers.

✔ Awareness training and quarterly meetings, with financial reports and book reviews, foster understanding of TQM principles and benefits.

✔ Direct involvement by senior management in the managers' training was a key to success.

✔ Statements of Commitments, signed by senior managers, send a strong signal to midlevel managers regarding the commitment and support of the president and other senior managers.

✔ Allowing managers to have a vote in whether the organization goes forward with TQM can go far in advancing their commitment.

✔ Ensuring midlevel management commitment to TQM takes time, training, information, senior management support, and the opportunity for middle managers to influence the decision.

15
Seven Required Skills for Fast-Track TQM Success

Regardless of how skilled or capable your employees are, without effective leadership, you won't get the most from Quality advancement or from Fast-Track TQM. Leadership is the guiding force that directs and inspires employees to achieve goals beyond their own expectations. But what exactly is leadership? How can you choose the correct leadership style to promote TQM in your organization?

The earliest model of leadership comes from the military. It was and still is autocratic with a strict, hierarchical structure. Autocratic leadership is effective when employee involvement isn't necessary and people are expected only to fulfill assigned tasks exactly as instructed. This style of leadership utilizes fear and punishment as the inevitable consequences of nonperformance or performance that doesn't meet management-determined standards. Unfortunately, many businesses today still adhere to this archaic leadership style.

Under the TQM model, leadership becomes much more participatory. Employees at all levels are asked to contribute their ideas, insights, skills, and talents to advance Quality. In contrast to the autocratic style of leadership, which actually seeks to reduce or eliminate input from the rank and file workforce, TQM leadership rewards employees who go beyond normal expectations and take the initiative.

Success with TQM does not occur by chance. It requires active, unwavering leadership. In a successful TQM organization, leaders at all levels support and sustain the value and importance of Quality. They create a relentless drive for Quality in which every employee, supervisor, and manager has clear direction about the value and purpose of Quality. The leaders not only point the direction for Quality, they inspire and motivate. They provide the all-important processes—the "how" of TQM—that allow employees to participate and become actively involved in "making the good better."

Effective TQM leadership doesn't require 50 or 100 leadership skills. In fact, using the Fast-Track Method, you can develop effective Quality-driven leaders by using only seven key skills. The Fast-Track Seven Key Skills to Quality Leadership have emerged from 20 years of involvement in leadership development. I've carefully observed the skills and qualities of leaders who were extrodinarily successful with their staffs. For years I kept a log recording my observations, trying to answer the question, "Why are these leaders so effective?" From the hundreds of leadership skills and qualities observed and recorded, the list boils down to a key seven.

If you fully utilize the Fast-Track Seven, you will not only create exemplary leadership, you and your managers will be set apart from your peers. You'll join the rare few managers who are on the fast track with their careers. Not all of these managers who are fast-tracking to success have learned the Key Seven Skills from the Fast-Track Method. They may have learned them through experience, from mentors, or from other types of training. But the managers who are on the fast track to success are guaranteed to be using the Fast-Track Seven Key Leadership Skills.

Leadership skills are those actions and behaviors that relate to leading others, particularly immediate staff. They go beyond the obvious skills of self-management. The Fast-Track Seven Key Leadership Skills are presented on the assumption that managers already have essential self-management skills such as thoroughness, time management, organizational ability, and attention to detail.

As you read through the skill descriptions, compare and examine each of them from your own experience. For each one, ask yourself, "How well do I do that and could I do it better?"

Fast-Track Tip 76

Successful TQM requires a specialized type of leadership. Apply the Fast-Track Seven Key Leadership Skills to develop successful Quality leaders.

Key Leadership Skill 1: Results Leadership

Of the tens of thousands of managers who are asked, "What do you get paid for?" all but a few respond with a list of duties. They truly believe they are paid to perform duties. *Yet people are not paid to perform duties; they are paid for results.*

This is an important distinction. In one training session, a manager made the comment, "I could perform every duty in my job description and still get fired for lack of performance." How true! When you're paying people for duties and not results, that's exactly what you'll get—thoroughly carried-out duties rather than results.

Fast-Track Tip 77

Managers are paid for results, not for duties, and must be held accountable for achieving those results.

In Fast-Track TQM, we pay people for results. The obvious question follows: "If we get paid for results, which results are we paid for?" In Fast-Track TQM, people are paid for results that fall into the seven categories shown in Fig. 15.1. (In some organizations, affirmative action/ EEO might be listed as an additional results category.)

As managers define the results they are paid for in each of the seven categories, they begin to know where and how to better apply resources in their areas of responsibility to achieve those results. They are better able to apply their leadership skills to make those results happen. Take a moment and test yourself. What do you get paid for within the seven categories? Be sure you describe *results*, not duties.

---

1. Quality	5. Safety
2. Quantity	6. Service
3. Cost	7. Image/reputation
4. Timeliness	

Figure 15.1. Results managers get paid to achieve

1. **Quality of product or service within their area of responsibility:** The following are examples of statements describing the Quality results a leader may be expected to achieve.

   Honor all contracts and agreements with customers—external and internal.

   Ensure that all company benefits and compensation plans are administered and honored according to contract agreements.

2. **Quantity:** Regardless of the level of responsibility of leaders, they are expected to accomplish a certain quantity of assignments within the area of responsibility. These are examples of what a results-oriented manager might be expected to accomplish in terms of quantity.

   Consistently increase the revenue ton miles/market share.

   Support all customers' needs to help them accomplish their goals and commitments.

3. **Timeliness:** The on-time requirement to complete a particular project or assignment is key to achieving expected outcomes. The following are examples of results relating to timeliness.

   Provide products and services within established time frames.

   Ensure that coordination of operations minimizes delays and meets customers' schedules.

4. **Cost:** Every leader responsible for a budget is expected to operate within established parameters and use resources effectively. The following are examples of results statements relating to cost.

   Ensure we operate within the established budget.

   Maximize passenger sales revenues in the most efficient and cost-effective manner.

5. **Safety:** Safety is an important result for every manager. Results-oriented leaders ensure the safety of employees, customers, and the public. These are results statements relating to safety.

   Ensure the safety of all personnel, the public, and property.

   Ensure that designs, procedures, and activities comply with corporate safety goals.

6. **Service:** In this context, service is defined as the exchange that takes place at the point of contact with internal or external customers. The result relates to the level of personal courtesy. These are examples of results relating to service.

   Ensure that customer service is delivered in a courteous and respectful manner.

Ensure that our customers' expectations for courteous service are consistently met.

7. **Image and reputation:** Every leader has the responsibility to enhance and build the company's image (what people see about an organization) and its reputation (what people tell others about it). These are results statements relating to image and reputation.

Ensure that the reputation of the company is consistently positive.

Project and reinforce a "caring" image.

Fast-Track Tip 78

Effective TQM leaders are results oriented. They know the required parameters and are accountable for demonstrating success.

Caution: Don't confuse results statements with goals. In most cases, goals are accomplished within a specific time frame. They change over time as they are accomplished and new goals are set. In contrast, results statements (describing what a person is paid for) remain relatively unchanged from year to year as long as the job classification and responsibilities are the same.

Fast-Track Tip 79

Results statements define and clarify what people get paid for, but they remain stable from year to year.

Once managers identify their results, it's vital that they meet with their immediate supervisor to clarify and confirm this understanding—that is, to ensure that these are in fact the agreed-upon results for which the manager is being paid. Very often, after having this meeting with the immediate supervisor, a manager will say, "That was the most important discussion I've ever had with my boss. Now I not only understand what I'm paid for, but now I know how and where I should be applying my effort and resources."

Clarifying results through the results statements can also help in rating performance. In many organizations, the results that people are paid for become the criteria for evaluating their performance. Using result-oriented criteria also takes the question out of merit pay increases. Those who produce results are rewarded. Those who do not, aren't.

Key Leadership Skill 2: Performance Agreements

Agreements are what make our lives work. In times of happiness and joy, we keep agreements with others; the agreements with others are in place and working. In difficult, stressful, discordant times, agreements with others have been violated or disrupted. So it is in our work lives. Whatever success leaders accomplish through their staff begins with the establishment of a performance agreement. In an effective agreement-setting process, each party—staff and manager—is clear about the expected outcomes, the time frames, and the place the outcome is to occur.

It's imperative for managers to clearly understand how important it is to honor and keep their performance agreements. If a manager says he/she will have a project completed on a specific date and time, that agreement must be honored, *no matter what it takes*. The only acceptable reason for violating a performance agreement is that something occurs beyond the manager's control.

An *excuse* is nothing more than failing to perform when the manager has control. In Fast-Track TQM, tolerance for excuses and performance failure are slim to zero. And there's an excellent reason: In organizations where management's credibility is weak, it's usually caused by managers' not following through and doing what they've agreed to do.

Being able to lead for Quality means being trustworthy. Employees must be able to count on management and what they say. To successfully lead for TQM, managers must value their agreements and take every action possible to keep their actions and words consistent and trusted.

Fast-Track Tip 80

For managers to lead effectively for Quality enhancement, they must be trustworthy and have credibility with employees. Honoring performance agreements establishes trust and credibility. Failure to honor them seriously impairs the advancement to Quality.

It's a vital skill for TQM leaders to be able to set and honor their performance agreements. Establishing clear and precise performance agreements can mean the difference between TQM success and TQM failure. Follow this Fast-Track Three-Step Performance Agreement process:

1. **Establish a clear understanding of the expected outcome.** In labor negotiations, this step can take weeks, months, and even years to accomplish. When asked, "How long does it take to reach agreement in a labor contract?" managers usally respond, "A long time." But in reality, it only takes three or four seconds. I ask, "Will you sign now?" You respond with a "yes." Only a few seconds have passed. The agreement-setting process encompasses only a small window of time. The weeks or months leading up to the request for agreement are used to confirm understanding and to prepare each party for the "yes" or "no" response.

2. **Go for the "yes."** There is something almost magical in the word "yes." Typically, people are reluctant to give a clear "yes" to their portion of a performance agreement. They may say, "yep," "sure," "absolutely," "of course," or "without question." All imply yes. If you don't hear a clear yes in negotiating a performance agreement, ask, "Does that mean yes?" You may have to ask the question several times to get to yes. The person may answer, "of course," "sure," or "that's what I said"— but still no clear yes. Ask again until you receive the magic word "yes."

   This may seem silly, but when people say "yes" to a performance agreement, you can be almost 100-percent guaranteed that they are making a personal commitment to keep and honor the agreement. Anything short of yes may result in questionable outcomes.

3. **Confirm commitment.** When people violate their performance agreements, they offer either an excuse or a reason. An *excuse* means the individual had control over the situation, but failed to perform. A *reason* for nonperformance is when the individual had no control over the situation and therefore couldn't perform. In Fast-Track TQM, successful leaders don't accept excuses and act to resolve the problems that caused reasons for nonperformance.

   Occasionally, it's important for managers to confirm employee commitment to honoring agreements at the time the agreements are made. By asking one simple question, you will know their commitment even before they walk away. Ask, "Is there anything that would keep you from honoring this performance agreement?" If they answer with anything besides a firm "no," their commitment to performing as outlined in the agreement is questionable. Some employees will make excuses for nonperformance even before they leave the agreement-setting process. It's vital for the manager and the employee then to reexamine the agreement and ensure that the employee is committed and has the resources necessary to fulfill the agreement.

Fast-Track Tip 81

Use the Fast-Track Three-Step Performance Agreement:

1. Establish clear outcomes.
2. Go for the "yes."
3. Confirm commitment.

Key Leadership Skill 3: Build Employee Commitment

Too often, managers know how to build commitment and motivation in others, but they forget to apply their knowledge in the pressured atmosphere of day-to-day work. They may have read about building commitment and motivating others, and they may understand the principles— but they fail to apply what they know. Even though applying a few simple principles can have a tremendous impact on the behavior of the workforce, managers have to learn and relearn motivational concepts, before they're willing to use them consistently in the workplace and in other areas of their lives.

What do you think is the number one people motivator? If you're like many managers, you probably said money. More than 50 years of psychological and management research have proven that, while money is important, it can't build long-term motivation and commitment. In fact, money ranks about ninth on the list of motivating factors. The top three are:

1. Consistent feedback and recognition.
2. Creating a sense of achievement.
3. Having influence.

Feedback and Recognition

Everyone wants feedback about his or her performance. People want to know how they did, where they stand in an organization. Think about yourself and someone you've enjoyed working for in the past. Did you always know where you stood with that person? Did he or she give you consistent positive and negative feedback about your performance? Chances are this was one of the qualitites you admired. Regularly letting people know how they're performing is absolutely vital in building commitment and motivating them to constantly improve.

Feedback is not just compliments, but rather giving recognition for performance. Compliments are like "atta boys" and "warm fuzzies." Recognition builds self-esteem through clearly stating the behavior that made the difference and how that behavior benefits the organization. Chapter 16 gives a clear description of the necessary processes to building employee commitment.

A Sense of Achievement

Everyone wants to be able to go home at night and say, "Wow! Look at what we achieved." One of the most effective tools you can use to create a sense of accomplishment is the graph. A graph allows employees to quickly get a visual image of performance—their individual performance, their work group's performance, or perhaps the performance of the company as a whole.

Having Influence

"Having influence" is another way of saying that people are understood and that others listen to their opinions. Allowing employees to have influence within the organization helps to build their self-esteem and self-confidence. "Having influence" does not necessarily mean that employees have a vote or can make management decisions. It does mean that they can offer their ideas and suggestions and that they will be listened to.

Think back to some of your own experiences when you were encouraged to give consistent feedback to your supervisor or colleagues. You knew you were making a difference; you felt valued and listened to. Did you feel committed and motivated? Of course, you did. Everyone does.

Much of what a leader does affects the self-esteem of employees. Self-esteem determines how they value themselves as human beings and how they see themselves valued within the organization. Using the three principles for building motivation and commitment can directly impact employee self-esteem individually and as a group. The stronger their self-esteem, the greater pride they take in a job well done, and the better able they are to tackle new skills and apply them to Quality enhancement.

Try a little experiment with your own family. If you're a parent, try applying the three motivating factors—feedback, a sense of achievement, and influence—on your children. You'll find these tools are quite powerful in every area of your life; they are whole-life tools.

Fast-Track Tip 82

To effectively involve all employees in Quality advancement, memorize the three statements for motivating and building commitment:

1. Provide feedback.
2. Create a sense of accomplishment.
3. Give employees influence.

As a manager leading to advance Quality, it does little good to simply insist that your staff commit themselves to performance agreements. Commitment must become an intrinsic force within each employee. Effective Fast-Track managers know how to build commitment. They use the three commitment-building factors identified by researcher David McClennen more than 40 years ago:

1. Recognition
2. A sense of achievement
3. Influence

Key Leadership Skill 4: Effectively Lead Meetings

There is a close link between being an effective leader and having good presentation skills and effectively leading meetings. As managers or supervisors address their staff, the employees are continually evaluating—what is their vision and strengths? Do their speech patterns and mannerisms effectively communicate what they are trying to say? An important part of Fast-Track TQM Training is the development of presentation skills before groups and in one-on-one conversations. Many effective presentation skill training programs are available and can be incorporated into the process of developing TQM leaders.

It's distressing to see so many managers fail miserably in leading meetings. But it is a leadership skill that must be learned and practiced to effectively advance Quality. Effective meetings begin with a clear, understandable agenda.

The Fast-Track Meeting Agenda Format

Most meeting agendas merely list the topics for discussion or review. Fast-Track TQM managers break meeting agendas into three major categories:

1. Information items
2. Discussion items
3. Decision items

If you consistently apply the Fast-Track Three-Step Agenda-Setting Process, you can reduce meeting times by as much as 50 percent and get more accomplished.

Information Items.   In a typical meeting, an inordinate amount of time is spent—wasted, actually—sharing and exchanging information. In most cases, information can be exchanged via written communication prior to the meeting or distributed at the meeting. Less than 10 percent of the meeting time should be devoted to information sharing.

Discussion Items.   These include topics that need to be discussed for clarification for future decision making or action by the group or its members. A large portion of the meeting should be devoted to discussing topics for future decision making.

Decision Items.   The agenda should include a list of the decisions that must be made at the meeting. The leader and the group participants must be clear about exactly who is making the decision, whether it is the leader, another manager, or the group itself. It's important not to surprise meeting participants and have them later complain, "I thought we had made the decision. What happened?"

Other Tips for Effective Meetings

There are other ways to make meetings useful and as brief as possible.

For one thing, effective meeting leaders keep storytelling and extensive examples to a minimum. Managers can express their ideas, concerns, and information without taking valuable time telling "war stories."

Second, make sure all the participants are clear about the purpose of the meeting. Whether the group's purpose is to exchange information, share ideas, or problem-solve, all the members should be clear on their mission. A group of managers who met weekly were once asked, "What is the purpose of your meeting together on a weekly basis?" No one could say. After considerable discussion, the group concluded that they were no longer focused on their original purpose. They'd veered off track and were meeting more out of habit than out of a clear purpose. Instead of weekly problem-solving meetings, the group members decided to meet once a month to share ideas.

Third, don't allow hidden agendas. Keep the focus of the meeting only on the planned agenda items. To establish an agenda for the next meeting, you can ask for manager input at the beginning or end of the current meeting.

Fourth, one of the greatest time-wasters during meetings occurs when the leader says, "Let's go around the group and hear from each participant." Several years ago, I sat in meetings at which the group leader routinely asked each participant to report. Week after week, I prepared something to say, because I knew I'd be called on, or because I didn't want to be stuck with nothing to say. Others at these meetings did the same and felt the same. Clearly, attending meetings at which everyone reports—whether they have something to contribute or not—wastes hours of valuable time.

In addition to having an effective agenda, a skilled TQM leader must be able to ask the right questions during meetings. Leading for Quality isn't a matter of telling people what to do. It's a matter of asking questions that will stimulate understanding, build commitment, and encourage others to examine options and alternatives. Before you go to your next meeting, review your agenda and identify the key questions that should be asked. You'll find that your staff members have the solutions to advancing the department or organization, if only you have the insight to ask the right questions.

Fast-Track Tip 83

Save up to 50 percent of valuable meeting time by eliminating needless storytelling, being clear on the meeting's purpose, avoiding hidden agendas, and skillfully asking power questions.

Key Leadership Skill 5:
Build Teams

The difference between a mob and a team is very slight, yet very significant. A mob acts without purpose or direction. A team has a common goal and focus for achievement. A team focuses its energies cooperatively on achieving/accomplishing that goal. Good examples of this are crises or life-threatening situations in which people exceed all normal expectations in working cooperatively. The common goal of survival becomes a unifying force. Every cooperatively functioning team has a common goal or target to align their energy, resources, and commitment.

An important aspect of Fast-Track Awareness Training involves bringing managers and supervisors together and forging a common goal together. That goal may be to build and enhance Quality within their assigned areas. As managers and supervisors come to realize the importance of a common goal in building a team, they examine their own priorities and begin making plans to build more unity in their work groups. Chapter 6 describes a proven questioning process to build unified work teams.

Recognized leaders effectively create a focal point for employees to support. In the case of Fast-Track TQM, that focus is Quality advancement. There's no more laudable goal than being the best in providing Quality products and services. Employee energy and resources become focused on the common goal of enhancing and building Quality to meet and/or exceed customer expectations.

Fast-Track Tip 84

Successful TQM leaders build teams using Quality management as the focal point and common goal.

Key Leadership Skill 6:
Empower Employees

So much has been written about empowerment that it's become almost a cliché. But employee empowerment is a vital part of Fast-Track TQM. *To empower someone is to give them the belief that they can accomplish something either alone or with others.* But how can you give someone such a gift? The answer lies in the Five-Step Empowerment Process as described in Chap. 17.

Fast-Track Tip 85

Use the Fast-Track Five-Step Empowerment Process to strengthen employees' self-esteem, and give them the belief and confidence that they can improve Quality.

A fundamental component of Fast-Track TQM is that every employee must have an understanding, a belief that they can take action to meet or exceed their customers' expectations. They are empowered to create customer satisfaction.

Key Leadership Skill 7: Create
Positive Working Relationships

To build an effective TQM organization, people working together must be positive, supportive, and cooperative with one another. It's the leader's responsibility to ensure that the working relationships between managers, supervisors, and employees are congenial and strong.

The basis for positive working relationships or for any relationship is trust. Every person in the organization must be able to trust that each will support the other, and will act in the best interest of the organization. Leaders directly impact trust by ensuring that they honor and keep the performance agreements as discussed in Key Leadership Skill 2. By consistently honoring and keeping your own performance agreements, your employees will come to trust you as a respected leader. Beware, however, that if you violate an agreement, months or even years of trust and credibility can be damaged. In organizations where employees question the credibility of management, you can be sure that the managers have violated established agreements. Honoring or violating agreements has a direct and dramatic impact on a leader's effectiveness.

To demonstrate just how powerful agreements are, take the example of the employment agreement. When someone is hired for a job, they must agree to accomplish certain tasks. Barring other conditions beyond the employee's control such as a downturn in the economy, his or her continued adherence to the performance agreement means continued employment. If the person violates the performance agreement, firing may result.

Friendship is another example. All of us at one time or another have lost friends or even relatives over the violation of an agreement. What a tragedy! While the specific agreements themselves may have never been discussed, individuals make inferences about how each will behave in the relationship. Violate those inferred agreements and the relationship is damaged, perhaps even lost altogether.

It's vital for you as a TQM leader to carefully examine your performance agreements. Are you sure you can honor and keep the agreements? Are you willing to do whatever is necessary to keep your agreements with your staff? If you can answer yes to both of these questions, you're on your way to leading for Quality.

Fast-Track Tip 86

Cooperative working relationships are built on trust. Honoring and keeping performance agreements directly build trust and management credibility.

Fast Track at a Glance

✔ Successful TQM requires effective leadership.

✔ Autocratic styles of leadership are contrary to TQM success.

✔ Effective TQM leaders invite and even reward employee involvement at all levels.

✔ Leaders who are successful in implementing and building TQM in their organizations use seven key leadership actions: (1) employ results-oriented leadership, (2) establish performance agreements, (3) build employee commitment, (4) lead meetings effectively, (5) build strong teams, (6) empower employees, and (7) create strong working relationships.

✔ Results-oriented leaders understand they are paid for achieving results, not for performing duties. Results statements clarify those results.

✔ Performance agreements define who will do what and in what time frame. Effective TQM leaders use a three-step method for setting performance agreements: (1) establish clear expected outcomes, (2) go for the "yes," and (3) confirm commitment.

✔ Honoring performance agreements will increase a manager's trustworthiness and credibility with employees.

✔ Leaders are responsible for building employee commitment and empowering employees to meet and exceed their customers' expectations.

✔ Too often, meetings waste valuable time. Meeting agendas should be divided into (1) information items, (2) discussion items, and (3) decision items.

✔ Effective meeting leaders (1) keep storytelling and examples to a minimum, (2) ensure everyone is clear about the meeting's purpose, (3) do not tolerate hidden agendas, and (4) stick to the established agenda.

✔ Improving group and one-on-one presentation skills can positively impact a leader's ability to lead for Quality.

✔ Quality leaders build teams by making Quality the focus and common goal.

✔ To motivate and build employee commitment to Quality advancement, leaders must (1) provide consistent feedback, (2) create a sense of accomplishment, and (3) allow employees to have influence in the organization.

✔ Employees can be empowered to act by using the Fast-Track Five-Step Method.

✔ Managers who fail to keep and honor their performance agreements lose the credulity and trust of employees.

16

Four Steps to Building Employee Commitment

One of the unique factors of Fast-Track TQM is the way employees are recognized and valued. Of course, employee recognition is important to any TQM effort, but in the Fast-Track Method recognition is given in a way that works simply and almost instantly. The original basis for this process began more than 25 years ago with a little program called "crediting," which Xerox Corporation started with the sales staff. Since then, many consultants and organizations have used variations of the process. In Fast-Track TQM, the process has evolved from merely giving credit to truly building employee value and self-esteem.

More Practical Than Theory

Over the years, I've asked thousands of managers, "Think of someone who works for you that you'd identify as a high performer. How does this person value himself, or herself? How would you describe the person's self-esteem?" Invariably, managers say the high achiever has high self-value—high self-esteem.

If you could enhance or improve an individual's self-esteem, what impact do you think it might have on his or her performance? Chances are excellent that performance would improve. That's the simple theoretical basis for the Fast-Track Method of building commitment and improving performance: Focus on building the self-esteem of individuals and groups through a process of recognition. While it may sound a little far-fetched, it's worked for hundreds of organizations and for thousands of employees.

Fast-Track Tip 87

Improve employee self-esteem and you improve performance: the higher the self-esteem, the higher the performance.

Defining Self-Esteem

I once conducted an off-site planning session with a group of medical doctors, each of whom was chief of a specialty area such as surgery, pediatrics, or internal medicine. Our task was to define the qualities they were looking for in a new medical director for the hospital. In the course of discussion, someone suggested the person selected should have high self-esteem. I turned to the chief of mental health and asked him to give us a layman's definition of self-esteem. He said there are three aspects of the self:

■ Self-image
■ Self-confidence
■ Self-esteem

Self-image, he explained, is how individuals see themselves. It's their picture of themselves as a performer and as a human being. In athletics, athletes often create a mental picture of themselves succeeding in an event. Research has shown that such positive mental images markedly improve performance. People in difficult circumstances, such as prisoners of war, have used self-images to survive. By picturing themselves successfully engaged in activities requiring concentration such as playing golf or typing on a typewriter, they were able to maintain their mental focus and capabilities.

Self-confidence is the inner strength that lets some people perform and achieve in settings that require extra effort. Individuals going for a personal interview or speaking before a group need self-confidence to enable them to perform. Succeeding in competitive activities can build self-confidence.

Self-esteem, the most important aspect of the self according to most mental health professionals, is how individuals value themselves as human beings. It is how they value themselves, how they consider themselves as being of value to others. Studies have shown that students who drop out of school typically have a low self-esteem. They do not see themselves as having value.

Sometimes we're fooled into thinking of a person who is outgoing and expressive as having high self-esteem. That's not necessarily true. Being outgoing and expressive is more a dimension of self-confidence. Some people who have a high level of self-confidence and outwardly appear to be highly capable may do self-destructive things, such as use drugs or alcohol excessively. Such behavior usually reveals low self-esteem. Self-destructive behaviors may be efforts to compensate for low esteem and to artificially build up one's personal value.

More Powerful Than Dollars

Assuming you can improve employees' performance by increasing their self-esteem, would you be interested in a proven way to build and strengthen that esteem? If you're like most managers, you are. Self-esteem does not arise from money. In fact, as already mentioned, money is far down on the list of factors that build commitment and motivation. If you still believe money is the great motivator, think for a moment about your present job. Very likely, you stay with it for one or more of the three factors: (1) personal recognition, (2) a sense of achievement, or (3) having influence. Each of these factors directly affects the development of your self-esteem.

So it is with others. We all have a personal need and desire to be valued—to build our self-esteem. We cling to those parts of our lives where we get a sense of being valued. When people in an organization build the self-esteem of the employees, the employees respond in kind. They work hard to express their appreciation and even reflect value back to us, strengthening our own self-esteem.

Fast-Track Tip 88

Don't rely solely on money and benefits to build commitment and motivation in your staff. More powerful motivators are recognition, a sense of achievement, and influence—a feeling that, "What I do matters."

TSBT

In Fast-Track TQM, I can improve an employee's performance with only 40 seconds of effort. Let me describe the process and demonstrate how easy it is to build self-esteem by giving an employee recognition for an accomplishment. Use a stopwatch to time the process. Put yourself in the position of the employee receiving recognition from your boss. The recognition will be given in two different ways. Then you be the judge. Compare the two and the potential impact they might have. The first example should last 10 to 12 seconds.

First Method

Mary, I want to thank you for your effort on the project over the last few weeks. It gives me a great deal of pride to see that kind of work coming out of our department. Thank you again for a quality piece of work.

How would you respond to hearing that message from your boss? Most people say, "I'd feel great. Wonderful. What do you want me to do next?" Now reset the timer. This example will take 35-40 seconds.

Second Method

Mary, the report you've been working on for the last three months is really a quality piece of work. It gives me a lot of pride to see that kind of work coming out of our department. The graph you prepared on page 23 of the report was very impressive. I put your name on the bottom of that page, made photocopies, and took them into the management meeting last Friday. Because of your skill in preparing the graph and how you displayed the workload versus staffing in our department, it looks like we're going to have a reduction in our workload and an increase in our staff. Mary, I want you to know that your skill in preparing that graph has made a real difference and I want to thank you for a quality piece of work. Again, thanks. You're making a difference.

Now how do you respond? If you're like most people, you'll say, "Even better." Besides the fact that the second message took approximately 40 seconds, what else was different? The second message was specific and outlined the benefits that Mary's work produced.

Success in improving employee self-esteem and performance involves a simple four-step process:

1. **T**hanks: It begins with offering Mary thanks for a great job.

2. **S**pecific: The boss is specific about what Mary did that made the difference—preparing an excellent graph.

3. **B**enefit: The benefit was identified to the boss, to the department, or to the organization. In the example, Mary's work benefited the boss and the department by reducing their workload.

4. **T**hanks: Close with another "thanks."

Thanks, specific, benefit, and thanks become a TSBT.

Fast-Track Tip 89

TSBTs can improve performance by building self-esteem. If you're willing to invest 40 seconds, you can improve employee self-esteem with TSBT.

It may seem too simple, but the Fast-Track TSBT formula for employee recognition is an incredibly powerful tool for building employee self-esteem. Let's look at how TSBT can be used to build performance or commitment to achieve a particular task.

1. Share your thanks for the employee's contribution.

   I want to thank you for...

   I appreciate your...

2. Describe the specific behavior you valued.

   You asked several good questions.

   Your directions were very clear.

3. State how it benefits you, your department, or the organization.

   Our organization needs employees who know how to handle...

   Our department really benefits from...

4. Give an overall statement of thanks.

   I really appreciate it.

   Thanks a lot for the effort. You're making a difference.

TSBT in Everyday Life

It's amazing how effectively the TSBT concept works in everyday life. You can impact and influence the performance of others by using TSBT whether you're in a restaurant, in a taxi cab, with your family, with an employee, with a colleague, or with your boss. Regardless of where you are, 40 seconds invested can build self-esteem and improve the performance of people around you. With a small investment of time, you can change personal relationships in a dramatic way.

When I travel, it's fun to see how giving TSBTs impacts people from all walks of life. I like to watch the reaction of complete strangers who are providing service when something they've done is recognized as their best effort. The responses are amazing. It makes me feel good too. It's like looking into a mirror—you get back what you send out. When you start building value with others, they respond by building value with you.

What a powerful tool you have to change the world and your organization.

Perhaps the most important place you can use TSBT is at home with your family. Many of you probably have children or teenagers at home, and you'd like to build and strengthen your relationship with them. TSBT may be the most effective way to do it. While you may be skeptical, you'll find TSBT the same great value that thousands of others managers have found in building the self-esteem and performance of others.

Recognition vs. Complaints

There's a big difference between giving effective recognition and giving compliments. Look back at the 10- and 40-second examples. The 10-second version offered nothing more than a compliment to the employee. It offered nothing specific. It did not address the benefits the work created for the individual, the unit, or the organization. Compliments create "warm fuzzy feelings," but they do little to build intrinsic value.

TSBT focuses on building individual self-esteem in a lasting way. When you talk with your staff about giving recognition, avoid using the word "compliment." It implies "atta-boys" and "warm fuzzies." It's stronger and more impacting to refer to it as "building value" and "building self-esteem."

Fast-Track Tip 90

Compliments don't really say anything. They create a "warm, fuzzy" feeling, but do little to improve self-esteem. Building self-esteem requires recognition that specifically identifies the behavior and outlines the benefits of that behavior to the individual, the department, and/or the organization.

Rules for Offering TSBTs

To create success and have immediate impact using the Fast-Track TSBT Method, it's important to follow these rules.

1. Be sincere: Anytime TSBT is offered, it must be a sincere gesture. Never offer a TSBT in a flippant, casual way. It should always be given with full sincerity and dignity.

2. Offer it soon: TSBT should be offered as soon as possible after the event occurs. The longer the delay, the more diminished the impact and sincerity.

3. Focus on behavior, not results: Correct behavior yields correct results. If you reinforce and build specific behaviors through giving recognition, employees will repeat those behaviors with positive results.

4. Recognize best effort: If you wait until the "best results" occur before offering TSBT, it will never happen. Use the reinforcement of TSBT to grow best results and improve performance over time.

5. Reinforce in private: Other employees who overhear TSBT may wonder why they aren't receiving feedback. Just because you're reinforcing someone's behavior does not mean the person's doing outstanding work. It simply means they are being given recognition for the behavior that is the best for them at the time.

TSBT—How Often?

Give TSBT to employees only as often as you can maintain sincerity. In Fig. 16.1, three levels of performance are listed. The performance of average employees is typically somewhere between "acceptable" and "good."

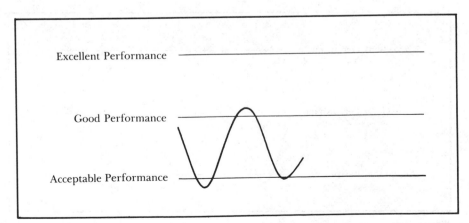

Figure 16.1.

Of course, you want to advance the performance of each employee to the excellent level as shown in Fig. 16.2. The tick marks along the line showing the progress to the excellent level represent the frequency of giving TSBTs; notice that the tick marks aren't equally spaced. At the beginning, there are more TSBTs. As the performance gets better and better, the frequency of TSBTs can decrease. If you wait for an employee's performance to be excellent before you offer a TSBT, you probably will never give one. Instead, give TSBTs along the way as employees perform work that is their *best effort and best accomplishment for them.* It may not be excellent performance, but it is their best. The performance improvements may be small, but they will continually improve as you give TSBTs.

By analogy, it's like moving a big steel ball. In the beginning, you need a lot of energy to get it moving. But once it starts moving, sustaining advancement becomes only a matter of maintenance. So it is with TSBTs. Initially, you may need to apply this tool more frequently. As employee performance gets closer to achieving the excellent level, your TSBTs can become less frequent and still maintain the high level of performance.

Fast-Track Tip 91

Only offer recognition in the form of TSBTs as often as you can maintain sincerity. Initially, it will require more recognition; as performance improves, the number of TSBTs you must give to maintain good performance decreases.

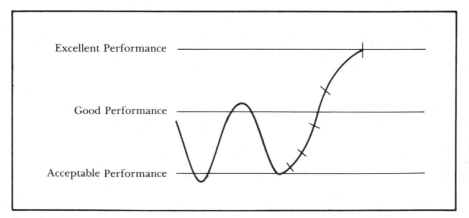

Figure 16.2.

Verbal vs. Written TSBTs

Are TSBTs more effective if they're verbal or written? You can build an effective case for either. A verbal TSBT is more immediate and, some might argue, more personal. And you can back it up with a written TSBT later. Others insist that a written TSBT shows a greater level of sincerity, that you value the employee's actions so much you'd take the time to put it in writing. One of our clients, the president of a utility, has made a personal commitment not to leave his office on Fridays until he has written a minimum of five TSBTs to employees throughout the organization. He's set up a system where every manager and supervisor is empowered to keep him informed about employees whose behavior is of special benefit to the company. Then he takes time to write a TSBT to those deserving employees. Far more than compliments, these TSBTs build self-esteem and personal value in his employees.

In a Fast-Track TQM training session, one of the participating managers told this story: After learning about the value of TSBTs, the manager had sent a written TSBT to one of his employees. The day after the employee received the letter, he came into the manager's office and said, "I've worked for this company for 20 years. This is the first time anyone has ever given me a letter recognizing my good performance." The employee's eyes filled with tears and he headed toward the door. Before he left, he turned and smiled at the manager, saying, "You will be repaid many times over."

Preparing and offering TSBTs isn't a natural part of being a Quality manager. It isn't something you naturally think of doing. It requires special effort to build personal value with staff. It's a lot like learning to drive a car. When you first got behind the wheel, you felt awkward and uncomfortable. But the more you practiced and developed skill, the more natural it felt to be driving. So it is with offering employees TSBTs. At first, it will feel awkward and uncomfortable. But with practice it will feel quite natural.

Fast Track at a Glance

- ✔ High achievers have high self-esteem.
- ✔ If you can improve employees' self-esteem, you can improve their performance.
- ✔ Self-esteem is how people value themselves and are valued by others.
- ✔ Giving recognition, a sense of achievement, and a feeling of influence are more powerful in creating commitment and building self-esteem than money and benefits.

✔ The Fast-Track formula for giving recognition is TSBT—thanks, specific, benefit, thanks.

✔ TSBTs can be effective in increasing self-esteem and improving performance in all areas of your life, not just at work. To be effective in offering TSBTs (1) be sincere, (2) give it soon after the event, (3) focus on behavior, not the result, (4) recognize best effort, and (5) reinforce in private.

✔ Give TSBTs only as often as you can be sincere.

✔ Give TSBTs frequently when first improving performance, less frequently as performance approaches excellence.

17

Five Steps to Empowerment

Chapter 7 briefly referenced the importance of empowerment, but it is a far too powerful and vital force in Fast-Track TQM to be left at that.

I once needed to make a ticket change at an airport. My ticket had me departing from an airport at an adjoining city, but I wanted to leave from the airport I was in. The airline agent first told me that I couldn't change the ticket. Then she said I could make the change, but it would cost an additional $75. I asked to speak to her supervisor. Reluctantly, she asked her supervisor to talk with me. Within a few seconds, the problem was resolved to my satisfaction. The ticket was reissued without additional charge departing from my current airport.

What was the difference? Why did one employee tell me she couldn't solve the problem to my satisfaction, while another settled the problem quickly and pleasantly? The difference is empowerment. When the ticketing supervisor gave me my altered ticket, she said, "We have been empowered by our president to make decisions that will best meet the needs of our customer. I'll be glad to change your ticket." The term "empowerment" intrigued me. I asked her what she meant by it. She answered quickly, "We have permission to make decisions that will satisfy our customers."

Giving employees permission to make decisions that will satisfy their customers is empowerment at its best. It enables employees, when confronted with difficult situations, to be able to make choices to satisfy the customer. In turn, those customer-satisfying decisions go far in building a positive company reputation. Will I fly on that airline carrier again? Of course. Will I tell others about the service I received? Absolutely.

There was another lesson in this experience. The ticket agent who was not empowered to satisfy my needs acted frustrated and put out by my request. The supervisor, however, who was empowered, acted excited and enthusiastic about being able to solve my problem. She had obviously received some training and instruction in empowerment. Not only did she have permission to act, she firmly believed that she had the right and the responsibility to look for situations in which she could resolve customers' problems and meet their needs.

Fast-Track Tip 92

If you empower employees to resolve customer problems, you create satisfied customers and enthusiastic employees.

Empowering employees at all levels to take action to best meet the needs of customers is a fundamental principle of Fast-Track TQM. Specifically, I'm talking about satisfying all customers—both internal and external. It begins by changing rules and procedures to allow employees to have more choices in their decision making. Most TQM training systems focus only on this aspect of empowerment. The difficulty is in creating an intrinsic belief within employees that they truly have the power and the authority to look for situations in which they can take action assertively to meet their customers' needs. This is our emphasis in Fast-Track TQM.

To the Fast-Track employee, the empowerment process begins with assessing how employees are currently empowered. Consider your own staff. What are they presently empowered to do? After asking hundreds of managers this question in workshop sessions, I'm always startled at how few choices most employees are given to meet their customers' needs. Most managers say, "Yes, but the procedures, requirements, and rules we provide for employees, in most cases, allow them to act within the best interests of the company." In the best interests of the company, perhaps. But what about the best interests of the customers? If you're not meeting your customers' needs, you're not acting in the best interest of your organization.

Most rules, regulations, and procedures limit employee empowerment to act on the special and unique situations customers may bring. While 95 percent of all customer problems can be handled by applying the present rules and regulations, employees need additional options to enable them to meet the 5 percent of customers who present difficult problems. Consider my ticket change request at the airport. With only a small change in the rules, the ticket agent would have been able to accommodate me with no frustration and without having to involve a supervisor.

give away the store. Special circumstances and difficult problems relate to only a tiny percentage of your customer population. A small change in the airline's rules or an exception to the rule would have empowered the employee to immediately meet the needs of a customer who represented a very small, but very important, percentage of their customers.

Fast-Track Tip 93

Rules and procedures that don't ensure customer satisfaction aren't in the best interests of the organization.

Benefits of Empowerment

The obvious benefit of empowering employees to meet the needs of customers is having more and more customers satisfied. Yet there's a secondary benefit that is less obvious, but extremely powerful. It involves what happens to employees, how they feel and how they respond to solving problems quickly and efficiently and seeing their customers satisfied. *Empowerment builds self-esteem in employees.* It creates a sense that they are in control. It lets them know that they can cause, direct, and guide other people to be satisfied.

The mirrorlike results of increased self-esteem radiate throughout the company. What employees—or anyone for that matter—send out is reflected back. When employees build value and satisfaction within customers, the customers radiate it back to the employee. It's a win-win situation. As employees become better able to meet the needs of the customer, their willingness to take risks expands. They are more willing to look for unique and different ways of solving problems and meeting their customers' needs. Again, employees don't have to abandon the company's interests. But if they know they are not going to be demeaned or punished for actions they take, they become more willing to look aggressively for ways to meet customers' needs and build satisfaction. The more experience they have in meeting customer needs, the better their judgment becomes in resolving problems. As employees have more success in satisfying their customers, their personal pride grows and they become excited, eager employees.

Fast-Track Tip 94

Empowerment builds employee self-esteem.

The Structure of Empowerment

Having the right rules and procedures to empower employees involves a three-step process:

1. Identify the present rules and procedures.
2. Challenge the present rules and procedures with customer needs in mind.
3. Change/alter the rules and procedures.

Step 1 is to identify the current rules and procedures that allow an employee to meet the needs of customers (you can't change what you haven't identified). Begin by making a list of each of the options or choices an employee can take to meet customer needs. In most cases, the list is small—only three to five options. An easy way to walk through this process is to identify various situations an employee may be confronted with, and then list the various options they have to solve the problem.

Once you've identified the present rules and procedures, step 2 involves challenging each rule and procedure. Does it meet the needs of the customer in any situation you can identify? If the rules or procedures might result in customers' leaving dissatisfied or displeased with their experience, it's time to move onto step 3.

In this final step, examine any of the rules or regulations that might cause customer dissatisfaction, and then consider changes. To be effective, those rules must not simply be examined, but rewritten to ensure employees can operate in ways that satisfy their customers.

Fast-Track Tip 95

Use a three-step process to ensure that you have correct and proper rules and regulations to meet your customers' needs and expectations:

1. Identify the present rules and procedures.
2. Challenge the present rules and procedures with customer needs in mind.
3. Change/alter the rules and procedures.

Empowerment as a Belief

Now you've accomplished the easy part of empowerment—changing the rules and procedures. That's only the beginning. At this point, most organizations tell employees, "Now go and apply the new rules and create satisfied customers." Will it work? Probably, but with definite limitations.

Empowerment doesn't work unless you address the beliefs of employees. You must give them the belief that they can, by themselves or working with others, take action to accomplish the desired outcome.

Five Steps to Empowerment

Let's examine the five-step process in detail.

Step 1: A Common Need

Whether you're talking about empowering a salesperson, a ticketing agent, or a purchasing agent, there must be a common need identified, usually accompanied by a "pinch" or a "hurt." This pinch or hurt may be the frustration or the emotional reaction the employee has in dealing with a difficult, confrontational customer. The aim is to identify common needs, not common goals. An effective way of identifying these common needs is to meet with employees and ask them to identify difficult customer situations that they felt were beyond their ability to resolve.

Let's look at how "need" applies in another context. Think about how a pop star is created. Popularity is generated by identifying the social nature of the target audience, their "need." Rocker Bruce Springsteen had a hit album with "Born in the USA." At the time the album was released, his target audience needed the hero, the nationalism, the pride, and the blue collar values that the music represented. Contrast that with the later success of oldie crooner Henry Connick Jr. He built his success initially not by singing his own music, but by singing old tunes to which his audience could relate. His audience needed the romance, the nostalgia, and the old-fashioned values his music represents. Each singer is very successful with his respective target audiences.

The person doing the empowering must recognize a common, specific need, pinch, or hurt in the person or group being empowered, and seek to fulfill that need. The empowering process extends the belief that, alone or together, we can eliminate the pinch or hurt.

Fast-Track Tip 96

Employees feel a common need, a "pinch" or "hurt," that will motivate them to change how they serve customers.

Step 2: A Quick Success

If you can quickly demonstrate success to employees by eliminating one of the pinches or hurts, they become encouraged and hopeful that other difficult situations can be resolved. Like a snowball rolling downhill, this process begins small, but as it advances it gets bigger, faster, and more powerful. Giving employees the ability to have a quick success is like rolling a small snowball. Just watch it build.

Fast-Track Tip 97

Success is like a snowball. It builds on itself.

Step 3: Have the Required Resources

Don't set up employees for failure by not having the resources to continue eliminating problems that cause the pinch or hurt. The resources may include equipment, supplies, time to act, rule changes, or, in some cases, a direct change in corporate policy. Ensure the continued removal of the pinch or hurt by making the resources readily available.

Fast-Track Tip 98

Employees need to have the necessary resources (time, equipment, etc.) to serve customers. Without them, you doom the empowerment process to failure.

Step 4: Employee-Defined Success

Employees must be allowed and encouraged to define and describe success. What would the situation be like if the pinch and hurt went away in serving and meeting customer needs? This process begins by defining how a customer may respond to a "what-if" question. "What if the customer were satisfied?" "What would have to happen?" This not only defines the outcome, but confirms and identifies various options for consideration to ensure customer satisfaction.

It's imperative that management doesn't take this step for employees. The "what-if" questions guide the employees through the option-identifying process. It helps them create the attitude and belief that they can do what is needed and actually make a difference with their customers.

Step 5: Employee Evaluates Success

It's also important that employees be able to recognize the success they've created in building customer satisfaction. When employees recognize they've created satisfied customers, they begin to seek out dissatisfied customers so that they can apply their new skills and knowledge. They begin to actively build and create satisfaction in their customers. Personal satisfaction and success occur as the employees' vision in the "what-if" sessions becomes a reality.

The five-step Fast Track to employee empowerment process can be applied to individuals or to groups. It can even be applied to very large groups numbering in the millions. For example, you can apply the Fast-Track empowerment process to the entire American population. If you were to run for political office, the five-step process would prove invaluable in getting your constituents to support you and vote for you.

Here's how it would work.

Step 1: Identify a common need, a hurt or pinch among the people. What is it that is bothering your voters? What is causing them pain or discomfort?

Step 2: Identify what creates and builds quick success. Perhaps you could change a tax law or eliminate a complicated process that is causing voters problems.

Step 3: Make sure you have the resources available to cause that quick success to happen. In this case, perhaps the resources involve support from your colleagues at city hall, political clout, or financial resources.

Step 4: Help your constituents define success. You want them to recognize what things would look like if the pinch or hurt were removed.

Step 5: Have your constituents evaluate the success, to confirm it, and to tell others about it.

Empowerment is catching. One way to spread the empowerment bug is to have employees share their successes in resolving customer problems with one another in staff meetings. Ask, "Has anyone had a difficult situation over the past few days that they were able to resolve?" As employees conclude their descriptions, have everyone applaud. This gives the speakers the knowledge that they've made a difference and that their actions are recognized, valued, and appreciated.

The process is almost magical. As employees listen to situations in which others were able to resolve problems quickly and efficiently, they become excited about the customer satisfaction process. Soon they too are looking for ways to resolve customer problems and build success.

Fast Track at a Glance

✔ Empowered employees create and build customer satisfaction.

✔ For TQM to succeed, all employees at all levels must be empowered to act to satisfy both internal and external customers.

✔ Empowering employees involves changing rules and procedures and changing employee beliefs and attitudes.

✔ Use a three-step process to ensure rules and procedures are satisfying customers: (1) analyze current rules/procedures, (2) challenge rules/ procedures, and (3) change/alter those that don't satisfy customers.

✔ Empowerment not only creates satisfied customers, it also builds employee self-esteem.

✔ Use the five-step Fast-Track empowerment process: (1) identify a common need, (2) create quick success, (3) have the required re- sources, (4) have employees define success, and (5) have employees evaluate success.

✔ The five-step empowerment process can be used anywhere and with individuals or groups.

✔ Have employees share their successes at staff meetings and reward their efforts with applause.

18

Eight Communication Channels for Fast Tracking TQM

Once, while talking about the value of keeping employees informed about Quality processes in the organization, a company president said, "You can't communicate with your customers if you can't communicate with your employees." This manager is certainly an insightful leader. He recognizes the importance of keeping staff well-informed, so as to enable them to serve and communicate with their customers, particularly external customers.

Clear, consistent communication with employees builds and strengthens employee understanding about the Quality processes in the organization. It helps them see where they can actively participate in the Quality advancement process. Keeping employees informed also fosters personal commitment to TQM and to the company. It helps them catch the full vision of TQM and what it can do for the organization, for their department or work group, and for themselves.

Fast-Track Tip 99

If you can't communicate with your employees, you won't be able to communicate with your customers. Clear, consistent communication is a key to developing employees who are able to meet or exceed their customer's expectations.

Keeping lines of communication open with employees isn't a short-term process. It is something that must become ingrained into the very fabric of the organization as a way of doing business. Organizations committed to advancing Quality must be willing to devote the time and resources needed for clear, consistent employee communication if they are to succeed with TQM. Mid-sized to large companies often assign a full-time staff member or even a small department to the sole duty of employee communications. Some companies, particularly smaller ones, opt to hire independent communication consultants to handle employee communications rather than pay for full-time communication staff. Regardless of whether you use internal or external staff to get the job done, the extent and frequency of the employee communication program and its emphasis on keeping staff informed about Quality advancement will reflect the commitment of the organization's senior management—particularly the president or CEO—to TQM.

As with any effective communication process, no one vehicle or approach can ensure that the right messages are getting across consistently to every employee. Just as educators and psychologists have identified different types of learners, people receive messages in different ways. Some may respond to a general company communique like a newsletter, while others need a personal letter or a seminar. To ensure reaching everyone, you have to be willing to use a variety of communication channels. Some of the most effective communication channels for keeping employees informed and involved with the TQM process are discussed in the following sections.

Fast-Track Tip 100

Different employees respond to different messages. Use a variety of communication vehicles to reach everyone with the quality message.

Channel 1: Fax and Photocopiers

A group of senior managers were discussing their lack of effectiveness in communicating with employees. The problem was compounded by the fact that they have field offices in three states. Their concern was for more than being able to keep employees informed, but being able to provide immediate recognition to employees for special achievements. The solution was at their fingertips, yet overlooked. The solution was a special use of the fax machines located in each office. Together we designed a form with the heading in large, bold print, "News Flash." A border was included with adequate space to type or write in the hot news item. This made it easy for managers throughout the organization to fill in the news item and to quickly disseminate it throughout the organization.

By having a prepared form, each office became a distribution center to convey hot items describing employee accomplishment in advancing Quality. Photocopies of the fax received at each location were made to distribute the news item. To retain the identity of the "News Flash" to Quality advancement and employee recognition, senior managers agreed to limit its use to Fast-Track TQM.

Fast-Track Tip 101

Develop and use a "news flash" form to disseminate hot news items about employee achievements. Use a fax or photocopy machine to broadcast the news items throughout your organization.

Channel 2: Newsletters for Quality

Newsletters are certainly not the easiest channel of communication, but they are one of the most cost effective. Even small companies with 100 or so employees typically have some kind of in-house newsletter to keep employees informed about the activities of the organization. It's here that you can begin your Quality communication emphasis.

Fast-Track Tip 102

Newsletters can be one of the most cost-effective methods of consistently communicating the Quality message to your employees.

When Quality advancement is just beginning in an organization, it's common to add a special column or page devoted to advancing product or service Quality in the current in-house newsletter. Eventually, it will be important to have a separate publication for advancing Quality, whether it is an extension of an existing newsletter or an additional publication.

By giving Quality advancement its own communication vehicle, you send a strong message about its importance in the organization.

Too often, organizational newsletters are boring and seldom read by employees. You can avoid this if you follow two important rules:

1. Maximize the number of employee names listed in the newsletter.

2. Maximize the number of employee photographs.

Everyone likes to see his or her name and picture. Employees do too. Seeing their names and photographs in the Quality newsletter creates pride in employees, who come to identify with the company and with the TQM processes. Typically, employees featured in the organization's Quality newsletter share the newsletter with family and friends. They may save the issue in a scrapbook or post it on their office wall. While it may seem a small thing, being recognized in the organization's Quality newsletter builds and reinforces the value and importance of the employee to the organization and increases employee self-esteem.

Controversial topics can also add spice to the newsletter. You can have both sides express their opposing views on a chosen topic, and let employees reach their own conclusions. Not only does it build understanding of sometimes complex issues, it also fosters tolerance for differing opinions and sends the message that people don't necessarily have to agree to work cooperatively together.

Size, Frequency, and Format

The biggest mistake companies make with their Quality newsletter is that they become too ambitious. They start off with a publication that is too large and too frequent to sustain over the long run. Often, companies will produce a large, multipage newsletter and announce it will be published on a monthly or semimonthly basis. The first issue of a Quality newsletter is always easy to prepare. At this point, there is a lot of excitement and enthusiasm about the Quality process. New and unusual events have taken place, and it's easy to include articles about them in the first issue.

The next issues become more problematic. How do you keep the newsletter newsy and interesting for employees? If you talk to any staff member who has had to consistently produce a Quality newsletter, they'll tell you that the fun and excitement diminishes very quickly and that the publication can become a real burden.

A more realistic approach is to publish the newsletter on a quarterly basis and limit its size to a single 11×17-in. sheet, folded in half. This yields four pages and, in some cases, even this size can be very ambitious for a continued publication. Using plenty of high-quality photographs will make the publication graphically interesting, keep employee interest high, and use up space when news items are limited. The format should be two or three columns, with a balance of text and photographs. Give byline credit to employees who write special articles.

Keep in mind the publication of a Quality newsletter is a management performance agreement. Management has stated that they will publish this document on a consistent schedule. They've said that this vehicle is an important part of communicating with employees about the Quality process. If management doesn't follow through consistently on the publication, employees will question management's commitment to Quality, and the all-important trust and credibility between employees and management will suffer.

Fast-Track Tip 103

Don't be overly ambitious with your Quality newsletter. In the beginning, publish no more frequently than quarterly and keep the size down to four pages or less.

Newsletter Content

An established newsletter format makes subsequent issues easier to prepare. Often a template can be created on a computer that speeds up the placement of regular columns and features faster, and gives the newsletter a consistent look. Here are some of the topical areas that should be addressed regularly in each publication:

1. **Employee recognition:** A minimum of 50 percent of the publication should be devoted to names and photographs of employees in articles that describe their action and involvement in the Quality process. Whenever special events to improve Quality take place and employees are involved, their names should be included in the descriptive articles.

A word of caution: Often, organizations expect their managers and supervisors to be so excited about the Quality process that they will write and submit newsletter articles. It won't happen. While managers, supervisors, and employees are enthusiastic and want to see their department or work group featured, most have neither the time nor the skills to write newsletter articles. If you don't have someone with the necessary writing and editing skills on staff, you may have to hire an independent communications consultant to write and edit your publication. Whoever is responsible for publishing the newsletter must interview the managers, supervisors, and employees—and write the articles. The newsletter editor should ensure that not only are the articles professionally written, but also that the names of everyone mentioned in the newsletter are spelled correctly. While this may sound like a minor point, it's vitally important. A name is an important part of a person's identity and value. It's imperative that the publication—particularly a publication on Quality advancement—be free of spelling or other defects.

As mentioned, photographs play an important part in both employee recognition and in the professional look of the publication. It is important to have a camera available to ensure that photographs are taken of employees actually participating in Quality events. Nothing is more boring than having a series of "mug shots" of people not doing anything but smiling into the camera.

2. **Celebrations:** Include articles about celebrations both large and small that take place around significant accomplishments.

3. **Employee suggestions:** The newsletter can be the vehicle for a running dialogue between employees and management. Employees can make suggestions about advancing Quality, and management can respond with comments on how the suggestions were implemented or with explanations for not implementing them. Employees, seeing their ideas in print, are encouraged to make more suggestions. Publishing employee ideas also encourages "hitchhiking"—that is, tagging onto other ideas—thereby expanding and improving on others' suggestions.

4. **President's message:** Every issue of the newsletter should have space devoted to a message from the company president. While some senior officers may see this as a burden, it is an important part of their commitment to advancing Quality in the organization. It isn't necessary for the president to actually write the message him- or herself. The staff member or consultant producing the newsletter can interview the president or CEO, write the piece, and then have the senior officer fine-tune the article. Occasionally it's a good idea to use an interview question-and-answer format in the president's column. It

provides a quick and easy read, and can make for an interesting article because it is in the president's actual words.

5. **Schedule of events:** It's important to keep employees informed about activities going on in the organization that support and advance the Quality process. The schedule of events may include special classes, speakers, or seminars. The lack of a consistent flow of upcoming activities on a quarterly basis is a good indication that the organization isn't doing enough to advance Quality. It underscores that the time has come to reevaluate the organization's commitment to TQM. Keeping a consistent flow of Quality-oriented activities going takes special effort, but it's an important part of keeping the excitement and enthusiasm alive in the Quality-advancement process.

6. **Customer interviews:** A portion of each publication should be devoted to one or more interviews with external customers. This reminds employees that Quality advancement is really all about meeting or exceeding customer expectations. Seeing photographs of customers and hearing stories about the products and/or services they receive creates a real picture of customer service for employees. Customer interviews can help employees answer the question, "How well are we serving our customers?" Over time, customer interviews can help employees see the changes and improvements they're making in the company's products and services. They also give employees another form of recognition for a job well done.

7. **Employee interviews:** These features reinforce employee commitment and help employees get to know one another better. An easy format to duplicate is the one used by the *USA Today* newspaper that has a photograph of the person, a single question, and a brief paragraph of response.

Fast-Track Tip 104

If you don't have communications/public relations professionals on staff, consider hiring a professional writer/editor to produce your newsletter.

Channel 3: Letters from the President

In addition to supporting management forums, letters from the president can also be used at any time to provide the special recognition from the senior officer that is so important for TQM success. Word processing has made it very easy for presidents and CEOs to send a special letter in a mass mailing to all managers and employees, or to a select group of managers and employees. You can personalize the letter even further by having it addressed to the individual's home address.

Letters become a special form of recognition. They can announce an upcoming event or provide instruction and guidance about an activity taking place in the organization. While it may be a form letter, using the individual's name and having the president sign it makes it personalized. It's a good idea to have the president's signature in a different color to make it easy for the recipient to recognize that the president, in fact, took the time to sign their letter.

Channel 4: Computer Screen Messages

In organizations in which employees log onto a mainframe computer, it's easy to insert messages that appear on the screen as employees enter the system. This channel of communication must not be used in such a way as to suggest that "Big Brother" is keeping an eye on people. When used to communicate special announcements or upcoming events, or to recognize the particular achievements of an employee, it can be very effective. Cute or humorous sayings become tiring, and after a while become a form of derisive humor, particularly toward management. The computer screen is a channel for Quality information that may even replace employee bulletin boards in importance.

Fast-Track Tip 105

Computer screen messages can be effective at communicating with employees. But they must not be viewed as a "Big Brother" tactic. Limit the messages only to special announcements or recognitions.

Channel 5: Brown Bag Lunches

Several years ago, when I was the director of organizational development for a large corporation, a new president came on board who was anxious to get to know the employees and understand more about the organization. I arranged for him to meet informally with employees and managers in a series of brown bag lunches, each lasting about 45 minutes. The company supplied the lunches, as twice a week the president met with groups of employees and managers to share lunch. The informal lunches enabled the president to share his ideas and views and to answer questions. Even more importantly, they allowed employees to express their ideas and suggestions.

While having lunch with the boss may not seem particularly significant, the employees were amazed that the president would actually take the time to eat and talk with them. The informal setting encouraged candor and openness in both the employees' questions and the president's responses. It not only created a new level of understanding among employees, it gave the president real insight into the concerns of the employees and ways the company could be more effective in creating a satisfied workforce. The president's brown bag lunches were so popular that they evolved into an ongoing affair regularly scheduled throughout the year. It became a valuable forum for open dialogue between the president and employees.

You can easily adapt the brown bag lunch idea to your own organization to advance Quality and ensure open communication. Not only can the president establish brown bag meetings, divisional or department managers or work group supervisors can use this informal format on a regular basis. You'll find it's an effective way not only to stop unfounded rumors and gossip, but also to keep employees informed about the Quality process.

Fast-Tract Tip 106

The informality of brown bag lunches with management and employees can foster the open and honest exchange of concerns and ideas.

Channel 6: Payroll Stuffers

Announcements in payroll envelopes are effective ways to communicate with every employee in the company. But beware. Overusing this communication channel can quickly render it ineffective. Payroll stuffers should be limited only to special announcements or special recognition for employees who have made significant accomplishments.

Channel 7: Visual Identification of Quality Processes

Banners, posters, special mottos are all ways of making quality processes visible. But it's a communication channel that's frequently abused. Many managers become so excited about the Quality advancement process that they want to decorate the entire company with special banners and slogans. The danger is that Quality advancement will be seen as a special program, not as a way of doing business on an ongoing basis. If you choose to use visual identification of Quality processes in your company, keep it simple and don't overdo it. The message should be short, identifiable, and meaningful. The Ford Company's "Quality is Job One" is a good example. All employees, regardless of their positions in the company, can relate to it.

Fast-Track Tip 107

Be careful not to overuse banners, slogans, and mottos that can give the impression that Quality advancement is a program that will end.

Channel 8: Employee Bulletin Boards

Some organizations devote a special bulletin board or portion of one for announcements and information regarding Quality in the organization. The board can become an important communication channel for posting special announcements and scheduled events and for recognizing extraordinary employee efforts. But be aware that this is another one of those performance agreements—if you're going to start it, be prepared to sustain it. Lack of continued effort in employee bulletin boards will be seen as a decrease in the importance of Quality in the company. Keep the bulletin board new, fresh, and filled with ideas and information, and employees will see it as another message that Quality is important to you and to the organization.

Fast Track at a Glance

✔ Employees must be well-informed if they are to effectively serve their customers.

✔ Clear, consistent communication about Quality processes in the company clarifies employee understanding about how they can participate in Quality advancement, creates and strengthens personal commitment, and builds employee self-esteem.

✔ Use various channels of communication to ensure reaching every employee with the Quality message.

✔ Quality newsletters can be one of the most effective forms of employee communication.

✔ The Quality-advancement process should have its own publication within the company.

✔ To ensure employee interest in the Quality newsletter, maximize the number of employee photographs and names in each issue.

✔ Companies often make their Quality newsletters too large and too frequent to sustain over time. Limit the size to four pages and publish it quarterly.

✔ Include the following content items in your newsletter: (1) employee recognition, (2) celebrations, (3) employee suggestions, (4) president's message, (5) schedule of events, (6) customer interviews, and (7) employee interviews.

✔ Personalized letters from the president can be an important form of communication and recognition.

✔ Brown bag lunches with management and employees can foster open communication.

✔ Other ways to communicate the Quality message include (1) on-screen computer messages, (2) payroll stuffers, (3) visual messages like slogans or posters, and (4) employee bulletin boards.

✔ Whatever its format, keep employee communication consistent and regular. If you decrease or halt communication channels about Quality, employees will think the importance of Quality has dropped within the organization.

19

Ten Rules for Fast-Track Success

After working for more than a decade helping organizations improve their effectiveness with Fast-Track TQM, I could list several hundred factors that contribute to TQM success. But of the trivial many contributors, which are the vital few? What do you really need? What must you have to be truly successful with Fast-Track TQM? Hundreds of managers have asked me the same question.

My response is the ten Fast-Track Rules for Success. Use them, apply them thoroughly, and I guarantee you'll develop Quality and advance your organization to more success. The ten rules are:

1. CEO commitment.
2. Clarity on the reason for TQM.
3. Senior management commitment.
4. Team effort.
5. Effective leadership.
6. Avoiding the common hangup on SPC.
7. Easing employees into TQM.
8. Compressed training schedule.
9. TQM visibility.
10. Change in culture through accountability.

Rule 1: CEO Commitment

Much has been written and said about the importance of commitment to TQM on the part of an organization's CEO or president. In our culture, when people say they are committed, we often accept their words at face value and assume their commitment means active involvement. Technically the term "commitment" refers to what people do, not what they say. When a CEO or president makes the statement, "I am committed to TQM," it only describes *intent*. The proof of commitment is reflected in day-to-day actions. Show me an organization in which TQM has failed, and I'll show you an organization in which the president's or CEO's commitment to advancing TQM in the organization is questionable. The CEOs or presidents must be committed beyond words. They must demonstrate their commitment day in and day out by being not just observers, but active players on the Quality-advancement team.

So what does the truly committed CEO or president look like? How does he or she demonstrate through action a commitment to TQM? Here are some of the observable characteristics and actions:

- **Use of Quality language:** The first and foremost CEOs and presidents can demonstrate TQM commitment in how they talk about Quality and performance in their day-to-day language. They know and recognize the special efforts of employees throughout the organization. Above all, they are positive and seek out success.

- **Action at meetings:** Leaders demonstrate their commitment to Quality advancement by how they handle the topic of Quality advancement in management meetings. Successful TQM leaders place TQM at the top of meeting agendas. They allow adequate time to examine, discuss, and plan specific actions to advance Quality in the organization. They continually ask their staff, "What progress have we made in the last 30 days in advancing our products or service?" "What actions are contributing to the improvement of service to our customer?"

- **Willingness to attend meetings:** Successful Fast-Track TQM leaders get out of their offices and attend Quality meetings with all levels of employees. They visit with employees on the job and talk with them about their progress in building and strengthening Quality. They attend management forum meetings where employees give presentations on Quality progress. And they participate in the celebrations of success with employees to recognize and reinforce the accomplishments.

- **Establish clear expectations:** In addition to being involved in Quality meetings with staff, TQM-driven managers establish clear expectations with their staffs at all levels. Everyone in the organization at every level knows what he or she is expected to do to advance Quality in the company.

- **Allows participatory decision making:** An autocratic CEO who continues to make all the decisions in the traditional hierarchical manner does not understand the value and importance of participatory decision making in TQM. Leaders who are successful with Fast-Track TQM involve more individuals in the decision-making process at all levels of the organization. "Making decisions at the lowest possible level" is a reality for these leaders.

- **Willingly share information:** The old saying is that information is power. It's true. And with Fast-Track TQM, when you share information, you multiply your organization's power. Successful Fast-Track managers encourage and demonstrate open communication. They ensure that the lines of communications between departments and between individuals are opened and broadened. They encourage employees at all levels to ask questions of one another, share information, as well as cooperate in reaching solutions and in allocating resources.

- **Patience:** When organizations embark on a TQM track, their expectations are high and rightly so. But, while TQM can bring organizations terrific outcomes and benefits, realizing those high expectations often takes months or even years. Using the Fast-Track Method yields measurable results within six to nine months, but more far-reaching changes and outcomes require even more time. Successful TQM managers realize that building and advancing Quality is a process that requires long-term commitment and patience.

- **Allocation of resources and training:** Successful TQM CEOs and presidents demonstrate their commitment to the Quality process by making sure managers, supervisors, and employees at all levels have the training and resources they need to advance Quality. This doesn't just mean awareness and skill training in the early stages of TQM development, but ongoing training that enables them to continuously improve Quality within the organization.

Fast-Track Tip 108

The CEO or president must demonstrate commitment to TQM by doing—by actions—not just by words.

Rule 2: Clarity on the Reason for TQM

For TQM success, all managers and employees must clearly understand the "why" of TQM. Why do we need to advance Quality? What good will it do? How well you answer the "why" question relates directly to how successfully your organization will be able to establish and sustain TQM, and ultimately how successful you will be in leading your organization's growth. In some organizations, the rationale for developing TQM is clear—it's a matter of survival. But in other companies, the rationale may not be so obvious. Helping managers and employees understand the critical "why" can help build employee commitment not just to TQM but also to the organization.

In today's global marketplace, no company's growth or stability is guaranteed. Employees feel the instability and may be less inclined to "give their all" in such an uncertain world. By helping managers and employees truly understand the "why" for building and advancing TQM in your company through knowing and understanding TQM principles, you help them see that the company is committed to its success and to their success through Quality advancement.

Fast-Track Tip 109

Don't expect employees, supervisors, and managers to commit to TQM until they fully understand the need for Quality improvement—the "why"—and its benefits to them, to their work group, and to the organization.

Rule 3: Build Senior Management Commitment

As important as it is to have the commitment of the president or CEO, it is just as important for senior managers to become an extension of that commitment at the top. In the eyes of employees, any member of senior management represents all of senior management. So it's vital that all senior managers demonstrate their commitment and support to Quality advancement in their day-to-day actions. TQM success becomes questionable without the complete support of every member of the senior staff. All senior staff members must become active supporters and champions of TQM.

To build such a cohesive senior management team, sometimes the president or CEO is forced to replace one or more senior staff members. This may sound harsh, but it may become necessary. *All senior management members must be fully committed to the Quality process.* Trying to implement and build TQM without all managers fully on board is like a football team playing without key positions filled. The opposition will readily see the holes in the field created by the missing players. Opportunities will be missed. Plays will fail. And ultimately, the team without all the players will lose the game. So it is with a company who tries to build TQM without all of its first-string management players actively engaged.

Once, at a senior staff meeting, the company president said, "TQM is the single most important course we will lead our company on in the next decade." He went on to tell his staff of his expectations and how they would be directly involved in the process. He ended his comments by saying, "If you are not a strong supporter, you are clearly against our efforts." While this president didn't threaten his staff, he was clear in his intentions and in his expectations.

A key aspect of building management support and commitment is heightening senior staff awareness of TQM principles and benefits. As their knowledge and understanding about TQM grows, so does their commitment and their understanding of how TQM fits into their job and how it can benefit the company and them as individuals. Often I encourage managers to talk with their counterparts in other successful TQM organizations, even in companies in other industries. Sharing experiences about TQM can broaden their understanding and develop their TQM commitment.

Fast-Track Tip 110

All members of senior management must be on board the Quality train and fully "packed" for the trip before it pulls out of the station, or the trip won't be a success.

Rule 4: Build a TQM Team

Successful TQM requires a team effort. Every member of the organization must be an active TQM team member. Teams just don't happen; they're built. Every TQM training session can help advance the TQM team. The trainer or facilitator must have a clear understanding not only of TQM principles, but also about how to create and build unity of purpose with training participants. Some companies spend thousands or even millions of dollars building teams simply so that employees can have a sense of unity in working together.

A better, more cost-effective way of utilizing and building unity is to work together to support and enhance Quality. Strong teams need a common purpose, a goal to unify them. There's no greater goal than enhancing and building the Quality of the company's products and services. Quality itself becomes the vehicle to build the team. Over the long term, the Quality focus harnesses and strengthens the power of employees at all levels.

At a dinner with the president of a client firm, we were reviewing the company's Quality-advancing progress over the past few months and planning strategies for the future. He said:

> I had no idea that our becoming involved in TQM and developing TQM skills with managers and employees would have such an influence on building such a strong management team. Nearly every one of our training sessions has reinforced and built our unity and strengthened our ability to work together successfully.

Earlier I'd talked about teambuilding as an important outcome of Fast-Tracking but now he was finally seeing that the Fast-Track Method was changing his company's culture in ways that would support Quality advancement for years to come.

Fast-Track Tip 111

Let Quality advancement be the focus that unifies your employees and managers into an effective team.

Rule 5: Develop Effective Leadership

If an organization's culture is the way a company does business, then TQM requires specific changes in culture—in how business is conducted on a day-to-day basis and in how managers lead. Autocratic styles of leadership are ineffective in building TQM in an organization. Managers have to understand that heavy-handed "tell" messages don't work in building TQM success. Autocratic management, so popular in American business, almost guarantees TQM failure. In an effective TQM organization, *everyone* participates and provides input in how to advance and build Quality in the company's products and services. Unfortunately, most TQM training offered today focuses on developing TQM skills, but does little to develop effective leadership to support TQM and ensure its lasting success.

If you are going to develop Quality in your organization, one of the first things you must do is develop Quality leadership. Only then can you advance Quality. Whether you use the Fast-Track Method or some other, be sure the training you receive provides for the development of supervisors, midlevel managers, senior managers, and the CEO or president of the organization. Developing Quality leadership is so critical to TQM success that Chap. 7 is devoted to it.

Fast-Track Tip 112

Autocratic styles of management have no place in the TQM organization.

Rule 6: Don't Get Hung Up on SPC

Reams have been written about using Statistical Process Controls (SPCs) to advance and build Quality into organizations. Of course, SPC is important in advancing Quality, but it is only one of the many tools available.

For example, the managers of a fast food firm were discussing advancing Quality in their products and service. The managers had read a book on statistical process controls, and they were convinced this was the panacea. Over the following four months, I tried in vain to get them to put SPC in its proper perspective, but they would have none of it. They were sure that SPC was the ultimate weapon in winning the war to advance Quality. Despite extensive training and expense, their Quality outcomes were mediocre at best. Unfortunately, the real damage was the negative attitudes many of the managers developed about TQM. For some of them, it will take years to erase their less-than-successful experience with building Quality.

While statistical process controls are certainly important in building Quality, change in any organization must be implemented only after participants are ready to advance to the next level of understanding and skill development. So it is with the SPC tools. SPCs are included in the Fast-Tract TQM paradigm, but only after other steps have been taken to ensure that managers and employees have the insight and understanding to use them effectively. In their zeal to advance Quality, many organizations quickly jump into SPC as the tool to develop and train their employees. SPC should be taught and applied only after much groundwork has been done and employees thoroughly understand its need and applications.

Fast-Track Tip 113

Don't be fooled by statistical process controls (SPCs). They're only one of the many tools in your Quality-advancement kit.

Rule 7: Avoid Overwhelming Employees

You have to crawl before you walk, walk before you run. So it is with developing employee support for TQM. The fastest way to "turn off" employees and create fear and resistance is to rush too quickly into the principles of charting, data collection, and statistical process controls. First, employees need to clearly understand the "why" of TQM and its benefits to the organization, the work group, and to them personally. They need to understand TQM principles and how they can ensure long term success in the organization. Once they have a clear understanding of what TQM really is and how they can use it to meet or exceed their customers expectations, they begin to relate TQM to their own experience. Instead of just abstract principles and concepts, TQM becomes real to them. They start asking, "What can I do to have TQM?" "What do I have to do to get the TQM benefits?" At this point, employees are ready learners. They're willing to improve their own performance by applying TQM principles. This kind of readiness is developed through four- to eight-hour training sessions with every employee in the organization. It's even more effective if the awareness training sessions can be followed up with discussions within the work groups. These sessions should be facilitated by managers or supervisors who have received both TQM skills and leadership training.

Fast-Track Tip 114

Don't rush into Quality-enhancing actions. Employees must be fully trained in TQM awareness, principles, and skills before they begin taking action to improve Quality.

Rule 8: Compress the Training Schedule

Many organizations are cautious in advancing TQM. While the CEO/ president and senior management may say they are committed to the process, their actions demonstrate a lack of commitment. For instance, some organizations spread out the TQM awareness training, TQM principles training, and leadership development training over a 12- to 18- month period. The outcome is diluted and weak. It's much like giving an intense speech in five-minute increments over a week's time. No one can remember what you said the day before and the speech lacks impact.

Stretching out the training effort is a lot like spreading out an ocean wave over several miles. What hits the beach is little more than a ripple. If you take the same wave energy and compress it into a shorter expanse as it strikes the beach, the impact is dramatic.

The same is true with developing and training employees and managers for TQM. To create intensity and excitement, everyone in the organization should receive TQM training as soon as possible. As soon as managers and employees complete awareness training and have caught the vision of what TQM can do for them and the organization, they should quickly advance to skill training in problem identification and problem solving. You can't let the fire go out! Once your employees and managers are excited and "turned on" by TQM awareness and principles, they need to be given the skills—the tools—to make TQM a reality. If you wait and stretch out the training, the window of opportunity will be lost. It's a little like a surfer catching the crest of the wave. Wait even a few seconds too long, and the energy from the wave's crest is lost and the exhilarating ride to the shore doesn't happen.

At the same time employees are receiving TQM awareness and skill training, the leadership capabilities of managers and supervisors must be developed to support TQM. Now that employees are "fired up" about TQM, don't let undeveloped managers and supervisors pour water on that flame with poor leadership. In developing employees, supervisors, and managers to advance and build TQM, power comes from intensity. The more intense the training effort, the greater the impact.

Some may say, "You're moving too quickly." If that's your concern, try establishing a "pilot" group to examine the training. But once the pilot group has been trained and fine-tuned, it's time to allow the training effort to become intense and involve everyone. By compressing the training sessions into five or six weeks and having everyone involved, you create energy, excitement, and support for advancing Quality.

Fast-Track Tip 115

Maintain training intensity by keeping the training time frame to six weeks or so. Stretching out the training period lessens its impact.

Rule 9: Make TQM Visible

Employees, supervisors, and managers come to value what they believe is important. If they are led to believe that TQM has value and importance in the organization, they will become active TQM players and supporters. The longer and more intensely the message of TQM importance is given to them, the more intrinsic or internalized the message becomes within each person.

Often, organizations that are successful in implementing TQM become showplaces for other companies interested in advancing Quality. Managers and employees should participate in tours and visitor orientations, showing off their organization's commitment to TQM, and at the same time building their own pride in and their commitment to the company and Quality enhancement.

Fast-Track Tip 116

Underscore the importance of TQM by making Quality advancement the premier example in your industry. Reinforce for employees that your organization is different and, above all, special.

Rule 10: Change Culture
Through Accountability

With few exceptions, employees, supervisors, and managers perform and achieve in the areas for which they are held accountable. When asked whether they like being held accountable for their actions, thousands of managers and employees, without exception, have said that they do. People want to have responsibilities and to be held accountable for them. They want feedback about how they're doing and information that tells them what they're doing makes a difference.

An important aspect of establishing accountability are face-to-face meetings with managers and employees to discuss their progress and success, and, when needed, to make course corrections. These quarterly or semiannual meetings, held to share and confirm success, almost invariably lead to Quality improvements. As employees and managers are given the freedom to develop and use their skills and talents, it's amazing to see their enthusiasm and interest rise as they see their actions making a difference.

Fast Track at a Glance

✔ Follow the 10 Fast-Track Rules for Success to ensure that you advance and build Quality in your organization and reap all of the benefits available through TQM.

✔ CEOs and presidents must demonstrate their commitment to advancing Quality through actions such as appropriate language, giving Quality importance at meetings, attending employee Quality meetings, establishing clear staff expectations, supporting participative decision making, and encouraging the sharing of information and ideas.

✔ Employees, supervisors, and managers must be clear about the reason to pursue Quality advancement and the benefits it can bring.

✔ Senior managers must become an extension of the president's or CEO's commitment to Quality.

✔ All senior managers must commit to TQM for it to work.

✔ Some senior staff may have to be replaced if they cannot climb on board the Quality train.

✔ In a TQM organization, Quality becomes the focus that builds teams.

✔ Autocratic styles of management are incompatible with successful TQM because TQM requires participation from all employees at all levels.

✔ Many TQM training courses fail to effectively train managers to lead for Quality.

✔ Statistical process controls (SPC) are only tools. They are not the total answer for developing Quality. Too much emphasis on SPC can inhibit TQM success.

✔ Take time to train employees at all levels in TQM awareness, principles, benefits, and skills. All employees should have four to eight hours of training in TQM.

✔ Avoid stretching out training over several months. Instead, try to compress training into a five- to six-week period to retain its impact.

✔ Keep the importance of TQM in employees' minds by making it visible through company communications, in meetings, and through active participation of management.

✔ Make managers, supervisors, and employees accountable for Quality advancement in their areas and then give them the feedback to let them know how they are progressing.

✔ Plan quarterly or semiannual meetings to discuss Quality-advancement progress.

20

The Future of TQM

Now that you know how to implement and develop TQM in your organization, it's important to look at the Quality initiative in the context of current and future economic conditions. What's the next step for TQM? As the 1990s roll on, it's easy to see how the excesses of the rapid-growth 1980s are coming back to haunt American businesses. Large corporations such as TRW, IBM, and General Motors, among others, are drastically slashing staffs in an effort to pare down. All of this restructuring is an attempt to send the message to consumers that American businesses are tightening belts, becoming leaner, meaner, more competitive, and more profitable.

Of course, the realities of all this belt tightening have yet to be played out. American corporations may or may not become more competitive and more profitable. Not since the Great Depression of the 1930s has America experienced a recession as deep and as broad as the early 1990s. Even during the 1982-83 recession in which nearly 11 million people found themselves unemployed, America was still a powerhouse in international trade. Banks were stable and willing to lend money when the recession ended. Corporate America borrowed that money and moved forward.

The early 1990s find 7 million people unemployed and the world a drastically different place. Our financial institutions are feeling the pinch and are not as eager to lend the dollars thtat corporate America needs to move forward. Small and midsized American companies are faced with both domestic and international competition. While focusing on the negative side of business growth in American and the world can be depressing, it often takes difficult times to stimulate change. Now is the time that small and midsized companies must look within themselves to create a vision for growth in the future.

When an organization determines to develop Quality in its products and services, it creates a vision to be the best, to be the leading competitor, to set the standard far and above the competition. For a company to be successful in today's economy, that vision must be global and must include rapid, sweeping commitment to Total Quality Management.

Change usually involves some pain. Some business leaders might resist the change to Total Quality Management, saying it is too painful, too revolutionary, too rapid. But as Rosebeth Moscanter, editor of Harvard Business Review, points out, change looks revolutionary only in retrospect. When we talk about changing organizations so that they meet and exceed customer expectations by continuously improving everything they do all the time, we're talking about a road map of positive change for the future of American business.

An associate of mine is John Hayes, Ph.D., whose experience and insights can be valuable to small and midsized companies looking for ways to improve Quality and become global competitors. John has a scientific background in oceanography. When he was the director of Oceanography for the U.S. Department of Commerce, John developed a Quality focus for his organization. This was long before the term "TQM" was commonplace and before management magazines were full of articles on improving Quality. Because of his success in leading the Department of Commerce to a vision of Quality, John was selected by the then Secretary of Commerce, William Varrity, to become the first executive director of the Malcom Baldridge National Quality Award Program. The program was designed to reward corporations who achieve world class Quality. John later became the executive director of "Export Now," a presidential initiative to form, educate, and stimulate small and midsized corporations to seize the many opportunities in the global marketplace. Drawing on his unique background and perspective of world markets, John says the future of American business growth lies with small and midsized companies and that, to be truly competitive worldwide, these companies must become Total Quality Management organizations.

Most economists agree that companies not involved in global trade by the year 2000 will be out of business. It will be the small to midsized companies who are flexible, have low overhead, and are eagerly looking for new markets who will be the world traders of tomorrow. But to date, only a small number of U.S. companies are selling worldwide. Through 1987, 70 percent of all U.S. exports were sold by only 2000 American companies. The remaining 40,000-50,000 companies exported only infrequently.

Why don't more small and midsized corporations compete in the global marketplace? The answers are many and most of them are based on fear—fear of the unknown, fear of language barriers, fears about the financial system, the trade system, the custom system. Of course, these are all simply excuses. They are many of the same excuses brought up when the Total Quality Management process is talked about as a way for small to midsized companies not only to survive, but to successfully compete with foreign competition in a global market.

Five Steps to Global Quality Management

So how do we move forward into the next century and help small to midsized companies be successful? How do we help them build Quality-management processes that will make them competitive world business leaders? John Hayes and I both believe that the following five-step approach is clearly the answer.

Step 1: Total Quality Management Is Required.   Once organizations recognize they need to have Quality management with a customer focus, Fast-Track TQM becomes the obvious methodology to advance their organization. The Fast-Track Method to TQM is a proven, efficient, and cost-effective way for companies to develop and implement TQM.

Step 2: Partnering with the Customer.   In TQM, we often talk about exceeding customer expectations and going to any length to satisfy customers. Ultimately a partnership is needed with customers. The partnering process goes beyond the traditional method of trying to sell the customer what he or she needs. It is a very deliberate method of sitting down with a customer and working out an internal vision of assisting the customer to become successful in his or her business. Each becomes a business partner in the other's success.

A good example of customer partnering can be found in the telecommunications industry. It doesn't do any good for a telecommunications company to offer discount rates for international calls to small and midsized companies if those companies don't have customers in foreign countries. Through partnering, the telecommunications company offers new, innovative, and cost-effective ways for companies to penetrate foreign markets. The telecommunications company, in turn, gains new customers for its international long distance services.

It takes trust and understanding for companies to partner one another. Once that trust and understanding have been developed, each company can help the other grow and expand. Partnering becomes a win-win situation for everyone.

Step 3: Refine the Core Competence.   Part of the reason for the prolonged recession in America today is that many corporate executives fear experimentation. No one wants to take risks, even calculated ones in their "core competence"—that is, what they do well. Authors Gary Hamil and C. K. Proholid wrote in recent articles in Harvard Business Review about the importance of a company's core competence. They cited Sony Corporation as an example. The Japanese have conquered the miniaturization of electronics products. It is one of their core competencies. Sony has taken that core ability and put it into its products to meet customers' needs.

Just as a corporation spends time and effort with its senior managers defining their vision for Quality, they also need to specifically determine the company's two or three core competencies, those things the company does very well. Once those core competencies are well defined, it's easy to focus Quality improvements around them. It becomes a matter of refining and improving what the company already does well—making a good thing even better.

Step 4: Going Global.   This step really repeats steps 2 and 3, only on a global scale. In step 2, we partnered the customer. When your company goes global, customers speak different languages and come from different cultural perspectives. To be successful, you have to adapt to those differences.

John Hayes once described the difference between Asian and American cultures this way: When the Vietnam Memorial in Washington, D.C., was constructed many Americans found it difficult to locate the names of their lost loved ones on it. They expected to find the name of the first dead listed on the upper top left proceeding to the right, much like reading a book. But the memorial was designed by an Asian who listed the names of the first killed in the middle and proceeded outward in both directions. It replicated the Asian concept of connecting a line to form a circle, the circle or team of people being stronger than the individual. This is a very different concept from the American concept of individualism.

Sondra Snowdon is an author, lecturer, and consultant to Fortune 100 companies and a leading authority on cultural differences. She says the success comes in conducting business as comfortably around the world as you do at home. This level of comfort and competence requires a complete understanding of the cultural diversity of the countries with which your company does business. Just as you'd never think of attending a business meeting without wearing proper business attire, you don't want to go into a foreign country unprepared and unskilled in the way business is conducted. Become a world student. Learn about your customers' customs, language, and ways of doing business.

Once you understand and are comfortable with the cultural diversity of your global markets, you must redefine your core competencies so that they translate across cultural boundaries. You now have new customers with new and very different needs and expectations. You must rise a step higher to meet those needs and expectations. You must continually seek out and know those needs/expectations and define and redefine your company's core competencies to meet them.

Step 5: Never Stop.   Once Fast-Track TQM processes are begun in a company, there must be no turning back. You must continually move forward in satisfying customer needs and expectations. Your success and your profitability depend on it.

Likewise, once your company goes global, there is no turning back. TQM requires that all employees be involved continuously in improving every step of the way, ever focused on customer needs and expectations. In the global marketplace, all of these TQM requirements must be in place and continually applied. It is only when your company is constantly improving through Fast-Track TQM that you can be assured of remaining globally competitive.

Using these five steps, TQM, particularly if it is developed and implemented using the Fast-Track Method, can adapt your company's culture so that it is prepared to go global. It can offer your organization a vehicle to move forward and be successful in the world marketplace.

The global market is changing so rapidly we don't have time to wait for the handful of world class companies like Motorola, IBM, and Federal Express to teach us how to run Quality organizations and how to be successful on a global scale. We have to take the initiative to teach ourselves to be successful, Quality-driven organizations. The success of our individual companies depends on it, and the success of our country's economy depends on it.

21

Seven Key Actions to Fast Tracking TQM

Key Action 1: Prepare a Master Plan

You're a manager considering applying TQM principles in your organization. Here's my challenge to you: Are you willing to devote between 12 hours and 16 hours to working with your senior management staff to plan a process—if I can guarantee that the time invested will advance your organization and ensure your success with TQM? If you're like most managers, you are willing to make that investment. You know a good deal when you see one. And this good deal is what makes Fast Tracking so extraordinary.

First, let's be clear about what we mean by "senior management." It includes the president or CEO and the managers who immediately report to him or her, including the vice presidents of marketing, operations, finance, human resources, and legal counsel. Also included are the staff who immediately report to the vice presidents. The group could be between 15 and 30 senior managers.

Too often, organizations get ahead of themselves in the TQM process and sabotage their own success by failing to lay the necessary groundwork on which to build TQM. They charge forward with skills training and development before knowing how people will work together in applying those skills. Let me make a distinction here between content and processes.

Content includes the skills and training necessary to implement TQM. It's the "what" of Quality advancement.

Processes are the "how," the way managers will work together in a unified and cooperative way to lead the organization to TQM success.

For TQM success, you must have both the "how" and the "what" in place. And it's up to senior managers to determine the how and to make it happen.

At a training session, when I was talking about the "magic" of Fast Tracking, a manager challenged me. "There are no magical secrets in building a TQM organization," he said. Not true. While there may be no profound, earth-shattering secrets that will make your company an instant success, there are seven key actions that, when linked together, can assure dramatic success in building a TQM organization. These actions will develop a committed and unified senior staff. You may be familiar with some of them. They are not necessarily new. Their real power is unleashed by putting them together in a structured way. These actions will enable your senior management to build and create a direction and method to advance your organization to phenomenal TQM success.

Fast-Track Tip 117

Invest 12 to 16 hours in planning Fast Tracking for guaranteed TQM success.

Key Action 2: Build Win-Win Requirements

It's one thing to talk about Quality enhancement, but change requires action. TQM requires managers and employees to change their behaviors, how they perform on the job. Establishing a code of behavior will create a standard, a guideline for everyone in the organization. As with the other steps in the Fast-Track Master Planning Process, establishing a code of behavior will help senior managers clarify and understand how TQM principles will be applied in the organization. Once this code of behavior has been clearly stated, senior managers will share it with mid-level managers, who in turn will bring it to all employees. Ultimately, the "what" is defined as how managers and employees will work together in a win-win relationship. Everyone must come out a winner with no one feeling a loser or left out.

Fast-Track Tip 118

Fast-Track TQM success requires win-win management. Everyone must act to support themselves and others in advancing Quality.

Key Action 3: Set Relationship Agreements on How to Work Together as a Team

The process of setting up working agreements is much like that of setting the win-win requirements. In this case, you ask the group, "As you work together as the senior management, how do you want to work together to advance Quality in our organization?" This may sound basic, but it builds a foundation for effective working relationships. One manager in a training session complained, "This is like a bunch of Boy Scouts sitting around deciding how they'll conduct their weekly meetings." Even though we're adults who have years of experience and training, we still need to have a common understanding of how we'll work together. It's basic. It's fundamental. And it's as important and absolutely necessary as beams on which a beautiful house or sturdy bridge are built.

There may be nothing unique or startling in a list of agreements, but it's the *process* that's important. It not only establishes a common understanding about how the management group will work together, it also strengthens their relationships with one another. There's tremendous power in having people question and challenge one another about how they work together. It gives them permission to disagree and question one another. They discover that they can hold differing views and that those differences don't block or hinder their ability to work cooperatively together. They find the questioning process actually leads to higher-quality ideas, solutions, plans, and decisions.

The process also teaches valuable lessons in listening to and expressing ideas. It's amazing to see how much more cooperative managers become when they realize that others are actually listening. As the managers begin to realize that their performance and their effectiveness are going to be monitored by their colleagues as defined in the working agreements, their interest in being effective leaders is heightened.

As in the win-win process, after the managers have established their working agreements (preferably writing them out on wall charts for all to see), they should be asked, "Are you willing to apply and operate under the agreements that you've established?"

At that point have them sign the wall charts as a symbol of their commitment. At first, the chart signing may seem frivolous, a waste of time. However, it's amazing how effective it can be. Signing the chart is much like signing a contract. In effect, they are contracting with one another to behave and work together in particular ways. In the win-win process, they are saying they will act to ensure that individuals in the organization and the organization itself win. In the case of working-together agreements, they are contracting with the rest of the group that they will be the kind of manager the group has defined.

Some may still be skeptical about this process. Of those, all I ask is that you try it for yourself. It has worked with hundreds of groups of senior managers. It has built unity and created a bond within the management teams that has enabled them to lead cooperatively and effectively to build Quality within their organizations.

Key Action 4:
Establish/Confirm a Clear
Mission or Vision Statement
Regarding Quality

Most organization's have mission statements that describe the direction of the organization and establishes a clear priority. In the case of establishing and building a Quality-driven organization, it's imperative that the mission statement address Quality and its importance either to the customer or to the organization. If your organization's mission statement doesn't mention Quality, it's time to sit down with your senior managers and rewrite it. I realize that most mission statements end up in a notebook or on wall plaques in offices. Their practical usefulness in day-to-day operations is easily lost. But the power and importance of rewriting the mission statement with your senior staff aren't in the statement itself, but, again, in the *process*.

Instead of "mission statement," try calling this document a Vision Statement because it's the management's vision of where the company is going. If a company values Quality, then Quality must become a part of that Vision Statement.

Some CEOs or presidents prefer to prepare the vision statement by themselves. This is a mistake. You've lost the greatest benefit of the process—working together with your senior staff. The real value comes in senior management taking the time to reevaluate the organization's direction and priorities. It's a time when the managers can learn more about the president's or CEO's vision for the company and share their own ideas for the company's future.

It may sound ludicrous to you to have 30 or 40 top managers sitting around trying to write a statement that will probably be only one or two sentences. But again I say, "Try it." During the process, make sure the managers practice the win-win principles and working-together agreements they've already established.

Fast-Track Tip 119

Your Vision/Mission Statement must reflect the importance of Quality in your Organization.

Key Action 5: Establish Quality Values

This is another situation in which the process becomes more important than the resulting document. Establishing Quality values is a process of clarifying and confirming those values, those things the managers see as important to the organization and to the Quality of its products and services. The process creates a common understanding among the managers of the critical values.

Key Action 6: Set Quality Standards

Setting standards has a built-in catch. As soon as you set a standard and everyone achieves it, the standard automatically becomes mediocre. If everyone can achieve it, it can't be much of a standard. Given this pitfall, an important part of your 12 to 16 hours of meeting with senior managers should be spent in setting "ultimate" standards for the company.

What are "ultimate standards"? They are not goals or aspirations. Goals are something to which you aspire. Standards describe guideposts in measuring your performance. They clearly identify progress in moving an organization forward. In some cases, items identified as standards may be currently in place. For others, it will require considerable effort and time to achieve the standard. Ultimate standards describe what the organization will look like when your company is the best in its industry.

Like the other processes described in this book, setting ultimate standards requires a group effort with all senior staff participating. Each senior staff member must have the opportunity to provide input and apply each of the previously established principles to each standard as it is discussed. Does each standard, for example, fit with the organizational values the group has established? Does it mesh with the organization's vision statement? Do any of them violate the working agreements?

Typically, management groups come up with five to seven ultimate standards. The standards then become a benchmark against which to measure decisions and actions. Every action and every decision made in the organization by each manager should somehow lead to and support achieving the ultimate standards.

As an example, let's look at defect-free, a common ultimate standard for TQM organizations. Defect-free means that every customer is satisfied, every time. At first, many managers resist this standard. Industry managers say, "No way. This is blue sky thinking. My industry is too unique to achieve a standard of defect-free." Those in the service industries say, "No way. It's impossible to be defect-free when you're working with people."

Defect-free might be a monumental task, but it is not impossible. Whether in a manufacturing or service industry, the key is to strive for customer satisfaction in delivering both products and services.

Other examples of ultimate standards may include:

- Participation by everyone in the organization.
- Continuous Quality improvement.

Fast-Track Tip 120

Ultimate standards define what the organization will look like when it is the best in the industry. They serve as a guidepost for management actions, decisions, and allocation of resources.

Key Action 7: Confirm Accountability for Fast-Track Success

The senior management group should plan to come together every 90 days to review their progress and accomplishments. It's important to keep the wall charts that have been created during the initial 12- to 16-hour session and post them on the walls again. Then distribute 3×5 cards and, beginning with the chart on win-win requirements, ask each manager to identify any item they feel has not been successfully honored or supported in the previous 90 days. Repeat the process on a new card as you work through the same process with each chart—win-win, working-together agreements, the Vision/Mission Statement, Quality values, and ultimate standards.

Don't have them put their names on the cards. Collect the cards and place tick marks next to items on the chart listed on any of the cards. Invite the managers to openly discuss each item. What's working? What's not? Why not? What can you do differently? What support do you need for success?

In addition to reviewing/critiquing the leadership key action charts, each manager should be given the opportunity to report on his or her progress in improving the Quality of products of services in their area of responsibility. What challenges have you encountered? How can others in the group help? Share successes and celebrate the major accomplishments the group has made.

The importance of these follow-up senior management meetings cannot be overemphasized. They keep the TQM process on track by holding managers accountable for their leadership. The meetings perform a maintenance function, making sure each manager is applying the correct leadership to advance Quality in the organization. Later, as managers become more comfortable with their new styles of leadership, these maintenance sessions can be shortened to 30 or 40 minutes and incorporated into regular management meetings.

Fast-Track Tip 121

Conduct regularly scheduled management meetings to review progress in keeping performance agreements, win-win, value standards. This reinforces the importance of Quality and supports progress in advancing Quality.

Fast Track at a Glance

✔ Senior managers must meet to determine the processes, the "how" of implementing TQM.

✔ There are seven key actions to leading for success in Fast-Track TQM: (1) preparing a master plan, (2) building win-win requirements, (3) setting working-together agreements, (4) establishing a Quality-oriented Vision/Mission Statement, (5) establishing Quality values, (6) setting ultimate Quality standards, and (7) monitoring group progress in honoring agreements about how the group will function together.

✔ Successful TQM requires a leadership style that encourages win-win situations in which people collaborate and cooperate.

✔ Senior managers must define how they will work together to advance Quality.

✔ Mission/Vision Statements must reflect Quality as a priority for the organization.

✔ Organizational Quality values define what is important to the management and to the organization as it relates to advancing Quality.

✔ Performance standards are ever changing, ever increasing. Ultimate standards are unchanging. They reflect how the organization will look when it is the best in the industry.

✔ Follow up at senior management meetings in which each manager reports on the Quality-enhancing progress that his or her leadership has brought about. This creates accountability and ensures that the TQM process is sustained and continues to move forward.

PART 4

Fast-Track Success Working

It's one thing to talk about success; it's another to demonstrate it. In this final section of the book, I give you two examples from actual companies who have successfully used the Fast Track to Quality process. This section can give you an idea of what you can expect from the process and how you might adapt it to your own organization.

22

Fast-Track
Success at
Alaska Railroad

The Alaska Railroad Company (ARRC) came into being in 1914 when the United States Congress enacted the Enabling Act of 1914, which empowered the President to fund construction of a rail line from the southern tidewater port of Seward, Alaska, to the interior city of Fairbanks at a cost of about $35 million. By 1923, the line was completed as far north as Nenana. President Warren G. Harding traveled to Alaska in July of that year to drive a gold spike, which signaled the completion of a major part of the Alaska Railroad line.

The railroad remained under federal ownership until January 5, 1985, when it was transferred to the state of Alaska. The state legislature created the Alaska Railroad Corporation Act, which mandated that the state-owned railroad be structured similarly to other private rail lines and be governed by a seven-member board of directors appointed by the governor.

The statute mandates that the railroad function as a public corporation and be exclusively responsible for all of its financial and legal obligations. With its new responsibilities as a commercial enterprise, the corporation was also given the responsibility of fostering and promoting economic growth and development in the state. It wasn't long before ARRC's management realized that meeting its obligations and becoming a profitable enterprise would require some major changes in the way the railroad conducted its business. It was time to invest in Quality advancement.

The Decision-Making Process

Alaska Railroad's president, Bob Hatfield, made it very clear to his senior management staff that the decision to proceed with Fast-Track TQM would be theirs. If Alaska Railroad was going to become TQM-driven, everyone would have to confirm his or her commitment and willingness to participate. Before the big decision, the managers were given a variety of articles and other information about TQM. I gave them a presentation about TQM principles, the implications for management, and the benefits that they and their company could expect with TQM success.

After several weeks of meetings and discussions, the question was put to the group, "Should we proceed with Fast-Track TQM?" The managers weren't asked to vote yes or no, but instead were asked whether they were willing to declare openly to their colleagues their commitment to the process. By expressing their willingness to pursue TQM, they were declaring that not only were they personally committed to the process, but that they were willing to commit their staffs to actively applying the principles of TQM. Their declarations became public statements that they were willing to be TQM coaches, inspiring their employees, and serving as the driving force behind the effort to improve Quality.

Because Alaska Railroad's senior managers had thoroughly investigated Fast-Track TQM, all of them clearly understood their responsibility in the process. They recognized the changes TQM success would demand from the leadership. They knew that the process might mean changes in the company's personnel and even in the organization's structure itself. And they understood that they'd have to be willing to provide each of their employees with training on an ongoing basis to ensure that employees had the skills to implement TQM changes.

After a great deal of candid discussion, the group decided unanimously to proceed full steam ahead with Fast-Track TQM. The group decided to hire the Richard/Rogers Group to provide the necessary training and guidance to direct the TQM process. No time limits were set on the process. Instead, the group decided to pursue their commitment to TQM in an open-ended time frame. They agreed that their decision was one of the most important ones they would make in leading the railroad into the twenty-first century.

Over the next 12 months, we applied the Fast-Track Method for TQM. We defined and implemented a series of events to advance the organization and develop the necessary cultural changes necessary to make TQM principles an intrinsic way of doing business within the company. The following is a chronology of the events that occurred within the first year of Alaska Railroad's Fast-Track TQM experience and the impact each event had on their efforts to become a TQM-driven organization.

Executive Staff Master Planning

The president and his immediate staff participated in a two-and-a-half-day planning session which I facilitated. We met at an off-site location, stayed overnight, and worked together to clarify and confirm how management would work together to apply leadership to advance TQM and to prepare a master plan. This planning session was the culmination of several team-building sessions. Here they did the important work of clarifying their role in TQM, confirming their expectations, and deciding how they would measure their progress.

By the end of the session, the group had established a clear list of performance agreements, statements about how they would work together and apply leadership to advance TQM. They also drafted a set of standards, which they would later share with middle management and supervisors. The standards were left in draft form to enable managers throughout the organization to comment and give input before finalization. The final agreement set a standard that said Alaska Railroad would be a model, an example of what railroading at its best could be in the United States. The senior managers also revised the company's Mission Statement to include the new Quality emphasis. They called their new mission and value statement "All Aboard."

Because the seasonal changes in Alaska are so dramatic, they decided to complete the necessary training for managers and employees before June 1. They established a schedule to ensure that every employee, supervisor, and manager in the company would receive initial training in TQM principles before that date. June 1 became the target date because it is the start of the annual tourist season in Alaska, and the company wanted to be ready to better serve its external customers.

Senior Management Staff Training

The senior managers of Alaska Railroad easily recognized that TQM success is a management issue, not an employee issue. They knew they needed the leadership skills necessary to lead their company to TQM. So they became the first training participants, learning both about TQM principles and Quality leadership. The training group included the president and all department heads, including 16 key managers within the organization. During the training sessions, they focused on developing knowledge and skills about TQM principles and learning the different types of leadership skills they would need to advance Quality.

Perhaps more importantly, the training sessions forged a strong management team. The bond that was created between the members of the senior management team would become the driving force behind the company's TQM efforts for years to come.

Training All Managers and Supervisors

Every supervisor and manager in the company was scheduled to attend five days of TQM and Quality leadership training over a five-week period. Each manager attended one day of training per week. The schedule gave managers the opportunity to apply the new principles and skills they'd learned in classroom training the following week and then return to training for feedback. This allowed managers to test, practice, experiment, and finally internalize the principles they were taught in training sessions.

The managers and supervisors found that many of the principles and skills supporting TQM and Quality leadership ran counter to what they were used to. They found that, in many cases, implementing TQM meant going against previous instructions or expectations defined by the company's culture. The managers soon came to understand that successful TQM would mean more than simply learning a few new skills. It would mean changing the company from the inside out; changing the organizational culture to make Quality improvement and enhancement the focal point.

A total of 115 managers participated in TQM and leadership training. In addition, all of senior management received the training described in the previous sections and attended training sessions with their staffs.

All of the training materials for the company were custom-tailored to the specific and unique needs of Alaska Railroad. The participant training manuals were specially prepared to ensure the examples and situations described in them applied directly to the railroad industry. This customizing enabled the training participants to personally relate to the Fast-Track TQM training and let them see how it could be practically implemented in their company.

Training for All Employees

While the managers and supervisors were attending their five days of training over the five-week period, other employees throughout the organization became curious and even excited about the prospect of

TQM. When the employees learned that they too would receive TQM training, many of them expressed surprise. Veteran employees who had been with the company for 20 or 30 years said they couldn't ever recall a time when every employee in the company had the opportunity to attend training. Employees saw this as a change in managements' attitude toward them. Instead of being viewed as simply workers, employees now believed that management was interested in them as active participants in cooperatively building and strengthening the company. "We are in partnership together to enhance and build quality in serving our customers," became a common phrase around the company.

Having all Alaska Railroad employees attend TQM training was the first clear signal that a major change was truly taking place and that everyone would be involved in the change. All of the company's 452 employees participated in eight hours of training that included the principles of TQM and the role of employees in advancing Quality.

It's important to note that training all employees meant not only involving more than 400 people, but five different labor unions representing five separate trades. At the same time the training was being conducted, the company was involved in labor negotiations for each of the craft contracts. Early on, the company's managers had debated whether the time was right to implement TQM. Perhaps, some said, they should wait until the labor negotiations were completed and contracts established.

But Alaska Railroad's management took a proactive approach. They decided to go forward with TQM, using managers and employees working together to advance Quality as a model of what the future could bring to the company. After the labor negotiations were completed and three-year contracts signed, many of those involved said the TQM process had a positive impact on the labor process. Of course, there isn't any quantitative data to support that Fast-Track TQM did, in fact, help the negotiation process. But it certainly provided a clear message about management's commitment to unity, to working together with employees, and to serving customers.

A sign of this new unity was evidenced by employee participation in the annual company Christmas party. In the past, many employees had viewed the event as the "management's Christmas party" and had refused to attend. However, after working together for eight months learning and sharing about Quality advancement, the two groups came together and celebrated the Christmas holiday as a united group.

Another evidence of the company's unification was their involvement in the United Way campaign. In years past, certain groups within the company had openly rejected the campaign and had refused to participate. After becoming involved in TQM, these same groups became active, sharing participants in the fund-raising campaign.

We completed the first phase of training for managers, supervisors, and employees throughout the organization by the target date of June 1. Managers and supervisors left the training sessions with the clear mandate to work collaboratively with their staffs in applying the TQM skills to enhance and improve the delivery of service and products to their customers. They were also told to be prepared to give a five- to eight-minute presentation sometime in the fall on their Quality-advancement success.

First Management Forum

The summer passed quickly, and in October Alaska Railroad's first management forum was held. All supervisors and managers were given the opportunity to present their successes and accomplishments in advancing Quality to their colleagues and, more importantly, to the company president. The 115 managers were divided into four groups with each group scheduled for one day of presentations. The company president and all of the senior managers attended every day of the presentations. Their presence was a clear message of their commitment to the TQM process.

Initially, many of the managers, particularly entry-level managers, expressed fear and concern about having to give a presentation in front of the company president. But the anxiety soon faded as it became apparent that this wasn't a test, but a celebration of success. Some of the five- to eight-minute presentations were simple and brief. Others were more elaborate. Each manager had to be able to quantify, as much as possible, his or her Quality-advancing efforts and success.

It was gratifying to see how even entry-level managers became caught up in the excitement and vision of TQM at the forum. From their presentations and the discussions that followed, it was apparent that managers at all levels had caught the TQM vision and clearly saw that they could make a difference in serving customers by their active participation in the process. The Forum became the occasion for an active exchange of ideas, with managers and supervisors sharing their insights and ideas through overhead transparencies, graphs, charts, and handouts.

At the conclusion of each presentation, the president led a rousing round of applause to personally thank each manager for his/her efforts. Then they all participated in a celebration luncheon that culminated with a specially prepared sheet cake with a message that expressed thanks and appreciation.

Quality-Improvement Teams (QITs)

An important part of the initial training with supervisors and managers was the introduction of the concept of Quality Improvement Teams

(QITs). Managers at all levels in the organization were given the opportunity to become QIT sponsors. Alaska Railroad president Bob Hatfield, himself, became the sponsor for several QITs, as did members of his senior staff. Over a 10-month period, 45 QITs were formed and made Quality-advancing recommendations. In every instance, at least a portion and, in many cases, all of the QITs' recommendations were implemented.

When each QIT was formed, the group's sponsor clearly described how to identify the problem the QIT was to resolve, what resources were available, and the time frame in which they had to work. Because of the successes of Alaska Railroad's QITs, millions of dollars in performance improvements have been effected. The following are three examples of problems addressed and resolved by QITs.

1. Consider Alaska Railroad's existing traffic flows and current service levels and recommend what train operations should be and their costs. This enables ARRC to design the services that will meet customers' needs, yet remain within our financial capabilities to provide services.
   - Satisfy customer requirements.
   - Achieve 100-percent on-time service.
   - Operate trains efficiently.

2. Develop an efficient and effective process to pay all employees accurately and on time.
   - Reduce redundancy and duplication.
   - Reduce the number of time cards submitted.
   - Ensure that ARRC continues to comply with all related federal/state laws and regulations.
   - Minimize stress associated with processing biweekly payroll.

3. Develop a correspondence and telephonic communication manual.
   - Create a generic correspondence manual that fits the needs and image of the company.
   - Establish correspondence standards to be utilized by all clerical employees (internal and external).
   - Develop training programs to instruct employees how to make correspondence "reader friendly."
   - Develop training courses to instruct employees on telephone manners, techniques, and how to change an angry customer into a satisfied customer.

4. Review the ARRC's vehicle fleet requirements.
   - Reduce operating costs without sacrificing customer satisfaction.
   - Reduce the size of the fleet.
   - Meet both the customers' needs and the requirements of the company.
   - Investigate the feasibility of leasing versus owning.

An important part of the success of Alaska Railroad's QITs has been a company log that records the problems identified for resolution and the team members working on each part of problem. In addition, each employee and QIT manager/sponsor receives a personal thank you letter from the president, Bob Hatfield, commending them for their efforts in advancing Quality at Alaska Railroad.

The "New Disease" at ARRC

An important part of Alaska Railroad's Fast-Track TQM training was the process of enhancing and building employee self-esteem throughout the company. To build confidence and self-esteem, ARRC's managers and supervisors needed to do more than just give compliments or praise employee performance. They learned a powerful step-by-step process to validate employees. Many managers and employees jokingly referred to the empowerment process as a "new disease" at Alaska Railroad. The comment was essentially true in that building employee self-confidence and self-esteem seemed to "infect" every manager and supervisor, who in turn actively passed on the "germs" of empowerment.

The Fast-Track TQM validation process involves both verbal and written commendations by managers and supervisors. Letters of commendation are sent to employees, and copies are placed in their permanent personnel files. ARRC employees eagerly responded to the consistent feedback and validation. Many of them actually framed their letters and hung them on the walls at home or at work.

Employee Suggestion Program

As part of senior management's master plan to advance TQM in the organization, an employee suggestion program was implemented. The intent was to provide all employees in the organization with a quick and easy way to express their ideas, insights, and suggestions on how the company could improve Quality and better serve its customers, both internal and external. To personalize the process and let employees know how important senior management felt employee input was, the company installed a "hotline" in each of the cities served by the company and an 800 number for other locations throughout the state.

The company president, Bob Hatfield, was very clear that he wanted to be an active participant in the employee suggestion program. To that end, the recording on the hotline numbers asked employees to address their comments to "Dear Bob." The president recorded a phone message that said, "Hi, this is Bob Hatfield. You have reached the Alaska Railroad's Employee Hotline for Innovations for Quality. I am glad you care enough about the Railroad to offer your ideas for improving the company. It is important to me that you receive credit for your suggestion, so please leave your name along with your idea after the beep. Thank you very much." This personalized message makes sure the employees know they are speaking directly to the president.

The suggestions are transcribed daily and given to the president for his review. Within 48 hours, employees receive a personal response to their suggestion signed by the president acknowledging their contribution and letting them know where the suggestion has been forwarded for consideration.

In addition to the phone line, Alaska Railroad prepared a series of posters inviting employees to share their ideas (Fig. 22.1). The posters are changed quarterly to keep them fresh and interesting. A company newsletter reinforces the employee suggestion message in every issue. They've adopted the acronym "IQ" for "Innovations for Quality" as their slogan. Employees who offer suggestions via the hotline are given a button and a sticker to put on their hard hats that says, "Ask me about my IQ." Employees wear the buttons and the stickers with pride. Many employees have received multiple stickers, which they display proudly.

The hotline receives 50 to 60 suggestions per month. That's about 10 percent of the workforce offering suggestions at any one time. Since the hotline was established, the company has not received one profane or inappropriate call. Almost every suggestion offered is clearly thought out, and all are sincere. This is still another indication that employees take the Alaska Railroad TQM program seriously and willingly cooperate in its success.

Interestingly, Alaska Railroad's successful employee suggestion program offers no financial rewards to employees for their input. The button, sticker, and letter of thanks from the president give them the recognition and reward they need.

In some cases, employees receive an additional award of recognition for their ideas. The first one was received by an employee from the Passenger Service division who suggested a way to improve passenger baggage handling. The Alaska state governor, Walter J. Hickel, presented the award and personally thanked the employee for making a difference in the railroad and its success.

Figure 22.1. 617 Heads Are Better Than One

Customer Reaction to Alaska Railroad's Efforts

The proof of any TQM effort's success is in customer response, and Alaska Railroad has had plenty of positive feedback. Throughout the months that Fast-Track TQM has been in place at ARRC, both ticket-buying customers and employee customers have expressed their delight in the changes. In December of 1991, ARRC held its first customer appreciation reception in Fairbanks. More than 200 customers, managers, and employees attended the gala event to thank customers for using the rail line and for being a part of building a better and stronger Alaska. The catered affair was held in one of the company's depots, which gave many of the service contract customers an opportunity to see some of the facilities. In addition to managers and employees, members of the governing board of Alaska Railroad attended to show their appreciation to the customers.

More than half of Alaska Railroad's customers have made positive comments about the improvement in the services provided by the railroad. They've commented on the courtesy and help they've received from ARRC employees. Others have said they were pleasantly surprised to receive phone calls from the company inquiring about the service they received and their level of satisfaction. Customers have said things like, "I've noticed a change in the railroad's services. I don't know what's causing it, but whatever it is, they should keep doing it!"

Following the reception, the chairman of the Alaska Railroad Board, Loren Lounsbury, made this comment:

> Customers have commented to me about how impressed they are with the change in attitude of our employees—everyone from the top to the bottom of the company. Many have said that Railroad employees have been making unsolicited calls to customers to satisfy their requirements in anticipation of freight movement rather than reacting after the customer contacts the Railroad. Another positive by-product since the implementation of the Quality process at the Railroad has been stronger bond between labor and management.

The Future of TQM at ARRC

Members of senior management at Alaska Railroad say that Fast-Track TQM has become a new way of doing business at the company. They've incorporated the principles and skills they've learned into a new management style. They intend to continue and expand their highly successful employee suggestion program. Employees will continue to receive personal recognition for their contributions. Plans are underway to establish an annual President's Circle, a special recognition for employees who provide multiple suggestions and for those who make significant contributions to improve Quality.

The planning stage of phase two for the manager and supervisory training is fully underway. Employees throughout the organization will receive an additional full day of TQM training. ARRC managers have said that continual skill training for managers, supervisors, and employees will become part of the way the company does business.

New employees receive a special orientation about Quality and how they can support and participate in ARRC's new TQM family. As the company becomes even more proficient in servicing its internal customers and improving Quality, the company anticipates even better service for its external customers, and eventually will include external customers in its Quality-enhancement activities through customer input.

The original design of ARRC's TQM process had as one of its goals the ability to ensure that the railroad could consistently provide Quality service to its customers before asking customers to become directly involved in the Quality-advancing process. The customer appreciation reception in Fairbanks became the launch point for involving customers directly. It gave customers an opportunity to understand, for the first time, the efforts the company was making to improve the Quality of its service.

Another way the company lets the public know about the changes at ARRC is through a series of ads in local newspapers. These quarter-page ads feature railroad employees, dubbed "track stars," and tell about their efforts and achievements to build a better railroad in Alaska. The company plans to feature employee track stars on a monthly basis in three cities along the railroad's service route.

Another change the company is planning is a complete revision of the employee evaluation system at the manager/supervisor level. The previous evaluation process incorporated many traditional benchmarks for job performance, knowledge, and skill. The new system will incorporate the advancement of Quality in the organization. Management performance will be evaluated in how well managers and supervisors are able to advance Quality and meet and exceed the expectations of their customers. Many management studies have criticized both manager and employee evaluation systems with good reason. Too many evaluation systems destroy management/employee unity and tear down rather than build up employee confidence and self-esteem. The new evaluation system being planned at ARRC will reinforce and enhance the Quality process, and encourage cooperation rather than competition between managers and employees.

Alaska Railroad president Bob Hatfield best sums up the company's experience with Fast-Track TQM:

> The success of TQM for us has been nothing short of astonishing. In 10 months, we've been able to demonstrate changes in our company culture, improvements in our services to our customers, and a stronger, more unified labor force. Beyond a question, Fast-Track TQM is building a stronger and more cooperative railroad serving Alaska.

23
Fast-Track Success at Western Growers Association

Western Growers Association (WGA), an agricultural trade association, has adopted a new way of doing business. Their new focus is on Quality utilizing the Fast-Track TQM process.

Western Growers Association is a regional trade group serving growers, packers, and shippers of fresh fruits, vegetables, and nuts in Arizona and California. The 2700-member association was founded in 1916 in California's Imperial Valley. Since its early days, its staff has grown from a handful of people occupying a single office to more than 270 employees located in 14 field offices in both states. Western Grower's annual income and assets are estimated at $100 million, including a self-funded, self-administered nonprofit accident and health benefits trust, a retirement and pension trust, a profitable worker's compensation company, a monthly business publication, the association services relating to the agricultural industry, and a legal corporation.

An elected board of directors, consisting of 42 growers who represent the farming regions of Arizona and California, sets policy for the association and directs its activities. WGA staff members meet formally with board members on a quarterly basis.

Fast Track Comes to WGA

The Fast-Track TQM process was first introduced to Western Growers vice presidents in January 1991 at their yearly planning retreat. I outlined the concept of Fast-Track TQM, its principles, benefits, and responsibilities for them.

A group of 29 managers were selected to participate in an intensive 40 hours of TQM training to be conducted over a five- week period beginning in June of 1991. The training sessions were held off site, and management attendance was mandatory.

All participants received Fast-Track TQM manuals and individual continuous leadership manuals to assist them in understanding TQM principles and in developing the necessary skills to lead employees for Quality advancement. In addition, throughout the training, the manager/participants used workbooks that were customized for Western Growers Association's particular needs and unique challenges.

The management training sessions, which were held before introducing the concept of TQM to the general staff, proved key in establishing important leadership qualities and were important in helping other employees wholeheartedly accept the process.

In mid-July, all the staff members at the headquarters office in Irvine, California, participated in one of two half-day sessions, which I facilitated. The seminar was videotaped for broadcast at field office meetings to be held the following week.

Defect-Free Week

After the staff's initial orientation to Fast-Track TQM, Western Growers declared a defect-free week, in which every staff member agreed and committed to providing defect-free service and products to the company's customers. Any defects that occurred during the week were documented. Then staff members reviewed the defects and their causes, looking for ways to prevent defect recurrence in the future. The emphasis was not on laying blame, but on detecting defects, resolving the problems that caused them, and planning for a defect-free future.

The original group of 29 managers who'd been trained in Quality leadership began meeting monthly in Quality Councils to discuss their progress, learn new concepts, and reinforce their commitment to TQM. They shared their achievements and challenges, and pooled ideas and insights they had gained from their experiences.

The managers organized Quality Improvement Teams (QITs) to examine and resolve identified Quality problems. As solutions to Quality issues were identified, the management implemented solutions that led to changes in the way the association conducted its business on a day-to-day basis. Each change implemented had to meet WGA's iron-clad objective: Did it improve the Quality of service or products for customers?

Implementing Changes

As a result of defect-free week, the QITs, and management meeting together regularly to discuss Quality improvements, Western Growers initiated a variety of changes in the organization. For example, in the Marketing Services Department, which helps association members collect accounts receivable, they were able to rework their procedures and cut 51 days off their collection cycle.

They also made positive changes in their health benefit plan processing. Before Quality improvements, it took WGA an average of 22 days to process new employer groups for health benefit plans. A Quality Improvement Team, led by a senior vice president and including team members from several departments, examined the problem and devised a new work flow. Now the maximum time it takes to process new members is six days. WGA customers appreciate the faster, more accurate service that enables them to provide better health coverage for their employees.

In addition to making changes to better serve their external customers, WGA turned its Quality advancing focus on internal customers. Staff members conducted Internal Quality Audits, interviewing internal customers to determine how to better meet their needs and ultimately how to produce defect-free products and services for external customers.

In its pursuit of excellence, WGA became committed to developing its people. In every staff meeting, employees are asked, "What can be done to make your job easier?" This people orientation led the association to create a successful employee suggestion program that has been instrumental in generating Quality-advancing solutions and empowering employees to seek their own solutions to problems. They also implemented an Employee Recognition Program that recognizes the Quality-advancing efforts of employees.

WGA also reevaluated its performance appraisal system with TQM principles in mind. Instead of assessing performance on more traditional benchmarks, WGA staff are evaluated with questions such as, "What Quality improvements do you plan over the next six months?" These questions are answered by both the employee and the executive.

To keep employee interest high in advancing Quality, the Personnel Department publishes a special Quality newsletter that highlights successes and acts as a continuing education program for staff.

The most noticeable Fast-Track TQM impact at Western Growers Association has been the unification of employees. Now everyone in the company works cooperatively to improve Quality. The "we/they" syndrome, in which departments criticized and competed with one another, has been replaced by "we together" and departments are now working cooperatively toward the common goal of improving Quality. QITs, which bring together staffs from departments throughout the organization, have had a powerful effect in bringing people together. And internal communications, spurred on by the need to improve Quality to both internal and external customers, has improved markedly.

TQM Payoff Equals Dollars

In mid-October, nine months from the time Fast-Track TQM was initially introduced to Western Growers senior management, the group met again at an off-site location to assess its progress. They analyzed factors such as increased profit, decreased waste, and less rework that has resulted from their TQM efforts. To their amazement, during the first four months of implementing Fast-Track TQM, from the first training in June until October, the association's combination of profit and performance increases totaled $1.5 million. The management group anticipated they were going to double that figure within the next eight months.

Appendix

Fast-Track Tip 1

The processes and techniques associated with Quality improvement have been around now for many years. Fast Tracking sets new priorities and eliminates the processes that waste time and resources.

Fast-Track Tip 2

Use the ten principles of Fast Tracking to quality as a checklist to confirm your understanding and direction in leading for quality advancement.

Fast-Track Tip 3

Be clear about your reason or purpose in getting involved in the Quality advancement process. Communicate your purpose to your staff clearly and frequently.

Fast-Track Tip 4

Don't try to define quality. Look to your customers for the real definition of quality in your products and services.

Fast-Track Tip 5

The word "defect" is a descriptive way of referring to an error, failure, or something broken without placing blame. The word "mistake" draws the question, "Who did it?" Change your language and begin using the term "defect" in conversations with your staff and colleagues. The change will foster cooperative solutions to problems without placing blame.

Fast-Track Tip 6

Memorize the three dimensions of quality:

   Fit for use
   Defect-free
   Perceived quality

Use these dimensions in your language as you discuss quality with your staff and your customers.

Fast-Track Tip 7

Clarify the correctness of TQM as the right business issue for your organization. Confirm your personal commitment to Quality improvement, and proceed only when you are willing to champion the Quality cause.

Fast-Track Tip 8

Be ready to show quantifiable "before-and-after" data on your Quality progress. Conduct a brief, semiannual climate survey with managers and supervisors to monitor behavior changes. Measured improvements in Quality will provide evidence to confirm advancements in organizational climate as Fast-Track principles are applied.

Fast-Track Tip 9

Challenge your staff to determine the cost of poor Quality.

- Have each work unit put a dollar figure on the cost of appraisal, mistakes, failure, lost business, and prevention.
- Record and total the figures. Then ask, "What is the message for our company?"
- Discuss each item, and challenge, "Is this acceptable?"

Fast-Track Tip 10

Avoid the inevitable employee question, "Why is change needed?" by stating the need for change and backing up the statement with hard data. Instead of simply announcing the change in a memo or meeting, hold discussion groups to confirm staff understanding and acceptance of the change.

Fast-Track Tip 11

Be open and clear with others regarding your vision of the organization. Instead of spending time describing the "how-to's" of your vision, involve your staff in the development of a "how-to" plan.

Fast-Track Tip 12

Apply the three key actions for visionary change:

1. Establish the vision.
2. Have a trusted person validate the need for, and the value of, the change.
3. Have an articulate messenger describe the change so that everyone understands the process.

Fast-Track Tip 13

No matter how much agreement there is on the need for change, in the end there will always be criticism of how the change took place.

Fast-Track Tip 14

To achieve dramatic, rapid organizational change, focus not on behaviors or attitudes, but on the processes that affect results. Change the processes, and you change the behavior and attitudes. Change the process, and you change the individual.

Fast-Track Tip 15

Be sure that you can answer these five critical questions:
1. Who are your customers?
2. What do you know about their needs and expectations?
3. How satisfied are they?
4. Can your organization become more responsive in servicing customers?
5. What actions are needed to improve customer satisfaction?

Fast-Track Tip 16

Your service and products must be good enough to create customers for life.

Fast-Track Tip 17

The reward for spending the time getting to know and understand your customer is the ability to identify actions to take and increase customer satisfaction, heighten market share, and produce additional sales.

Fast-Track Tip 18

It costs many times more to gain new customers than it does to keep old ones.

Fast-Track Tip 19

Be honest in your assessment. Are you giving lip service or hard service when serving your customers?

Fast-Track Tip 20

Fast-Track TQM includes a different way of doing business, requiring consensus decision making. As more people are involved in the decision-making process, and implementation time is shortened. Increased employee influence on decision implementation builds team unity and team spirit.

Fast-Track Tip 21

Through accountability, measurable results can be achieved within six to nine months.

Fast-Track Tip 22

To effectively lead for quality, autocratic managers have to significantly alter their personal leadership style.

Fast-Track Tip 23

Only continuous training can ensure that managers and employees have the skills and motivation for continuous Quality advancement.

Fast-Track Tip 24

For successful TQM, all employees must be directly involved in the Quality-enhancement process.

Fast-Track Tip 25

Schedule Fast-Track TQM skill training over several weeks to give participants the opportunity to try out new concepts and skills in a work setting, and then return to the training classroom for feedback and more skills.

Fast-Track Tip 26

Employees develop positive beliefs about TQM if you clearly demonstrate the personal benefits, the benefits to their immediate work group, and benefits for the organization as a whole.

Fast-Track Tip 27

Managers must be allowed to question and challenge the 20 Fast-Track TQM principles. Only when they have resolved all their questions and concerns, and have accepted the principles, are they ready to proceed with TQM.

Fast-Track Tip 28

Know your customer's strengths and weaknesses—and how you compare.

Fast-Track Tip 29

A shared TQM language enables managers to talk about Quality enhancement, and acts to solidify groups into effective teams.

Fast-Track Tip 30

To understand how to lead for Quality enhancement, managers must define the specific behaviors and actions that they can apply to advance Quality in their own organization.

Fast-Track Tip 31

If managers have the responsibility, they must have the authority to act, or at least a clear understanding of their level of authority.

Fast-Track Tip 32

Improving a manager's group and one-on-one presentation skills directly influences his or her effectiveness in leading for Fast-Track TQM.

Fast Track 33

Don't waste your time and resources solving problems that have questionable value to improving your organization's product/service Quality.

Fast-Track Tip 34

- Keep data collection formats simple and usable.
- Limit data collection to only three or four areas.
- Gather data only in areas over which you have direct control.

Fast-Track Tip 35

Utilize the minimum performance standard in setting standards, and let employee work groups set the standards for their areas. Avoid imposing management-generated performance standards.

Fast-Track Tip 36

Waiting for the "perfect time" to initiate Quality improvement is a mistake. That time will likely never come.

Fast-Track Tip 37

An effective TQM design should be able to demonstrate measurable performance improvements in six to nine months.

Fast-Track Tip 38

To improve Quality, first improve the Quality of management. Then improve the management of Quality.

Fast-Track Tip 39

Use the experience of an outside Quality consultatnt in the planning and training of senior managers.

Fast-Track Tip 40

Managers will support what benefits them personally or what benefits their department, division, or company. It's imperative that managers understand their role and the support that they will receive in actively participating in Fast-Track TQM.

Fast-Track Tip 41

The process of Fast-Track Master Planning is important in creating unity and common understanding among managers. It is a process of involvement.

Fast-Track Tip 42

Create a simple, relevant mission statement that all managers and employees can understand, relate to, and support.

Fast-Track Tip 43

Establish organizational values that all employees and managers can support.

Fast-Track Tip 44

Managers strengthen their unity and their leadership effectiveness as they clarify how they will work together.

Fast-Track Tip 45

Master Planning facilitators need special skills and abilities to ask penetrating questions.

Fast-Track Tip 46

Regularly reevaluate your customers' ever-changing needs and expectations.

Fast-Track Tip 47

Managers and select employees are directly involved in identifying and clarifying customer needs and expectations.

Fast-Track Tip 48

Conduct a Fast-Track Quality audit only if you are truly serious about improving Quality to customers.

Fast-Track Tip 49

Request specific examples of areas in which your product or service is not meeting customer needs or expectations.

Fast-Track Tip 50

Whenever possible, conduct customer Quality audit interviews face-to-face in a private setting.

Fast-Track Tip 51

Fast-Track TQM succeeds only when management and employees work as a team. Involve all your employees in Quality improvement planning and in the necessary changes to processes.

Fast-Track Tip 52

Don't be fooled by the value of statistical process controls (SPCs). They are only one of many tools in your TQM toolbox. With only a small investment in training, employees at all levels can successfully utilize SPCs.

Fast-Track Tip 53

It's vital to the success of Quality Advancement that Management Forums be held 60 to 90 days following Fast-Tract TQM and leadership training. This ensures accountability and the opportunity to recognize exemplary achievements.

Fast-Track Tip 54

Management Forums not only create accountability; they sustain excitement and interest in advancing Quality. They become times of celebration and congratulations.

Fast-Track Tip 55

Management forums should be structured to encourage questions from the audience and the sharing of ideas. A cooperative rather than competitive atmosphere must be established.

Fast-Track Tip 56

The performance dollar figures generated during the presentations enable management to easily determine the return on TQM investment.

Fast-Track Tip 57

All your TQM strategies should be directed toward achieving two goals:

1. Customer satisfaction
2. Defect-free products and services

Fast-Track Tip 58

While Quality consultants can offer Quality-advancing strategies, only you can decide when to apply those strategies for your organization.

Fast-Track Tip 59

Success with Fast-Track TQM is predicated on employee involvement and appropriate risk taking at all levels.

Fast-Track Tip 60

Self-managed work teams collaborate to determine outcomes, along with the best methods, strategies, and actions to best achieve those outcomes.

Fast-Track Tip 61

Quality improvement teams (QITs) must have the direct involvement and support of midlevel managers to guide the problem-solving process.

Fast-Track Tip 62

By competitive benchmarking, you set your sights on others who are "the best" in what they do. If they can be the best, why can't you? The target is to become world class in your industry.

Fast-Track Tip 63

In TQM, suppliers become business partners, actively involved in the advancement of the Quality of your products and services.

Fast-Track Tip 64

Continuous skill training for managers, supervisors, and employees is needed if you're to have ongoing Quality improvement.

Fast-Track Tip 65

Consistent organizational direction, communicated clearly and frequently to employees, helps them know how and where to invest their time and energy most effectively.

Fast-Track Tip 66

Don't play the Quality game unless you're willing to keep score of your efforts. Without scorecards, people cannot know how well they're doing, and they soon lose interest.

Fast-Track Tip 67

Graphs provide an immediate visual image of progress in becoming defect free.

Fast-Track Tip 68

It's easier and less costly to design Quality into processes, products, and services than it is to rework for Quality improvement.

Fast-Track Tip 69

Carefully prepared instruction manuals give employees consistent and specific direction in how to serve customers.

Fast-Track Tip 70

Properly structured employee suggestion programs can involve and encourage employees to actively participate in Quality improvement.

Fast-Track Tip 71

Midlevel managers are the most resistant to buying into TQM. What makes them achieve midlevel management status is often what makes them fail with TQM. Without midlevel management support, however, TQM success is questionable.

Fast-Track Tip 72

Building midlevel managemer commitment to TQM requires a clear understanding of the benefits they can realize.

Fast-Track Tip 73

Having senior management—the president and vice president(s)—directly involved with the sharing process with middle managers conveys the important message of commitment.

Fast-Track Tip 74

Giving midlevel managers a vote in the decision to pursue TQM gives them "influence" in the organization, one of the proven keys to building commitment.

Fast-Track Tip 75

Agreement statements between senior and midlevel managers outline the commitment of senior managers to Quality enhancement and the responsibilities of middle managers in advancing Quality.

Fast-Track Tip 76

Successful TQM requires a specialized type of leadership. Apply the Fast-Track Seven Key Leadership Skills to develop successful Quality leaders.

Fast-Track Tip 77

Managers are paid for results, not for duties, and must be held accountable for achieving those results.

Fast-Track Tip 78

Effective TQM leaders are results oriented. They know the required parameters and are accountable for demonstrating success.

Fast-Track Tip 79

Results statements define and clarify what people get paid for, but they remain stable from year to year.

Fast-Track Tip 80

For managers to lead effectively for Quality enhancement, they must be trustworthy and have credibility with employees. Honoring performance agreements establishes trust and credibility. Failure to honor them seriously impairs the advancement to Quality.

Fast-Track Tip 81

Use the Fast-Track Three-Step Performance Agreement:

1. Establish clear outcomes.
2. Go for the "yes."
3. Confirm commitment.

Fast-Track Tip 82

To effectively involve all employees in Quality advancement, memorize the three statements for motivating and building commitment:

1. Provide feedback.
2. Create a sense of accomplishment.
3. Give employees influence.

Fast-Track Tip 83

Save up to 50 percent of valuable meeting time by eliminating needless storytelling, being clear on the meeting's purpose, avoiding hidden agendas, and skillfully asking power questions.

Fast-Track Tip 84

Successful TQM leaders build teams using Quality management as the focal point and common goal.

Fast-Track Tip 85

Use the Fast-Track Five-Step Empowerment Process to strengthen employees' self-esteem, and give them the belief and confidence that they can improve Quality.

Fast-Track Tip 86

Cooperative working relationships are built on trust. Honoring and keeping performance agreements directly build trust and management credibility.

Fast-Track Tip 87

Improve employee self-esteem and you improve performance: the higher the self-esteem, the higher the performance.

Fast-Track Tip 88

Don't rely solely on money and benefits to build commitment and motivation in your staff. More powerful motivators are recognition, a sense of achievement, and influence—a feeling that, "What I do matters."

Fast-Track Tip 89

TSBTs can improve performance by building self-esteem. If you're willing to invest 40 seconds, you can improve employee self-esteem with TSBT.

Fast-Track Tip 90

Compliments don't really say anything. They create a "warm, fuzzy" feeling, but do little to improve self-esteem. Building self-esteem requires recognition that specifically identifies the behavior and outlines the benefits of that behavior to the individual, the department, and/or the organization.

Fast-Track Tip 91

Only offer recognition in the form of TSBTs as often as you can maintain sincerity. Initially, it will require more recognition; as performance improves, the number of TSBTs you must give to maintain good performance decreases.

Fast-Track Tip 92

If you empower employees to resolve customer problems, you create satisfied customers and enthusiastic employees.

Fast-Track Tip 93

Rules and procedures that don't ensure customer satisfaction aren't in the best interests of the organization.

Fast-Track Tip 94

Empowerment builds employee self-esteem.

Fast-Track Tip 95

Use a three-step process to ensure that you have correct and proper rules and regulations to meet your customers' needs and expectations:

1. Identify the present rules and procedures.

2. Challenge the present rules and procedures with customer needs in mind.
3. Change/alter the rules and procedures.

Fast-Track Tip 96

Employees feel a common need, a "pinch" or "hurt," that will motivate them to change how they serve customers.

Fast-Track Tip 97

Success is like a snowball. It builds on itself.

Fast-Track Tip 98

Employees need to have the necessary resources (time, equipment, etc.) to serve customers. Without them, you doom the empowerment process to failure.

Fast-Track Tip 99

If you can't communicate with your employees, you won't be able to communicate with your customers. Clear, consistent communication is a key to developing employees who are able to meet or exceed their customer's expectations.

Fast-Track Tip 100

Different employees respond to different messages. Use a variety of communication vehicles to reach everyone with the quality message.

Fast-Track Tip 101

Develop and use a "news flash" form to disseminate hot news items about employee achievements. Use a fax or photocopy machine to broadcast the news items throughout your organization.

Fast-Track Tip 102

Newsletters can be one of the most cost-effective methods of consistently communicating the Quality message to your employees.

Fast-Track Tip 103

Don't be overly ambitious with your Quality newsletter. In the beginning, publish no more frequently than quarterly and keep the size down to four pages or less.

Fast-Track Tip 104

If you don't have communications/public relations professionals on staff, consider hiring a professional writer/editor to produce your newsletter.

Fast-Track Tip 105

Computer screen messages can be effective at communicating with employees. But they must not be viewed as a "Big Brother" tactic. Limit the messages only to special announcements or recognitions.

Fast-Tract Tip 106

The informality of brown bag lunches with management and employees can foster the open and honest exchange of concerns and ideas.

Fast-Track Tip 107

Be careful not to overuse banners, slogans, and mottos that can give the impression that Quality advancement is a program that will end.

Fast-Track Tip 108

The CEO or president must demonstrate commitment to TQM by doing—by actions—not just by words.

Fast-Track Tip 109

Don't expect employees, supervisors, and managers to commit to TQM until they fully understand the need for Quality improvement—the "why"—and its benefits to them, to their work group, and to the organization.

Fast-Track Tip 110

All members of senior management must be on board the Quality train and fully "packed" for the trip before it pulls out of the station, or the trip won't be a success.

Fast-Track Tip 111

Let Quality advancement be the focus that unifies your employees and managers into an effective team.

Fast-Track Tip 112

Autocratic styles of management have no place in the TQM organization.

Fast-Track Tip 113

Don't be fooled by statistical process controls (SPCs). They're only one of the many tools in your Quality-advancement kit.

Fast-Track Tip 114

Don't rush into Quality-enhancing actions. Employees must be fully trained in TQM awareness, principles, and skills before they begin taking action to improve Quality.

Fast-Track Tip 115

Maintain training intensity by keeping the training time frame to six weeks or so. Stretching out the training period lessens its impact.

Fast-Track Tip 116

Underscore the importance of TQM by making Quality advancement the premier example in your industry. Reinforce for employees that your organization is different and, above all, special.

Fast-Track Tip 117

Invest 12 to 16 hours in planning Fast Tracking for guaranteed TQM success.

Fast-Track Tip 118

Fast-Track TQM success requires win-win management. Everyone must act to support themselves and others in advancing Quality.

Fast-Track Tip 119

Your Vision/Mission Statement must reflect the importance of Quality in your Organization.

Fast-Track Tip 120

Ultimate standards define what the organization will look like when it is the best in the industry. They serve as a guidepost for management actions, decisions, and allocation of resources.

Fast-Track Tip 121

Conduct regularly scheduled management meetings to review progress in keeping performance agreements, win-win, value standards. This reinforces the importance of Quality and supports progress in advancing Quality.

Index

About the Author

Roger Tunks is president of the Richard-Rogers Group, a
management consulting firm specializing in total quality
management training. He is an acclaimed educator and
much sought-after TQM consultant and speaker nationwide.
Mr. Tunks has 22 years of experience as a consultant to a
variety of industries across America.